MODELING OBJECTS AND ENVIRONMENTS

PRINCIPLES OF COMPUTER-AIDED DESIGN

A Series by
Yehuda E. Kalay
School of Architecture and Planning
State University of New York, Buffalo

Graphic Introduction to Programming
Computability of Design
Modeling Objects and Environments

MODELING OBJECTS AND ENVIRONMENTS

Yehuda E. Kalay

School of Architecture and Planning
State University of New York
Buffalo, New York

WILEY

A WILEY-INTERSCIENCE PUBLICATION

JOHN WILEY & SONS

New York / Chichester / Brisbane / Toronto / Singapore

Library of Congress Cataloging in Publication Data:

Kalay, Yehuda E.
  Modeling objects and environments/Yehuda E. Kalay.
    p. cm—(Principles of computer-aided design)

  Bibliography: p.
  Includes index.
  ISBN 0-471-85388-7
  1. Computer-aided design.   2. Computer graphics.   I. Title.
II. Series: Kalay, Yehuda E.   Principles of computer-aided design.
TA174.K34   1989
620′.00425′0285--dc19   88-26872
                                                  CIP

Printed in the United States of America

10 9 8 7 6 5 4 3 2 1

SERIES PREFACE

Computers have made their debut as design tools in many engineering disciplines, providing designers with flexible means to represent design products. In that capacity they have already demonstrated their utility in improving the productivity and the quality of the production end of the design process, much like word processors have improved the production of documents in offices.

A growing number of researchers, developers, and users of computer-aided design (CAD) systems, however, have reached the conclusion that the utility of computers in design is far from what it might become, if their use were extended over the design process as a whole, including the complete, accurate, and efficient representation of the designed artifacts and the processes that are employed in their conception and creation.

This series of five books is intended to help realize the potential of CAD, through the introduction—in an integrative form—of principles, methodologies, and practices that underlie CAD. It is intended to be used by people who wish to engage in the process of research, development, and maintenance of the new generation of CAD systems. Since the current cadre of people involved with R&D in CAD is relatively small, the series assumes that the reader has no particular knowledge of the field and thus it can be used as a text for beginners. The topics it introduces progress, nevertheless, rapidly toward the frontiers of CAD and thus make the series useful as a text for advanced courses and as reference for professionals.

The first volume, *Graphic Introduction to Programming*, introduces the basic concepts of computing that are needed to master the tool—namely, the computer. These concepts include programming, structured problem solving, and interactive computer graphics. Programming is the means through which computers are instructed how to perform the desired tasks. Structured problem solving, through algorithm design and analysis, encourages a disciplined approach to the design process as a whole and to computer-aided design software development in particular. Given the established manner of communicating design between humans, and because of the ease with which graphic and pictorial information can be disseminated compared with text and numerals, computer graphics have become the standard means of interaction with CAD systems. These three topics have been integrated and are covered through learning the programming language Pascal. This language has certain features that qualify it for this task, which include ease of comprehension, enforcing good programming practices, availability on most computers, and provision of dynamic memory management facilities.

The second volume, *Modeling Objects and Environments,* introduces the concepts of modeling real-world phenomena in the computer's memory. It covers a set of methods and techniques for representing the physical environment as symbol structures that are understood and can be manipulated by computers. The book includes the study of data structures that are particularly suitable for representing two- and three-dimensional artifacts and for operating on these structures in a way that preserves their semantic integrity. The book covers the formative and other attributes of objects, such as topology, geometry, transformations, assemblies, and general database query/update operations.

The third volume, *Modeling Design Processes,* is concerned with the representation of design as a problem-solving process. The two essential components of CAD covered include the generation and the evaluation of alternative design solutions, represented through the modeling concepts introduced in the second volume. The study of solution generation covers all design phases, including preconcept, conceptual, and detailed design. It is introduced through techniques such as knowledge representation and search strategies and relies on selected practices from artificial intelligence, database theory, operations research, and optimization theory. All of these topics are covered in sufficient detail for the comprehension of the central topics in the book, though of course they do not attempt to be substitutes for formal texts in their respective disciplines. The theoretical treatment of the topics covered by the book is complemented by examples written in PROLOG, a programming language that has some powerful features useful for logic representation and manipulation. For the benefit of readers who are not familiar with PROLOG, an appendix introduces the basics of this language.

The fourth volume, *Performance Measurement Applications,* presents an assortment of task-specific applications that draw upon the model of the designed artifact and provide the designer and the knowledge-based CAD system with a variety of evaluative, simulative, and tabulative measures of the artifacts' expected performances. Written by noted experts in their respective disciplines, the applications present both state-of-the-art knowledge in specific fields relating to CAD and an integrative approach to employing computers as design consultants.

The fifth volume, *Computability of Design,* completes the series by reviewing the key topics that were presented and by raising the fundamental issues of design computation: How can design processes be mathematically modeled? What is design knowledge, and how can it be computed? How can the design process as a whole be computed? Alternatively, how can particular design tasks be computationally assisted? This volume is based on a symposium that was held in Buffalo, New York, in December 1986, where noted experts discussed the feasibility, utility, and desirability of various approaches to the computation of design.

The series as a whole is concerned with the principles of CAD rather than with an exhaustive survey of techniques, practices, and existing systems. Its goal is to educate students, researchers, and professionals, who will develop the CAD systems of the future and who will maintain them. It is intended to be used by designers in many disciplines, rather than by computer scientists alone. It may, however, be of considerable interest to computer scientists, too, by exposing them to the computational concerns of design professionals.

It is recommended that the books be used in sequence, but this is not a prerequisite for their utility. Neither is adherence to the programming languages Pascal and PROLOG a prerequisite; those languages are used to exemplify the theory. It is the concepts and principles presented in the series that are of primary importance, and they transcend the technologies and techniques used for their implementation.

Yehuda E. Kalay

Buffalo, New York
February 1987

PREFACE

Design, in the context of this book, is considered to be the process of specifying the properties (shape and other attributes) of an as yet nonexisting artifact to guarantee that it can be built (or manufactured) and that the product will meet certain performance criteria. *Computer-aided design* is a means to augment the design process by bringing computational techniques to bear on solving design problems, representing the designed artifact, and simulating its expected performances.

Computers, however, can operate only on abstract, symbolic (mathematical) structures. They cannot deal with the physical realities themselves. Therefore, in order to use computational means to facilitate the process of design, a technique called *modeling* must be employed. This technique allows us to represent physical realities in the computer's memory in the form of mathematical symbol structures. Once so represented, the computer can manipulate the structures, transform them into new structures, display them graphically, and perform various types of analyses on them.

The symbol structures that computers use for modeling the designed artifacts are free from the laws which govern the physical realities they represent. Therefore, they could be manipulated in ways that will violate these laws and render the model nonrealizable. In order for the manipulative actions to be meaningful in the context of physical design, both the symbol structures and the operators that manipulate them must comply with some strict constraints that guarantee the semantic integrity of the model.

This book discusses the principles of representing physical artifacts and environments in the computer's memory, subject to semantic integrity constraints, and the manner in which designers can create, visualize, and manipulate the symbol structures, such that they correspond to the advancing phases of the designed artifact.

The study of modeling comprises an understanding of both general principles and techniques of representing physical artifacts in the computer. They include, in particular, abstraction and hierarchical data structuring. *Abstraction* is a method that allows the grouping of symbol structures, representing the modeled artifact, and the operators that manipulate them into one computational entity. This grouping allows treating them as one whole, freeing the designer/programmer to concentrate on the role of the entity and its relationships to other entities rather than on the details of its implementation. *Hierarchical structuring* is a method that facilitates modularity of model building, whereby the abstract entities discussed earlier can be combined into larger, more complex entities, which can themselves be regarded as unitary elements of the model.

The objects and the environments to be modeled for the purposes of design have many attributes, such as form, location, materials, color, and cost, to name a few. Many of them must be modeled if the model is to be complete and general. This book deals with many attributes, but is concerned mainly with the modeling of *form*. The form that objects take is by far the most complicated attribute to model and in many cases is the most important one, too. *Form* is what we see and touch. It determines many of the functional and other characteristics of objects and environments. The book deals with form modeling at two levels: first in two dimensions, then in three. A *polygon-based* approach to form modeling is used. This approach lends itself to both representation and manipulation of area-enclosing shapes (polygons) and volume-enclosing shapes (solids). It allows the concepts of topology and geometry to be introduced in a simpler manner first (as they apply to polygons) and their interrelationships to be explained. Once this basis is firmly established, the book proceeds to discuss the much more complex roles of topology and geometry as they pertain to three-dimensional, volumetric shapes (solids). Almost all artifacts and environments are made of many objects that are closely linked (physically or functionally) and which interact in many ways. An engine is made of parts, and a building is made of walls, floors, windows, doors, and other components. Such collections of objects are known as *assemblies* and must be modeled together with the individual parts that form them. The study of assembly modeling in this book relies on principles used in database management systems that deal with large collections of interrelated components. In addition, techniques, such as *attribute inheritance* and *instancing,* that reduce the amount of data and enhance its integrity are adopted from object-oriented programming languages, such as Smalltalk.

The book comprises five parts. The first four parts deal with modeling issues: the *construction, placement,* and *association* of computationally represented objects. The first part deals with the principles of modeling the *form* of objects in two dimensions (polygons), and the second part deals with the principles of modeling the *form* of objects in three dimensions (solids). The third part discusses issues concerning the absolute and relative *placement* of objects in space and in assemblies of objects. The fourth part is concerned with the *association* of the formative attributes with nonformative attributes to complete the representation, management, and query of the model. The fifth part of the book deals with the two-way *communication* between the model and the designer. Three appendices provide additional information concerning geometrical and data structuring concepts, which are important to modeling but are tangential to the main body of the text.

It cannot be emphasized enough that the approaches and programs presented in this book represent only a few of the many ways to accomplish the tasks discussed in it. As a book concerned with *principles of CAD,* in-depth treatment of the issues was preferred to exhaustive coverage of techniques and methods. References at the end of each chapter direct the reader to additional approaches.

This book and the concepts it presents are the cumulative and refined results of more than 14 years of my involvement in researching and teaching geometric modeling. I am indebted to my mentors, colleagues, and students who proposed, criticized, tested, and otherwise helped shape the methodologies presented here and the format of their presentation. In particular I am grateful to Tony Cheng, Charles Eastman, Jang Jia Bin, Harvey Lichtblau, Bruce Majkowski, and Lucien Swerdloff. Carl Nuermberger deserves special thanks for aiding me in producing the book, a process to which he contributed both in form and in content. I am also grateful to the departmental, school, and university administrations for providing much needed support. In particular, I am indebted to Robert Shibley for his consistent help and encouragement. Last but not least, I am thankful to my wife, Riki, who put up with the endless hours through which this book came to be and who was always there when I needed her most.

Yehuda E. Kalay

Buffalo, New York
March 1989

CONTENTS

PART TWO   3D CONSTRUCTION

PART THREE   PLACEMENT

PART FOUR ASSOCIATION

PART FIVE   INTERFACE

APPENDICES

MODELING OBJECTS
AND ENVIRONMENTS

INTRODUCTION

Computer models of real-world phenomena are, in effect, *languages of represen-tation* composed of symbol structures and grammatical rules to manipulate them. This chapter establishes the role of computer models as a language of design and discusses some ways for implementing them. The advantages and disadvantages of particular versus generalized models are explored, together with the possible combinations of such models. All models should have four ba-sic properties: *well-formedness, completeness, generality,* and *efficiency.* The difficulty of developing models that have all these properties is explained, and two techniques that can be used to alleviate the problem—*abstraction* and *hier-archical structuring*—are proposed.

□ MODELING: THE LANGUAGE OF REPRESENTATION

Our knowledge of the world in general, and of abstract concepts in particular, comes through the mediation of *language,* which comprises two components:

1. Symbol structures that represent objects and concepts in that language
2. A mapping that defines the meaning of particular symbol structures through rules that relate them to each other and to the phenomena they represent

Computers are symbol manipulators—machines that can create, copy, and destroy symbols very rapidly and consistently, according to a given set of gram-matical rules. The symbols, or more precisely, the structures they make, how-ever, have no meaning of their own. In order for them to acquire meaning, and thus be interpretable in the world outside the computer's own memory, the sym-bol structures must be considered *representations* of some real-world or abstract phenomena.

1

For the purpose of aiding design processes, the symbol structures are often considered representations of objects and environments or the forces that shape them. Once so designated, the symbol structures can be subjected to various qualitative and quantitative simulated tests, in lieu of the represented artifacts themselves. A new form of a car, for example, can be tested for stability and crash worthiness. A new building can be cost-estimated, code-checked, and even appreciated aesthetically through its graphic presentation.

Like the symbol structures themselves, their interpretation as representations of real-world phenomena is, nevertheless, artificial. Much care must, therefore, be taken to maintain a meaningful correlation between the symbol structures and the real world, by controlling not only the symbol structures themselves but also the operators that manipulate them. Structuring the symbols in the computer's memory in a manner that supports their meaningful interpretation and their manipulation, such that this meaning is preserved, is the subject of this volume in the series on the principles of computer-aided design (CAD).

Computers were introduced in the process of designing physical artifacts in the late 1950s, when engineers found that computers could be used to simplify, or even eliminate, many of the complex mathematical calculations that accompany various engineering and design tasks. The early use of computers in design was, therefore, aimed at solving what was then the major engineering concern— the accurate solution of large and complex equation systems. Accordingly, the design process was carried out manually, as it has always been, except that at certain intervals data were taken off the drawings and presented to the computer for the performance of numerically intensive calculations (which have become known as "number crunching"). The results of these computations were interpreted manually, and the drawings updated accordingly. Because each analysis program required data in their own particular formats, and because little or no effort was made to improve data entry, this early computer-aided design cycle of manually generating design alternatives and their evaluation by means of computer programs was necessarily slow, tedious, and inefficient (Figure 1).

With the improvement of the accuracy of computer-aided engineering analyses, designers shifted their attention to improving the communication between the manually generated design alternatives and their computerized analysis. It became obvious that further benefits could accrue only if the computer was somehow made to "know" what was being designed and if it could perform the required analyses by getting its data directly from the designed artifact without the need for manual quantities take-offs. A machine that could "watch over the designer's shoulder" and "understand" the emerging artifact, such that it could analyze its various qualities upon request, was needed.

The solution to this problem began to emerge in the early 1960s, when the concept of computer models of real-world artifacts and phenomena was introduced by Steven Coons and Ivan Sutherland at MIT. It was not before the early 1970s, however, that computer-aided design systems became available that "understood" volumes, mass, materials, and other properties of objects. Progress was slow because it required a fundamental change in the way design was being

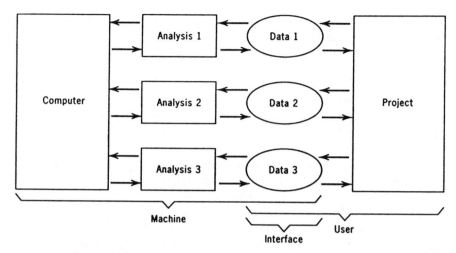

Figure 1. Schema of an early computer-aided design process.

practiced. Because it was impossible to have the computer recognize and comprehend design activity that occurred outside itself, design had to happen in the computer in its entirety. Methods, tools, and practices have since been developed that place the computer at the center of the design activity, as a *design environment*, rather than as a peripheral tool.

At the heart of this revolution is the design data and knowledge base, which together form a *model* of the designed artifact and the forces that shape it (Figure 2). This model, which is typically an accurate, manipulable, two- or three-dimensional, attribute-laden symbolic representation of the artifact, provides

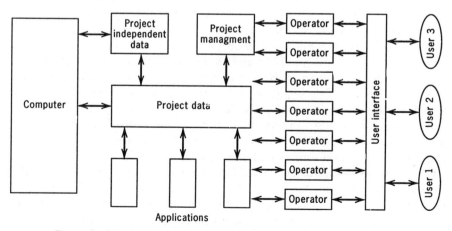

Figure 2. Schema of an integrated computer-aided design system.

the common grounds where designers and the computer meet. Designers can create, manipulate, and visualize the emerging artifact, while the computer can comprehend it, analyze its expected performances, and in some cases modify it appropriately. The core model is augmented by many analyses and application modules, each capable of a different task, yet all deriving the required data directly from the same source. Designers have access to this model through various interface modules, which display the data graphically or in tabular form. Such integration does not only eliminate the former need to manually extract particular data from the emerging artifact and present it to the computer for analysis, but also enhances the consistency of the design process as a whole and expedites communication between the design team specialists, since all the participants deal with the same pool of information.

Cognition scientists have demonstrated that the ability of humans to perform depends on internal models, built over many years by learning and experiencing. Social customs, morality, and even the perception of space are prime examples of behavior dependent on such internal "models." Likewise, models are needed if computers are to perform feats that we call "intelligent," such as estimating and advising us about the habitability of a building or the road performance of a new automobile. Without modeling, the potential of computers to aid the process of designing physical artifacts would be severely limited.

The primary function of models is thus to *represent* in the computer's memory an artifact, environment, or phenomenon, such that the computer can *reason* about it and consequently *operate* on it. This representation allows us to investigate the properties of designed artifacts and natural phenomena in ways that would otherwise not be feasible due to time or cost constraints.

A model of the atmosphere serves to represent a natural phenomenon for the purpose of investigating its properties and reasoning about its behavior (forecasting the weather). A model of an oil well serves to represent an environment for the purpose of simulating and testing alternative courses of action, which will result in maximizing petroleum recovery. A model of a new car serves to represent an artifact for the purposes of evaluating and estimating the characteristics it will have when it is built, such as its road handling capabilities and its crash survivability without loss of property or human life.

Nevertheless, the utility of computer models transcends their role as tools for simulation and investigation. Models also help designers to *visualize* artifacts that do not yet exist in reality in ways not afforded by traditional drawings and which are easier to construct and modify than physical scale models. A model of a new house, for example, can be walked through and appreciated aesthetically, and the visual impact it will have on its surroundings can be inspected. In this respect, the model performs metaphorically like a telescope—an instrument that allows scientists to view objects not visible to the naked eye. The model, unlike the telescope, can be made to respond to design changes, to reflect modification called for by the earlier evaluation. It thus becomes an active partner in the design process, bringing Donald Schon's metaphoric "reflective practitioner" closer to reality.

☐ TYPES OF MODELS

The large amounts of information needed to represent artifacts, environments, and phenomena typically limit the generality of models. Models are, therefore, typically task-specific. A model capable of supporting the design of electrical circuits, for example, may not be suitable for supporting the design of aircraft. Some models may, however, be more specific than others. For example, it is conceivable that a model of a building can support energy loss analysis, but cannot answer questions concerning circulation, privacy, or construction costs. On the other hand, a more general model could be developed that can do all these and more, although perhaps less efficiently compared with the highly specialized thermal transfer model. There is no clear preference for one kind of model over the other. A model for simulating the reentry orbit of a space shuttle should probably be extremely specialized. A model used for the design of buildings may, on the other hand, be more general and open-ended.

Variety and open-endedness can be accommodated if a distinction is made between the *core* of the model and the *applications* that use it; a generalized core could support numerous specialized applications (Figure 3). This way, neither the core nor the applications need to be overly compromised. Moreover, more applications can be easily added, and old ones can be replaced with new, improved applications. For example, a core model could contain all the information about a building, such as its geometry, materials, and site conditions. Specific applications could then be added to support energy analysis, structural analysis, habitability, and cost estimation. Each of the added applications would find the information it requires in the core model, which is essentially a superset of the information required by all applications. Furthermore, various applications can be developed by specialists within their respective disciplines and interfaced with the core model, creating an integrated CAD system.

The separation of the core model from applications that use it relies on the ability to find some common denominator for both operandi and operators among different tasks. For example, *lines* can be used to represent building floor plans, integrated circuits, and machine parts. Their particular use for any one of these tasks requires higher levels of data structures and operators, such as the

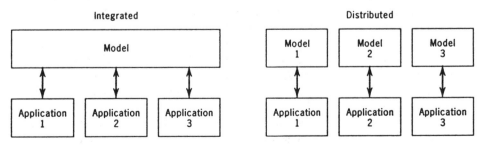

Figure 3. Integrated versus distributed models.

cost of building parts, properties of electrical components, or manufacturability constraints. Yet, the basic structures for representing line segments and the operators that create, modify, and display them on the screen are the same. Different core models may still be needed when no such common denominator can be found between the applications. For example, the line-based model will not be suitable for weather forecasting applications or for predicting the behavior of the stock market.

In this book we focus on the core model, particularly of the type used to represent physical artifacts and environments. What are its properties? How are such models built?

☐ PROPERTIES OF MODELS

In order to facilitate the symbolic representation and manipulation of real-world artifacts and environments in the computer's memory, a model must have the following four properties:

1. Well-formedness
2. Generality
3. Completeness
4. Efficiency

Well-formedness is the property that guarantees the correspondence between the model and the physical or abstract object it represents. The Klein bottle (Figure 4) is an example of an ill-formed model, because the entity it represents cannot be realized in the physical world.

Generality is the property that makes the model capable of representing a wide variety of objects. A model capable of representing only two-dimensional shapes, for example, has limited generality, because it cannot be used for modeling volumetric objects. A model that is capable of representing volumetric forms, but only ones bounded by planar surfaces, cannot be used in the automotive or aerospace industries.

Completeness is the property that makes the model useful for many applications, because each supported application can find all the data it requires in the model, either explicitly or implicitly (through computation). If, for example, the model represents all the geometric properties of a building but none of its material properties, it cannot support energy analysis or cost estimation.

Efficiency is the property that enables a model to be implemented in a computer using a reasonable amount of resources (time and space). If a model is well-formed, general, and complete but takes 20 minutes to answer a query, its usefulness is very much in doubt.

A model possessing all these qualities is, perhaps, impossible to achieve, because some of the desired properties conflict with others. In particular, *generality* is often difficult to reconcile with *efficiency* and with *completeness*. To

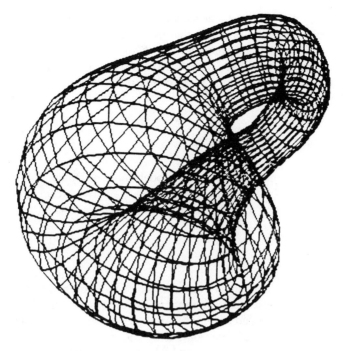

Figure 4. The Klein Bottle—an unrealizable shape.

achieve generality, a model must be simple, resorting to the least common denominator between its applications. This simplicity, in turn, reduces the efficiency of the model, because the semantic expressiveness of each element will be limited. A model consisting of line segments, for example, could be used to represent many artifacts, such as walls of a building or logic gates in an integrated circuit. However, the limited semantic meaning that can be derived from line segments makes this model inefficient when energy analysis of buildings is contemplated, which relies on the representation of walls as objects possessing material attributes and three-dimensional geometries. Likewise, the model will not be able to support logic simulation when it is used to represent an integrated circuit, because the lines cannot be automatically interpreted as logic gates. Both of these diverse applications could benefit from more sophisticated symbolic representation of the objects they deal with, but such higher level representation will prohibit the use of a single model for supporting both applications.

The quality most commonly compromised by models is, therefore, *generality*. Models that can represent logic gates of an integrated circuit, for example, cannot be used to represent walls and spaces in a building and vice versa unless the *completeness* requirement is relaxed for both applications.

The decision of which requirements should be relaxed and by how much makes the development of well-balanced models a difficult task, with significant ramifications. Not only do these decisions affect the complexity and efficiency of the applications that will use the model, but once developed and used for some applications, the model is extremely difficult to modify and fix, unless all the applications that use it are fixed as well. In contrast, the modification of a single application is a relatively simple task, compared with the modification of the core model itself.

□ MODELING TECHNIQUES

Two techniques can make the design of models more tractable: *data abstraction* and *hierarchical structuring.* These techniques are derived from research in the design of programming languages in particular and software engineering in general.

Data Abstraction

A model for representing some reality consists of an appropriate *data structure* capable of symbolically representing that reality in the computer's memory, and *operators* to manipulate and access that data. Together, the data structure and the operators constitute what has come to be known as an *abstract data type.* It is analogous to data types provided by high-level programming languages such as Pascal. For example, the data type INTEGER in Pascal stores whole numbers such as 15, but not 15.0. An integral part of this type definition is a set of operators to manipulate the stored integers. These operators allow the programmer to create, modify, access, and delete integers while guaranteeing the semantic integrity of the data. They include such operators as assignment, addition, substraction, and multiplication, but not division, which given two integer operandi might produce a value of type REAL. Instead, Pascal provides operators that are specific to the type INTEGER, called DIV and MOD, which perform a function similar to division but their product is guaranteed to be an integer number. DIV and MOD are, therefore, part of the INTEGER type definition in Pascal.

The operators that are provided with the model to create, modify, access, and delete the data are the only legal means to operate on that data, because their use guarantees the data will indeed correspond to the simulated reality.

Hierarchical Structuring

Hierarchical structuring is a technique used for developing large and complex software systems. By using this technique it is possible to develop low, intermediate, and high-level operators that rely on lower levels in the hierarchy. By developing a low-level "tool kit" of operators that are complete and robust, higher level operators become easier to develop. In most cases, the low-level operators are responsible for the creation of primitive data entities, their deletion, and the addition (or removal) of components in existing entities. The arithmetic operators of addition and subtraction can be considered such low-level operators. High-level operators use various combinations of low-level operators to perform more complex functions. They are, nevertheless, relieved from the need to know the specific details of how the low-level operators work, and in many cases even the detailed structure of the data itself. Multiplication and division can be considered such high-level operators; they use addition and subtraction as their primitives. Exponentiation can be considered an even higher level operator; it uses multiplication and division as its own primitives.

The hierarchical structuring technique makes development of models easier, enhances their integrity, promotes their conciseness, and most important, promotes the independence of operators in different layers. An operator in any layer may be modified, as long as this change does not affect other operators. Even the structure of the data itself may be modified, affecting only the lowest level of operators that manipulate it directly. An example to such layering is the ability of most software systems to run on many different computers, because the so-called "device drivers," which are specific to each hardware, have been put in a layer all by themselves and can easily be replaced by another set of drivers.

□ BIBLIOGRAPHY

Akin, O., "Representation and Architecture," in *Representation and Architecture,* Akin and Weinel, eds., Information Dynamics Inc., Silver Spring, MD, 1982.

Bronowski, J., *The Origins of Knowledge and Imagination,* Yale University Press, New Haven, CT, 1978.

Coons, S. A., "Computer-Aided Design," *Design Quarterly,* pp. 7–14, December 1966.

Cox, B. J., *Object Oriented Programming,* Addison-Wesley, Reading, MA, 1987.

Minsky, M., *The Society of Mind,* Simon and Schuster, New York, 1986.

Negroponte, N., *Soft Architecture Machines,* MIT Press, Cambridge, MA, 1975.

Schon, D. A., *The Reflective Practitioner,* Basic Books, New York, 1983.

Sutherland, I., "Sketchpad—A Man-Machine Graphical Communication System," Technical Report #296, Lincoln Laboratory, Massachusetts Institute of Technology, Cambridge, MA, 1963.

PART ONE

2D CONSTRUCTION

1

MODELING SHAPES

The shapes that artifacts assume are, in most cases, their most important design parameter. The shape not only determines how an artifact looks, but also forms the basis for many of its other properties. Shape information is difficult to model computationally because it consists of many intricately connected symbols. This chapter establishes the two classes of shapes we will be concerned with throughout the book and the properties of their representation and manipulation: *polygons*, which are area-enclosing shapes, and *solids*, which are volume-enclosing shapes. In modeling such shapes, we shall distinguish between their *topology*, which defines the components used to make shapes and the relationships between them, and *geometry*, which defines the placement of these components in the space embedding the shape.

Instead of attempting to represent the infinite number of points from which shapes can be thought to be made—a task that can only be accomplished if a crude sampling technique (called *spatial enumeration*) is used—we shall model only the *boundary* of shapes, which under certain conditions (which we will call *well-formedness conditions*) is sufficient to represent the shape itself. We shall develop operators to *construct* symbol structure that represent shapes, *place* them in space, and *associate* them with other (nonshape) attributes, as well as with other shapes.

☐ THE NATURE OF SHAPES

The design of most artifacts is a process that employs different symbolic representations (in various levels of abstraction) of the emerging product, for the purpose of exploring and communicating the designers' intentions to clients and to craftsmen. For example, sketches are used in early phases of the design process to capture ideas. They are developed into volumetric models and later elaborated in annotated and symbol-laden, two-dimensional drawings. Specifications are added to explain nongraphical aspects of the designed artifact and to convey instructions about the fabrication or construction processes.

Predominant among these symbolic representations is the *shape* that the artifact will assume when it is built or manufactured. Although shape is only one the many attributes possessed by artifacts, it is, in many cases, the most important one and the most difficult attribute to represent and manipulate by computational means.

Shape information is different from all other attributes of objects. Not only does it determine how an object appears to the observer, but shape properties also determine most of its functional performances, such as stability and habitability. The specification of the particular shape an object must take, such that it will respond to multiple performance criteria, is, therefore, fundamental to the design of most physical artifacts. Much effort has been devoted to computationally aiding the design of shapes. In fact, the modeling of shapes and their properties comprises a significant branch of computer-aided design known as *geometric modeling*.

Shape information is complex and verbose, and its various components are thoroughly interdependent. It is, therefore, not surprising that *geometry* and *topology*, the components of shape information, have been the subject of study by mathematicians and engineers throughout history. Euclid, Pythagoras, Archimedes, Euler, Möbius, Polya, and Lakatos are but few of the great names associated with the study of shapes. The complexity and the intricacy of shape information was reaffirmed when computers were applied to their modeling. The amount of data needed to adequately model even modest shapes exceeds disproportionally the amount of data needed for modeling most other properties. Even nonredundant representation of shape information may require thousands of bits of data. For example, a hexahedron (a rectangular box) requires, for its complete and explicit representation, 26 topological elements (6 faces, 12 edges, and 8 vertices) and at least another 24 geometric elements (the three-dimensional cartesian coordinates of each vertex). In addition, a complex network of links between the elements must be carefully maintained to ensure that the collection of faces, edges, and vertices will enclose a volume (Figure 1.1). The high interdependency of its elements makes shape manipulation an intricate and subtle task. For example, if one face of the hexahedron is moved, the adjacent faces, edges, and vertices must be adjusted accordingly, to maintain closure. The shape of a building is made of many thousands of such hexahedrons and of more complex shapes, making its computational modeling a formidable task.

□ TYPES OF SHAPES

There are many different types of shapes. In this book we shall be concerned with modeling *rigid* shapes: shapes whose proportions, angles, and size are independent of the shape's location and orientation in space. Thermodynamics, on the other hand, deals with nonrigid shapes, such as gases and liquids. Further-

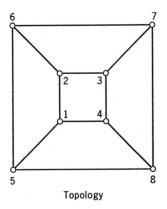
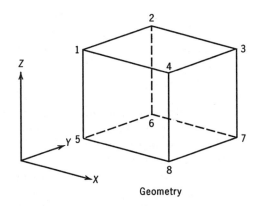

Topology   Geometry

Figure 1.1. The topological and geometric properties of a hexahedron.

more, we are interested in particular classes of rigid shapes that bound an *area* or a *volume*. Thus, we exclude from consideration such shapes as symbols (characters, electrical symbols, etc.). Area and volume enclosures give shapes a much richer meaning compared with shapes that lack these properties. It enables them to be used for the purpose of calculating physical phenomena, such as area and volume themselves, moment of inertia, and so on. These calculations can later be used, in conjunction with other attributes, to compute the weight, the thermal conductivity, and other object-specific information, as well as to derive inter-object information, such as spatial interferences and collisions in space.

In two dimensions we will be concerned with a class of formal shapes known as *polygons*, and in three dimensions, with shapes known as *solids*. The area- and volume-enclosing properties of polygons and solids make them particularly suitable for representing designed artifacts, whether architectural or mechanical. Of particular interest is that polygons and solids are not independent types of shapes; under certain conditions, assemblies of polygons in three-dimensional space can be (and often are) used to represent the boundary of solids. Many operations that we may wish to perform on solids, such as graphic display, sectioning, and shadow casting, are operations that involve polygons. It is not surprising, therefore, that many of the principles of modeling shapes are shared by both polygons and solids, and in many instances we can make direct inferences from one to the other. It is also obvious that solids encompass a much richer domain of rules and operations than do polygons because of their additional degree of dimensional complexity.

□ PROPERTIES OF SHAPES

Shapes share several universal properties that are applicable to the definition of all shapes, whether a building, a process plant, a machine part, or molded plastic consumer product. The first of these properties is *geometry*, which concerns the relative placement of points within the shape or its embedding environment. The other property is *topology*. It concerns the adjacency relationships between the elements of a shape. For example, a cube made of rubber could be inflated into a ball. Its geometry would change, but not its topology; the adjacency relationships between its edges, faces, and vertices (its boundary elements), and between the points that make up its interior, remain the same as before. Topology and geometry, nevertheless, are not completely independent of each other; at the limits, a change in geometry may cause a change in topology. For example, both the geometry and topology of the inflated rubber cube would be affected at the point of rupture. Interestingly, when modeling shapes, the data structure can typically rigorously represent the topology, because it deals explicitly with *relationships*. Geometry, on the other hand, is represented by the *values* assigned to various components of the data structure. Obviously, to completely represent a shape, both topology and geometry must be modeled, because one cannot be deduced from the other (Figure 1.2).

Computer-aided design systems must, therefore, be capable of symbolically representing shapes and be able to operate on these symbol structures. The symbol structures must be concise, so they fit within the constraints of computing resources, and must correspond to the physical objects they represent uniquely, unambiguously, and correctly. The operators that are applied to the symbol structures must not destroy this correspondence and must facilitate the generation, modification, and deletion of the represented shapes.

☐ THE MODELING OF SHAPES

The problem in modeling shapes arises from the very definition of the concept of *shape*. The most general, formal definition of a shape is a set of contiguous points in two- or in three-dimensional Euclidean space. For computational purposes, this point set must be represented mathematically by means of some symbol structures. It is quite obvious that such a computational symbolic structure could not be simply constructed by representing each and every one of the points in the Euclidean space that belongs to the represented shape. Instead, some abstraction must be employed, which will enable a finite symbol structure to represent an infinitely large set of points. What are the properties such a symbol structure must have in order to suit geometric modeling? Are there different ways of representing shapes? If so, are there some that are better than others? Let us first enumerate the properties such representations must have, then examine possible representation methods.

The Properties of Shape-Representing Symbol Structures

The rules underlying the symbolic representation of real-world objects and phenomena are typically defined by sets of mathematical properties known as *well-formedness conditions*. They comprise the set of semantic integrity constraints

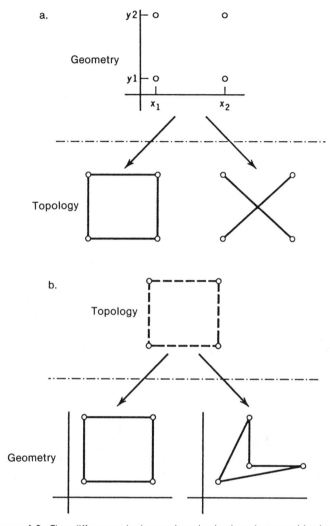

Figure 1.2. The difference between topological and geometrical properties.

that provide a basis for making assertions about the validity of the model at various stages of its manipulation.

The mathematical properties regarding the well-formed representation of shapes are defined in general topology and homology theory. They have been reformulated and adapted for solid modeling by Eastman and Preiss; Requicha; and Baer, Eastman, and Henrion (see bibliography at the end of this chapter).

To be considered well-formed, a computational symbol structure must have the following properties:

1. It must comprise a finite subset of the Euclidean two- or three-dimensional space, such that any given point in those spaces can be identified

unambiguously as being part of that subset or not (i.e., inside or outside the represented shape).

2. Points in the subset must be connected by a path comprising only points which belong to the subset itself (i.e., the represented shape may not comprise isolated points or multiple separate point sets).

3. The symbol structure must be constructed over a finite (digital) alphabet.

The first property is known as *solidity*. It supports the (computational) distinction between the *interior* of the represented shape and its *exterior*, such that it is possible to tell those points that belong to the shape from those points that do not. The second property in known as *continuity*. It excludes from consideration symbol structures that allow disconnected shapes. In addition, the symbol structure must be concise enough to allow its storage and manipulation by reasonable computing resources. It must, therefore, have the third property: *finite describability*.

Methods of Representation

Two major methods have, so far, been developed, which comply with the listed properties. They are known as spatial occupancy enumeration and boundary representation.

Spatial occupancy enumeration is a rather literal representation of shapes defined as sets of points in two- or in three-dimensional space. This method imposes a grid on the represented space and uses a symbol structure that lists all the cells in that grid occupied by the object (Figure 1.3). These cells are usually squares or cubes of a fixed size. The grid they belong to is known as a *spatial array*. This representation has two important advantages: it allows easy spatial addressing (accessing a given point in space), and it assures spatial uniqueness (no two objects can occupy the same space at the same time). It also has two grave shortcomings: it lacks object coherence (there is no explicit relationship between the points of an object), and it is extremely expensive in terms of storage space, because it is highly redundant—any cell is likely to have the same state of occupancy (inside or outside the object) as the cells adjacent to it. Only at the boundaries of the shape is this not so.

The *boundary representation* method recognizes this likelihood and uses a symbol structure that represents explicitly only the boundary of shapes (Figure 1.4). This boundary, which must be closed and must not self-intersect, partitions the points of the space in which the shape is embedded into ones internal to the represented shape and ones that are external to it. Although this method is much more concise than the first one in terms of the storage space it requires, it is more difficult to construct, manipulate, and query, because the enclosed area or volume is represented by inference rather than directly, as by the spatial enumeration method.

The verbosity of the spatial enumeration method, however, limits the number of cells that can be used for the purpose of representing shapes and, conse-

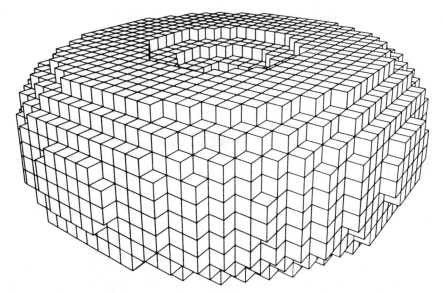

Figure 1.3. The spatial enumeration method of representing shapes. "Blocked Puzzle" approximation to a doughnut by A. J. H. Christensen from ACM SIGGRAPH '80 Conference Proceedings. Courtesy of the Association for Computing Machinery.

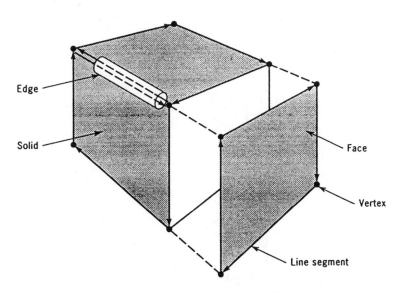

Figure 1.4. The boundary representation method of shapes.

quently, the accuracy of the representation. It is used, therefore, for applications that require only limited object resolution, such as tomography, or for modeling digitally acquired images, where the resolution of the shape is compromised to begin with. In this book we shall use the boundary representation method, which can support the design of complex and potentially large artifacts at a high degree of accuracy.

□ MANIPULATING SHAPE REPRESENTATIONS

To reflect the temporal and transient nature of design processes, symbol structures representing real-world objects must be operated upon by the modeling system in ways that transform them into representations of new (or different) object, as the design process unfolds. This can be accomplished by the following three classes of operations (Figure 1.5):

1. Operations that *construct* new shapes, by combining or subdividing the basic building blocks that comprise shape information (e.g., points and lines) into area- or volume-enclosing structures (e.g., polygons and solids)

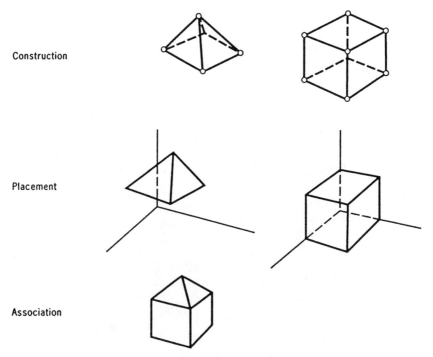

Figure 1.5. Classes of shape-manipulating operations.

and by combining existing shapes through Boolean operations (union, intersection, and difference) into more complex shapes

2. Operations that *place* shapes in two- or three-dimensional space, through translation, rotation, and scaling

3. Operations that *associate* shapes to form assemblies of interrelated shapes

In order to provide modeling capabilities for shapes of every type, we must construct suitable data structures, operators that manipulate shapes in meaningful ways, and user interfaces to access the operators and to apply them to the desired shapes. Although implementations differ widely, some principles and techniques have become common practices. For example, the topology of shapes is commonly represented by the structure of the data, in terms of the records it is made of and the links between them. The geometry of shapes is commonly represented by the values stored in these records, in the form of Cartesian coordinates. In the following chapters, we discuss the data structures, the operators, and the user interfaces for each type of operator, starting our discussion with polygons and proceeding to solids.

☐ BIBLIOGRAPHY

Baer, A., C. Eastman, and M. Henrion, "Geometric Modeling: A Survey," *Computer-Aided Design* **11**(5):253–272, September 1979.

Eastman, C. M., and K. Preiss, "A Review of Solid Shape Modeling Based on Integrity Verification," *Computer-Aided Design,* **16**(2):66–80, March 1984.

Giblin, P. J., *Graphs, Surfaces, and Homology,* Chapman and Hall/Halsted Press, New York, 1977.

Requicha, A. A. G., "Representations for Rigid Solids: Theory and Systems," *Computing Surveys* **12**(4):437–464, December 1980.

2

THE PROPERTIES
OF POLYGONS

A polygon consists of an infinite number of points bounded in some finite, continuous region of a two-dimensional space. To be modeled computationally, this infinite point set must be represented by a finite, one-dimensional symbol structure. The *principle of reduced dimensionality* is employed to represent the area by its *boundary,* subject to certain well-formedness conditions. These conditions include *closedness, non-self-intersection,* and *orientability.* Given a polygonal boundary comprising a circuit of alternating *segments* and *vertices,* which abides by the well-formedness conditions, it is possible to compute the area of the polygon (and from it deduce whether the boundary encloses the polygon itself or one of its holes). It is also possible to determine whether any given point of the two-dimensional space in which the polygon is embedded is inside the region bounded by the polygon or outside it.

☐ THE DEFINITION OF POLYGONS

A polygon can be defined as *a finite, contiguous region in some two-dimensional Euclidean space (E2).* Accordingly, a polygon comprises a bounded set of infinitely many contiguous points that lie in that space. These points can be distinguished from other points in the same space that are not part of the polygon. Although the number of points forming the polygon is infinite, they are "packed" in a finite region of E2. The finiteness of such a region, which is a property known as *boundedness,* means that we can literally draw a closed line around the points that comprise the polygon, which will have some finite length. We refer to this line as the *boundary* of the polygon. A polygon may have more than one boundary if it contains holes (Figure 2.1).

The *contiguity* property, which has been mentioned in the definition, ensures that the points comprising the bounded region are connected. More formally, we say that *there exists a path between any two points that are part of the polygon,*

Figure 2.1. A polygon is a bounded set of points in two-dimensional space.

which is made exclusively of points that are themselves part of the polygon (Figure 2.2). This property excludes shapes having isolated "islands" from being considered a single polygon. It also establishes exactly *one* of the boundaries of the polygon as the outermost, "exterior" boundary, which contains all its other boundaries (if there are any). Consequently, all holes can be treated equally (i.e., there are no holes that contain an exterior boundary of the same polygon or contain other holes of the same polygon).

□ THE PRINCIPLE OF REDUCED DIMENSIONALITY

How can we translate this abstract definition of a polygon into a form that can be represented in the computer's memory? More specifically, how can a two-dimensional entity (an area), which comprises an infinite number of points, be represented by a one-dimensional (sequential), finite symbol structure? The answer lies in applying *the principle of reduced dimensionality,* which, as we shall see throughout this book, plays a central role in geometric modeling.

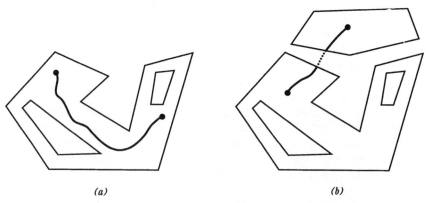

(a)   *(b)*

Figure 2.2. The area bounded by a polygon is contiguous: (a) A path exists between any two points in the polygon; (b) a path cannot connect points in isolated regions.

The principle of reduced dimensionality states, among other things, that *many geometric problems of a similar nature can be solved more easily in spaces of lower dimensions than in higher ones.* For example, it is easier to determine whether a point is part of a line in the one-dimensional Euclidean space (E1), than to determine whether it is part of a polygon in the two-dimensional Euclidean space (E2). Similarly, it is easier to determine whether a point is part of a polygon in E2 than whether it is part of a solid in three-dimensional Euclidean space (E3). This principle applies also to the representation of the shapes themselves. For example, it is easier to represent a bounded line segment by its two end points, a polygon by its bounding line segments, and a solid by its bounding surfaces, than attempt to represent them directly.

Yet, because dimensionality reduction involves loss of the information carried by the higher dimension, any attempt to apply it requires augmentation of the dimensionally reduced representation by additional constraints. For example, if a bounded line segment is to be represented by its end points, it must be straight. If a polygon is to be represented by its bounding line segments, these segments must comprise a closed circuit and must not self-intersect. If a solid is to be represented by its bounding surface, this surface must be bounded, non-self-intersecting, and consistently orientable. We call these constraints *well-formedness conditions.* They define the semantic integrity rules by which both operandi and operators must abide.

In addition to well-formedness conditions, the application of the principle also requires a particular *semantic interpretation* of the results. For example, there must be an understanding that the two end points of a bounded line segment represent all the (infinitely many) points that belong to that line segment, that a circuit of non-self-intersecting line segments represents the area it encloses, and that a bounded, non-self-intersecting and consistently orientable surface represents the volume it bounds. More formally, there must exist a *unique and unambiguous interpretation* of the dimensionally reduced model, along with its well-formedness conditions, in order for it to represent some higher dimensional entity.

□ THE PROPERTIES OF POLYGONAL BOUNDARIES

The principle of reduced dimensionality, when applicable, allows us to reduce the complexity of a problem by representing it in simpler terms. The two-dimensional area that constitutes a polygon can thus be represented by its one-dimensional boundary, if the representation of the boundary meets the following three well-formedness conditions:

1. The boundary is closed.
2. It does not self-intersect.
3. It is orientable in some consistent way.

The first condition guarantees that the region of the two-dimensional space enclosed by the boundary of a polygon is finite. The second condition guarantees that this region is contiguous. The third condition allows us to distinguish between the area of the polygon itself and the area outside it, using the boundary as the sole data. Compliance of the polygonal boundary model with these conditions guarantees its interpretability as a representation of some physical artifact, unlike those depicted in Figure 2.3.

Informally, the boundary of a polygon can be described as a one-dimensional shape made of line segments, joined at their end points, pairwise sequentially (Figure 2.4). Notice how in compliance with the first well-formedness condition the line segments form a *circuit*, otherwise they would not form a closed boundary. In compliance with the second well-formedness condition, the enclosed area is contiguous. The third well-formedness condition can be interpreted as an *ordering* imposed on the line segments that form this boundary.

We shall call the lines that compose the boundary *segments* and their endpoints *vertices*. Notice that the number of segments is equal to the number of vertices, a property that distinguishes a closed circuit from a sequence of segments and vertices that does not enclose an area.

This terminology (segments and vertices), and the well-formedness conditions, can be used to construct a more formal definition of the polygonal boundary:

A polygonal boundary is a circuit of n vertices, V_1, V_2, V_3 . . . V_n, joined pairwise sequentially by *line segments*, such that the last vertex is joined with the first one:

$$G_1 = (V_1 V_2), G_2 = (V_2 V_3) \ldots G_n = (V_n V_1)$$

The geometry associated with the segments of a polygonal boundary may consist of straight or curved lines. For the sake of simplicity and clarity, in this book

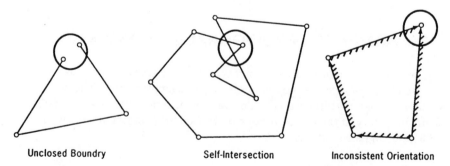

Unclosed Boundry   Self-Intersection   Inconsistent Orientation

Figure 2.3. Ill-formed polygonal boundaries destroy the model's ability to represent physical (realizable) artifacts.

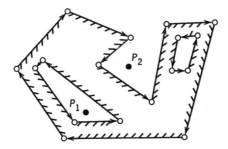

Figure 2.4. The polygonal boundary is made of closed, ordered sequences of alternating segments and vertices.

we shall generally restrict our discussion to straight lines that lie in one plane. The principles of polygon modeling are, nevertheless, extendable over curved lines and nonplanar shapes.

Given that the elements forming the boundary of a polygon are segments and vertices, the three well-formedness conditions can be restated as a set of well-formedness rules:

1. *Closure:* Every segment must be adjacent to exactly two vertices, and every vertex must be adjacent to exactly two segments.
2. *Non-self-intersection:* Adjacent segments may intersect only at vertices, and nonadjacent segments may not intersect at all.
3. *Orientability:* Segments must be directed, and their direction must be consistent.

Compliance with the first rule ensures that all segments are connected at both their vertices to other segments and that no more than two segments meet at any vertex. Compliance with this rule also guarantees that there are no "dangling" segments or vertices (i.e., not attached to other segments or vertices). Compliance with the second rule, coupled with the first one, ensures that nonadjacent segments do not intersect. Compliance with the third rule ensures that segments have a sense of direction and that this direction is consistent for all segments of the polygonal boundary and for all the boundaries of a polygon. By traversing the segments in the given direction, all the segments of one boundary are "visited" exactly once. Furthermore, during such traversal the "inside" of the polygon will always be on the same side of the traversed segments. The particular orientation is not important as long as it is maintained consistently. In this book we use the "right-hand" rule for orientation, which can be viewed as clockwise orientation in the two-dimensional Euclidean space: if someone were to "walk" on the segments facing their given direction, the "inside" of the polygon will always be on the person's right, as shown in Figure 2.4.

The closure and non-self-intersection properties imply that a polygonal boundary partitions the two-dimensional space in which it is embedded into *at least two* well-defined regions, *exactly one* of which is *inside* the polygon and the others are *outside* it. This partitioning is the primary reason for our interest in polygons (and later in solids), because it enables them to model physical entities.

The compliance of the polygonal boundary with the well-formedness rules enables us to use it to distinguish between the area which is inside the polygon and the rest of the two-dimensional space in which the polygon is embedded. Typically, we denote the enclosed area as "positive" and the areas outside the polygon as "negative."

The orientation of the boundary also facilitates representation of polygons with holes. Such polygons are enclosed by more than one boundary, as depicted by Figure 2.4. Using the right-hand rule, it is easy to verify that the orientation of the boundary of holes is *opposite* to that of the exterior boundary of the polygon. For example, if the exterior boundary is oriented clockwise with respect to point P_1 in Figure 2.4, then the orientation of the hole's boundary surrounding point P_1 is counterclockwise.

The terms "clockwise" and "counterclockwise" are not well suited for the purposes of modeling polygons, as can be readily seen in the case of point P_2 in Figure 2.4. A much more suitable distinction between the exterior boundary of a polygon and the boundaries of its holes can be established by means of *area calculation:* the area enclosed by the exterior boundary of a polygon is always positive; the areas enclosed by the boundaries of its holes, on the other hand, are negative. Accordingly, we shall henceforth designate the exterior boundary as *positive* and all hole boundaries as *negative*.

☐ CALCULATING THE AREA OF A BOUNDARY-REPRESENTED POLYGON

The area enclosed by a polygonal boundary can be computed as the sum of the areas of the triangles it comprises. Triangles can be defined when the vertices of the polygonal boundary are paired sequentially with an arbitrary reference point in the plane. That is, we may take any point in the plane and construct line segments between it and every vertex of the polygon's boundary (one boundary at a time). The area of the polygonal boundary is the sum of the areas of all clockwise triangles, less the areas of all counterclockwise triangles, when the orientations are defined by taking one segment of the polygonal boundary at a time, in clockwise order (Figure 2.5).

The area of each triangle can be derived from the determinant of the matrix formed by its three vertex coordinates, divided by two:

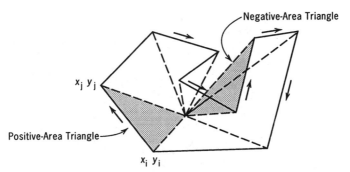

Figure 2.5. Triangulation of a polygonal boundary for the purpose of computing the area its encloses.

$$\frac{\det}{2} \begin{bmatrix} x_1 & y_1 & 1 \\ x_2 & y_2 & 1 \\ x_3 & y_3 & 1 \end{bmatrix} = (x_1*y_2 + x_3*y_1 + x_2*y_3) - (x_3*y_2 + x_2*y_1 + x_1*y_3)/2$$
$$= (x_1 - x_3)*(y_2 - y_3) + (x_2 - x_3)*(y_3 - y_1)/2.$$

An algorithm to compute the area enclosed by polygonal boundaries (both convex and concave ones) can be further simplified if the point of reference is taken to be the origin of the coordinate axes. This choice simplifies the computation, because one of the terms in the determinant is 0:

$$\frac{\det}{2} \begin{bmatrix} x_i & y_i & 1 \\ x_j & y_j & 1 \\ 0 & 0 & 1 \end{bmatrix} = (x_i*y_j + 0*y_i + x_j*0) - (0*y_j + x_j*y_i + x_i*0)/2$$
$$= (x_i*y_j - x_j*y_i)/2.$$

The algorithm can be embedded in a simple Pascal program, after a means for representing the polygonal boundary has been chosen. For the purposes of demonstrating this algorithm we use an array to represent a polygonal boundary of n vertices, where each vertex is a point in the two-dimensional Euclidean space:

```
coords  = (x,y);
point   = array [coords] of real;
polygon = array [1..n] of point;  {n is an integer}
```

Function POLY_AREA can then be written to compute the area enclosed by a given polygonal boundary P.

```
function poly_area (p : polygon) : real;
{Compute the area bounded by the polygonal boundary represented
 by P. A positive area signifies that the boundary encloses
 the polygon itself. A negative area signifies that it bounds a
 hole.}

var   i,j : 1..n;
      a   : real;

begin
  a := 0;  {initialize area summation}
  for i := 1 to n do  {loop through all segments}
    begin
      j := (i mod n) + 1;  {index of next vertex}
      a := a + (p[i,x]*p[j,y]) - (p[j,x]*p[i,y])
    end;
  poly_area := a/2
end;  {poly_area function}
```

☐ POINT-IN POLYGON INCLUSION TEST

Determining whether an arbitrary point in the plane is part of the polygon or is not is known as the "point in polygon" or the "containment" test. Like the area calculation, it relies on closure, non-self-intersection, and orientation properties of the polygonal boundary. Three methods can be used to determine the containment condition of a given point in the plane with respect to a polygon represented through its boundaries (Figure 2.6).

If the polygon is known to be convex,† the coordinates of the point can be substituted in the line equation underlying each segment bounding the polygon. If the signs of all such substitutions are the same, the point is inside the polygon, otherwise it is outside it (given that the coefficients of all line equations have been chosen in a consistent manner).

If the polygon is not known to be convex, one of two other methods must be employed. One is based on determining the parity of the number of intersections between the polygon and a ray extending from the test point to infinity. The point is deemed "outside" the polygon if the number of intersections is *even* because, for each outside-in transition of the ray, there exists an inside-out transition. The point is deemed "inside" the polygon if the number of intersections is *odd,* which indicates that there is one outside-in transition less than inside-out transitions.

---

†A polygon is said to be *convex* if any straight line intersects it in, at most, one continuous segment of that line.

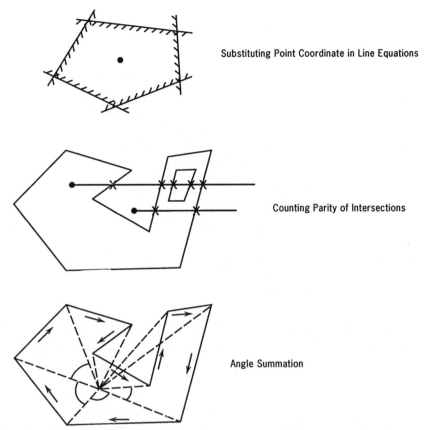

Substituting Point Coordinate in Line Equations

Counting Parity of Intersections

Angle Summation

Figure 2.6. Three methods for determining the containment of a point in a boundary-represented polygon.

The other method that is applicable to general polygons is based on computing the sum of the angles subtended by each segment bounding the polygon, as seen from the point being tested for containment. This sum is always an integer multiple of 2π, the multiple being, in fact, the *wrap-number* of the point (i.e., the number of times the point is encircled by the boundary of the polygon). The point is deemed "inside" the polygon if the wrap number is not zero; otherwise it is deemed "outside."

All these methods can be extended to handle polygons that include holes by simply repeating the test and correlating the results of each test for all boundaries (i.e., a point that is "inside" a hole is, of course, outside the polygon).

The Pascal function POINT_IN_POLYGON demonstrates an implementation of the angle-summation method discussed above, using the former array-based polygon representation. It uses the functions THETA and ANGLE to calculate the angles themselves.

```
function theta (pi,pj : point) : real;
{Compute the angle between the line segment defined by [pi,pj]
 and the positive x axis.}

const radians = 0.0174532925; {conversion factor}

var t     : real;
    dx,dy : integer;

begin
  dx := pj[x] - pi[x]; dy := pj[y] - pi[y];
  if dx = 0
    then t := 90*radians
    else t := arctan(dy/dx);
  if (dx < 0) or ((dx = 0) and (dy < 0))
    then theta := t + 180*radians
    else if dy < 0
      then theta := t + 360*radians
      else theta := t
end; {of theta function}

function angle (p1,p2,p3 : point) : real;
{Compute the angle from the line defined by points [p1,p2] to
 the line defined by points [p1,p3]. The lines intersect at p1.}

var t1,t2 : real;

begin
  t1 := theta(p1,p2);
  t2 := theta(p1,p3);
  angle := t1 - t2
end; {angle function}

function point_in_polygon (pnt : point;
                             p : polygon) : boolean;
{Return true if point pnt is inside polygon p. Use the angle
 summation method. Points on the boundary of the polygon are
 considered to be outside.}

var a   : real;
    i,j : 1..n; {n is global number of vertices}

begin
  a := 0;  {initialize angle}
  for i := 1 to n do  {loop through all segments}
    begin
      j := (i mod n) + 1;  {index of next vertex}
      a := a + angle (pnt, p[i], p[j])
    end;
```

```
if a = 0
  then point_in_polygon := false
  else point_in_polygon := true
end;  {point_in_polygon function}
```

☐ BIBLIOGRAPHY

Barton, E. E., and I. Buchanan, "The Polygon Package," *Computer-Aided Design,* **12**(1):3–11, January 1980.

Bentley, J. L., and W. Carruthers, "Algorithms for Testing the Inclusion of Points in Polygons," *Proceedings of the ACM's 18th Annual Allerton Conference on Communications, Control, and Computing,* 1980.

Kalay, Y. E., "Determining the Spatial Containment of a Point in General Polyhedra," *Computer Graphics and Image Processing,* **19**:303–334, 1982.

Lee, D. T., and F. P. Preparata, "Location of a Point in a Planar Subdivision and Its Applications," *SIAM Journal of Computing,* **6**(3):594–606, September 1977.

Shamos, I. M., and F. Preparata, *Computational Geometry,* Springer Verlag, New York, 1985.

3

THE REPRESENTATION
OF POLYGONS

How can the abstract definition of a polygonal boundary as discussed in Chapter 2, together with its associated well-formedness rules, be translated into a computational model? We must construct a *data structure* capable of representing polygonal boundaries and a set of *operators* to manipulate this structure in a manner that will comply with the well-formedness rules. Together, the data structure and the operators constitute an *abstract data type,* which we shall call a "polygon," and we shall use it for the purpose of *modeling* polygons. This chapter discusses several of the many possible ways in which the data structure for representing polygonal boundaries can be constructed. The following chapters discuss the operators for manipulating that data structure.

□ THE DUALITY OF VERTICES AND SEGMENTS

The boundaries of a polygon consist of two types of elements: segments and vertices. Therefore, the topological and the geometrical information associated with them is redundant: the information associated with the segments can be computed from vertex information and vice versa. In other words, segments and vertices are *dual* to each other rather than complementary. This duality can be traced back to the very definition of a polygonal boundary: a circuit of *n* vertices connected by *n* segments.

This definition does not give preference to vertices over segments or vice versa. A polygon representation could, therefore, be constructed using either one as its basis, while the other would be computed from it when needed. As such, we can construct a *vertex-based* data structure or a *segment-based* data structure to represent polygons. Although these structures are theoretically interchangeable, the choice we make is of considerable consequence for developing the operators that will manipulate the polygon model. If we choose a vertex-based data structure, operators that require explicit segment information will be more difficult to develop. Such operators will also require more time to execute, compared with operators using a segment-based data structure, because segment information is not readily available for their use, but must be computed. On the other hand, a segment-based data structure will make operators that require explicit vertex information less efficient.

The duality of segments and vertices applies also to geometrical information. We can completely determine the geometry of a polygonal boundary (made of straight segments) given the locations of its vertices, because pairs of consecutive vertices can be used to compute the line equations of its segments. Similarly, given the line equation associated with each segment, we can compute the location of the vertices as intersections between pairs of adjacent segments.

In modeling polygons we will need both explicit vertex information and explicit segment information. A third approach, then, would be to represent explicitly both segments and vertices. While this hybrid approach will expedite queries—operations that use the polygon information for a variety of calculations (e.g., area and center of gravity)—it will slow down update operations that modify the polygon, because each operation will have to be applied to both segments and vertices. Moreover, the redundant information must be kept strictly consistent to avoid possible errors.

☐ POLYGON REPRESENTATIONS

To appreciate the inherent differences between these options, let us use a notation of alternating vertices and segments to represent a polygonal boundary, as depicted in Figure 3.1.

A vertex-based data structure will thus have the following form:

$$-V_1 - V_2 - V_3 - \ldots -V_n-$$

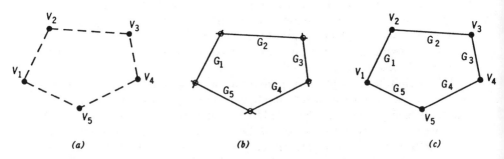

Figure 3.1. A polygonal boundary represented by (a) its vertices; (b) its segments; and (c) both its vertices and segments.

This structure can be implemented in Pascal by the following constructs:

```
vptr   = ^vertex;
vertex = record
              form  : point;
              vnext : vptr
            end;
```

where POINT is defined to consist of the following constructs:

```
coords = (x,y,z,w);
point  = array [coords] of real;
```

A segment, in this case, is represented implicitly by pairs of consecutive vertices:

$$G_i = [V_i, V_{i+1}] \qquad 1 \le i \le n.$$

(Note that $G_n = [V_n, V_1]$, because of the closure condition.)

A segment-based data structure can be similarly constructed, which will have the following form:

$$\text{-}G_1\text{—}G_2\text{—}G_3\text{-} \ldots \text{-}G_n\text{-}$$

This structure can be implemented in Pascal by the following constructs:

```
gptr    = ^segment;
segment = record
              form  : line;
              gnext : gptr
            end;
```

where LINE is a geometrical data structure, representing (in the parametric form $ax + by + c = 0$) the coefficients of the line equation that underlies the segment, and is defined as:

```
params = (a,b,c);
line   = array [params] of real;
```

(These and other geometric constructs, along with the operators that construct and manipulate them, are discussed in greater detail in Chapter 6).

A vertex, in this case, is represented implicitly by a pair of intersecting (adjacent) segments:

$$V_i = [G_i, G_{i+1}] \qquad 1 \leq i \leq n.$$

A hybrid segment-vertex data structure may have the following form:

$$
\begin{array}{cccc}
-G_1-G_2-G_3- & \ldots & -G_n- \\
| \quad | \quad | & & | \\
V_1 \quad V_2 \quad V_3 & & V_n
\end{array}
$$

This structure can be implemented in Pascal by the following constructs:

```
gptr     = ^segment;
vptr     = ^vertex;

segment = record
            form  : line;
            gnext : gptr;
            gvert : vptr
          end;

vertex  = record
            form  : point
          end;
```

To see the merits and drawbacks of each option, let us examine two operations that we will want to apply to polygons (and thus must manipulate the chosen data structure): PICK_VERTEX and PICK_SEGMENT.

These two operations are fundamental for interfacing between the designer and the model. Through them the designer can indicate which part of a polygon should be moved, deleted, or otherwise manipulated. PICK_VERTEX and PICK_SEGMENT are operators that search the database to find the vertex or the segment, respectively, that is closest to a given point which was indicated on the screen by the designer, as discussed in Chapter 30. The operators differ in the target of their search: PICK_VERTEX searches for a *vertex*, whereas PICK_SEGMENT searches for a *segment*. Both searches involve calculating the geometric proximity of the point indicated by the designer with all vertices or segments, respectively, in the database. PICK_VERTEX calculates the distance between that point and the location of each vertex, and PICK_SEGMENT calculates the distance of that point from the line equation associated with each segment. The relative efficiency of the searches and the calculation of distances depend on the particular data structure chosen for representing the polygons.

If a vertex-based data structure is chosen, PICK_VERTEX is easy to implement because the target of its search is explicitly represented. PICK_SEGMENT, on the other hand, is not; its target is implicit, represented only through pairs of adjacent vertices. Moreover, the geometry of the line that underlies the segment, to which the proximity of the point indicated by the user is measured, must be calculated for every search, a time-consuming effort, indeed.

If, instead, a segment-based data structure is chosen, the difficulties are reversed: PICK_SEGMENT is easy to implement, but PICK_VERTEX is not. Every vertex must be computed as the intersection of two adjacent segments.

If we choose the hybrid segment-vertex structure, then both vertex and segment data are readily available for the purposes of picking. However, their redundancy complicates the actual application of changes considerably. If the same geometric data are stored twice (once as vertex coordinates and once as line equations of the two adjacent segments), then both representations must be updated in a consistent manner.

In most respects, a vertex-based data structure is simpler to construct and manipulate than a segment-based data structure. Its most noticeable drawback, compared with the segment-based data structure, is its inability to accommodate polygons bounded by curves. If curvature is desired, then segments must be represented explicitly, and the choice of a suitable data structure includes only segment-based or hybrid segment-vertex representations.

☐ THE REPRESENTATION OF HOLES

Holes, as discussed in Chapter 2, are also considered polygonal boundaries. The only difference between them and the polygon's outermost boundary is their negative area. They can, therefore, be represented in the same way as the exterior boundary, provided their orientation is reversed to comply with the right-hand rule. Yet, to augment the data structure such that it can represent holes, we must add another record to represent the polygonal boundary as an entity in its own right and the means to connect polygonal boundaries in two-tier hierarchical structures. The following variant record is one possible way to link polygonal boundaries in two levels of nesting. The first tier represents the one and only exterior polygonal boundary, while the second tier represents a linked list of polygonal hole boundaries. Both exterior polygonal boundaries and hole boundaries are represented by the same Pascal record. The use of a variant record data structure facilitates the distinction between a polygon record representing an exterior boundary and one that represents a hole: if the variant part case selector HOLE is TRUE—the record represents a hole polygonal boundary. If it is FALSE—it represents an exterior boundary.

```
pptr    = ^polygon;
polygon = record
            pnext      : pptr; {nil-end list of polygons}
            glist      : gptr; {circular list of segments}
            case hole  : boolean of
              false :  (child : pptr);
              true  :  (parent : pptr)
            end;
```

The variant part of the record designates the exterior boundary as the "parent" of hole boundaries and hole boundaries as "children" of an exterior boundary. There is always exactly one exterior polygonal boundary, and this fact underlies the simplicity of the structure, which is capable of representing complex polygons, as depicted in Figure 3.2.

The list of segments (and vertices) does not depend on the designation of the boundary as exterior or as hole; therefore, one set of polygon boundary manipulation operators suffices to handle both. The only additional condition these operators must observe is that the relative (geometrical) orientation of the elements in the polygonal boundaries representing holes must be *opposite* to the orientation of the elements of the exterior boundary, in accordance with the right-hand rule discussed in Chapter 2.

Choosing a data structure that meets particular needs rests on analyzing the merits of each alternative representation scheme and the operators that will manipulate it. However, neither all the merits (and, of course, all the shortcomings) of a data structure nor all the operators that will be needed to manipulate it can always be anticipated before actual implementation has begun. Therefore, complex models (such as the ones used in CAD) are often designed iteratively, gradually improving them until a satisfactory scheme has been found. For example, the addition of the POLYGON record to the data structure, necessitated by the representation of holes, now requires us to go back and update the SEGMENT record by adding to it a back pointer GPOLY to the new POLYGON record:

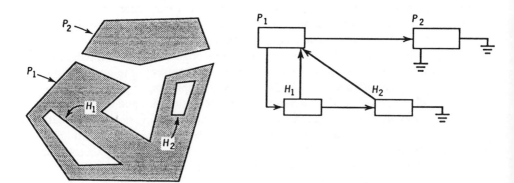

Figure 3.2. Representing polygons with holes.

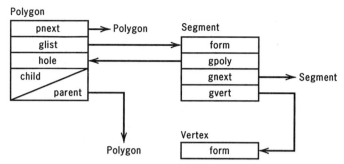

Figure 3.3. The complete POLYGON data structure.

```
segment = record
            form  : line;
            gpoly : pptr;
            gnext : gptr;
            gvert : vptr
          end;
```

This back pointer will allow us, in the future, to find the polygon, given a segment that belongs to it. This change was made apparent only *after* holes were considered and thus demonstrates our inability to construct satisfactory data structures without considerable generate-and-test iterations. The complete POLYGON data structure is depicted in Figure 3.3.

□ BIBLIOGRAPHY

E. E. Barton and I. Buchanan, "The Polygon Package," *Computer-Aided Design* **12**(1):3–10, January 1980.

W. Barton, "Representation of Many-Sided Polygons and Polygonal Lines for Rapid Processing," *Communications of the ACM* **20**(3):166–171, March 1977.

4

BASIC POLYGON OPERATIONS

Modeling operators access and manipulate the data structure for two purposes: for answering *queries,* and for *updating* the structure. The number and complexity of modeling operators require that a *hierarchical,* structured approach be used in their design. Hierarchical structuring facilitates development of low-level operators, which directly access the data structure. They can be used in different combinations for different purposes by higher level operators. These higher level operators, in turn, are isolated from the particular implementation details of the data structure and are, therefore, easier to develop and to maintain. This chapter introduces the basic polygon operators and discusses the properties of the primitive polygon data structure they create.

☐ CLASSIFICATION OF MODELING OPERATORS

The shape models discussed in this book are often used for two different purposes:

1. For answering questions concerning the represented objects
2. For constructing and modifying these objects

These two uses give rise to two kinds of operators: query operators and update operators. *Query* operators extract information from the data structure for use in applications that evaluate the designed artifact, for the purpose of establishing the artifact's expected performances in such areas as energy, structure, habitability, and cost. Query operators are also used to produce reports about the object itself and about the design process (such as part lists and schedules). Query operators do not modify the data.

Update operators, on the other hand, treat the data structure as a transient, temporal image of the artifact being designed; hence, they constantly modify it. To facilitate the modification and to guarantee the semantic integrity of the model, the operators must create, modify, and delete data in compliance with the well-formedness rules established earlier. Both query and update operators are needed for the modeling of shapes, constituting together with the data structure itself the abstract data type for modeling objects.

It is easy to see how the number of necessary operators of both kinds can grow quickly and how the task of managing them may become intractable. Moreover, the model must achieve two conflicting goals: it must minimize computation time and minimize storage space. In other words, the model should facilitate fast response time by minimizing the search that must be exercised to produce answers to queries or to apply changes to the data. This goal can be achieved by maintaining multiple redundancies of data and links. On the other hand, to achieve economy of storage space and to facilitate the model's self-consistency maintenance, the amount of stored data must be minimized, hence multiple redundancies must be avoided.

How can the task of developing correct and efficient operators be accomplished, given these conflicting goals? Clearly, we cannot satisfy both goals simultaneously. Rather, a solution must be found that does not compromise any goal more than is absolutely necessary.

The principal technique we shall use to accomplish the task of developing modeling operators that are correct, efficient, and manageable is *hierarchical structuring*. We will develop modules of operators that can be used in different combinations to accomplish different tasks. Such modules of operators can be developed in different levels of specifity, where lower level operators provide the functionality upon which higher level functions are built. Low-level operators, which perform very specific tasks, are combined by higher level operators to perform more complex tasks. The operators that orchestrate the combination of low-level operators to perform the complex operations are, by definition, higher level operators than are the ones they govern. For example, low-level operators can manipulate individual segments and vertices of a polygonal boundary. These low-level operators can then be combined to create, modify, and delete whole polygons. Furthermore, whole polygons can be used as building blocks for constructing even more complex polygons.

Combining operators of one hierarchical layer into a "module" and associating them with a set of semantics (rules) allow us to construct the complex and, in many cases, large sets of modeling tools needed to perform shape manipulations. A typical modeling hierarchy may thus consist of many layers, only some of which are of concern to us in this context.

The hierarchical structure of low, high, and still higher level operators can be likened metaphorically to an onion (Figure 4.1). At the core is the data structure itself, implemented in some programming language. The first layer, immediately in contact with the core, is composed of low-level (basic) operators and data

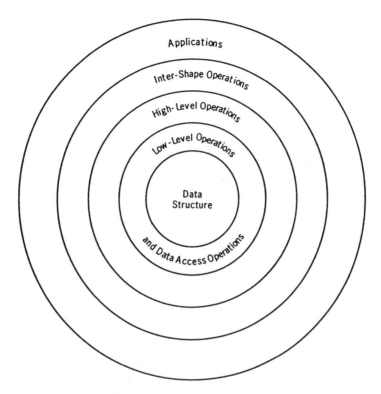

Figure 4.1. Schema of layered operators.

access routines that manipulate the data structure and query it. The second layer is composed of high-level operators that employ combinations of the first layer operators to accomplish their own tasks. At the third level are intershape operators that use both high and the low-level operators. At the outermost layer are application packages, such as energy and cost analyses.

Layering and modularity facilitate efficiency and consistency. Each operator must be implemented and debugged only once and later can be used by multiple higher level operators to accomplish different tasks. It is not always simple, however, to determine just the right level for each operator. If it is of too high a level, the operator may be overly specialized and not useful for other purposes. If its level is too low, the operator may be too primitive, requiring much augmentation in order to be useful for any particular purpose. Like the design of the data structure, operators must typically be designed iteratively several times before the "right" combination is established.

☐ HIERARCHY OF POLYGON OPERATORS

In Parts One and Two, we are concerned with operators that *construct* and *modify* individual shapes in two and three dimensions. We divide them into four levels:

1. Topological operators that initialize, create, delete, and dispose of shapes and their components. This layer also includes operators that access the data structure.
2. Operators that modify existing shapes by addition and removal of their constituent topological components.
3. Geometrical operators that place the elements in the two- or three-dimensional Euclidean space.
4. Operators that create new shapes from existing ones by "cutting" and "pasting" them and by means of the set-theoretic operators of union, intersection, and difference.

As discussed in Chapter 3, three data structure elements are involved in the representation of polygons: polygonal boundaries (including holes), segments, and vertices. The operators needed to span the range of all possible modeling actions that involve these elements are summarized and classified in Figure 4.2.

Developing all these modeling operators individually will lead to prolific and redundant efforts. Instead, we shall draw upon the similarities between the operations and build hierarchical tools that can be applied, in various combinations, to different aggregate elements of polygons and solids.

	vertex	segment	polygon	
init/dispose	X	X	X	[individual records]
create/delete		X	X	[data structures]
access		X	X	[data structure]
add/remove		X	X	[segs and polygons]
split/merge		X	X	[segs and polygons]
place	X	X		[geometry]
cut/paste			X	[polygons]
union/intersect			X	[set theoretic ops.]

Figure 4.2. Classes of polygon operations.

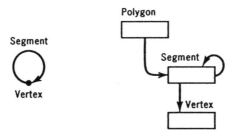

Figure 4.3. The Primitive Polygon.

□ BASIC POLYGON OPERATORS

The lowest level polygon modeling operators, which we call *basic* or "primitive" polygon operators, are composed of procedures and functions that initialize, create, delete, and dispose of polygonal boundaries and their components (polygons, segments, and vertices). These operators manipulate the data structures directly (they make up the innermost layer in the onion metaphor).

There are many ways in which these operators can be implemented. To minimize their number and to assign them the responsibility for maintaining at least some of the well-formedness conditions, we will require that they abide by the *closure* condition of polygonal boundaries. Non-self-intersection and orientation conditions cannot be guaranteed by the primitive operators, because they depend on geometrical conditions and can be tested only after such input has been acquired during run-time (i.e., the locations assigned by the user to vertices and segments).

Maintenance of closure implies that the simplest of all possible polygons, which is the starting point to all polygon operations, is made of a *single segment* and a *single vertex*. It is called, appropriately, the *primitive polygon*. According to the definitions in Chapter 2, this segment must be bounded on both its ends by the same (single) vertex, such that the structure forms a circuit, as depicted by Figure 4.3. This shape still complies with the definition of a polygon as an area-enclosing entity, although the area it encloses is of size zero.

The operators that create the primitive polygon must, therefore, not only create the records that compose it (in this case, a polygon, a segment, and a vertex records) but also link them so that the closure condition is maintained. The following procedures perform these functions. They have been divided into (1) operators that INITialize the records that represent vertices, segments, and polygons and (2) operators that CREATE data structures from combinations of these records.

```
type vptr    = ^vertex;
     gptr    = ^segment;
     pptr    = ^polygon;

     coords  = (x,y,z,w);
     params  = (a,b,c);
     point   = array [coords] of real;
     line    = array [params] of real;

     vertex  = record
                  form  : point
               end;

     segment = record
                  form  : line;
                  gpoly : pptr;
                  gnext : gptr;
                  gvert : vptr
               end;

     polygon = record
                  pnext : pptr; {nil-end list of polygons}
                  glist : gptr; {circular list of segments}
                  case hole : boolean of
                    false : (child : pptr);
                    true  : (parent : pptr)
               end;
procedure init_vertex (var v : vptr);
{Allocate new vertex record.}

var  ax : coords;

begin
  new (v);
  for ax := x to z do v^.form[ax] := 0;
  v^.form[w] := 1
end; {init_vertex procedure}
```

```
procedure init_segment (var g : gptr);
{Allocate segment record and initialize its fields.}

var  pr : params;

begin
  new (g);
  with g^ do
    begin
      gpoly := nil;
      gnext := nil;
      gvert := nil;
      for pr := a to c do form[pr] := 0
    end
end; {init_segment procedure}

procedure init_polygon (var p : pptr);
{Allocate polygon record and initialize its fields.}

begin
  new (p);
  with p^ do
    begin
      pnext := nil;
      glist := nil;
      hole := false;
      child := nil
    end
end; {init_polygon procedure}

procedure create_segment (var g : gptr; var v : vptr);
{Create new segment and new vertex records.}

begin
  init_segment (g);
  init_vertex (v);
  g^.gvert := v
end; {create_segment procedure}
```

```
procedure create_polygon (var p : pptr;
                          var g : gptr;
                          var v : vptr);
{Create a primitive polygon that consists of a circular list of
one segment and one vertex. Create the segment and vertex
records as well.}

begin
  init_polygon (p);
  create_segment (g,v); {note: this creates a vertex!}

  {connect segment to polygon, and vice versa}
  p^.glist := g;
  g^.gpoly := p;

  {make segment list circular}
  g^.gnext := g
end; {create_polygon procedure}
```

These INIT and CREATE operators† are complemented by a set of operators
that DELETE and DISPOSE of the data structures and the records of which
they are made.

```
procedure dispose_vertex (var v : vptr);
{Dispose of vertex record and set v to nil.}

begin
  dispose(v);
  v := nil
end; {dispose_vertex procedure}

procedure dispose_segment (var g : gptr);
{Dispose of segment record and set g to nil.}

begin
  dispose (g);
  g := nil
end; {dispose_segment procedure}
```

---

†These procedures are extended in later chapters to include additional primitive entities and
geometries.

```
procedure dispose_polygon (var p : pptr);
{Dispose of polygon record and set p to nil.}

begin
  dispose (p);
  p := nil
end; {dispose_polygon procedure}

procedure delete_segment (var g : gptr);
{Delete segment g and its vertex.}

begin
  dispose_vertex (g^.gvert);
  dispose_segment (g)
end; {delete_segment procedure}
```

(Note: The deletion of a polygon is not a low-level operation, because it involves deletion of all its holes and the segments that bound them. It will be introduced in Chapter 5, together with the operators that construct polygons and holes.)

□ DATA STRUCTURE ACCESS OPERATORS

The complexity of manipulating the data structure we have adopted for modeling polygons could be reduced if a few operators were added that would carry out the low-level, but frequent, data structure access functions. For example, our data structure includes an explicit pointer from the SEGMENT record to the VERTEX record, but not vice versa. This asymmetry was designed purposefully to avoid redundancies (which might lead to inconsistencies if the vertex would reference a segment other than the one referencing it). This makes it cumbersome, however, to find a segment given its vertex. To facilitate the identification of the segment, a data structure access function called GET_SEGMENT could be added to the model, which returns a pointer to the segment, given a vertex and the polygon to which it belongs.

```
function get_segment (v : vptr; p : pptr) : gptr;
{Return the segment of polygon p that references vertex v.}

var  g : gptr;

begin
  g := p^.glist;
  while g^.gvert <> v do g := g^.gnext;
  get_segment := g
end; {get_segment function}
```

Another purpose of the data structure access operators is to make the implementation of modeling operators easier to read, thereby easier to debug and to update. This utility is demonstrated by function OTHER_VERTEX, which returns the vertex referenced by the successor of a given segment (which is the other vertex bounding the given segment, in addition to the one it references directly). Although it is a very simple routine, the meaning of the operation performed by OTHER_VERTEX is expressed more clearly by its name than by its implementation.

```
function other_vertex (g : gptr) : vptr;
{Return vertex referenced by the successor of segment g.}

begin
  other_vertex := g^.gnext^.gvert
end; {other_vertex function}
```

A third purpose of the data structure access routines is to isolate the data structure from the modeling operators that manipulate it, such that it can be modified and updated without affecting them. By "isolation" we mean that the modeling operators do not manipulate the data structure directly, but rather through the access routines. For example, a function called PREDECESSOR, which returns the segment preceding its argument in the same polygonal boundary, would eliminate the need for the modeling operator employing it to know whether the segment list of a polygon is circular or a nil-ended.

```
function predecessor (g : gptr) : gptr;
{Returns predecessor of segment g in same polygon.}

var   gpred : gptr;

begin
  gpred := g^.gpoly^.glist;
  while gpred^.gnext <> g do
    gpred := gpred^.gnext;
  predecessor := gpred
end; {predecessor function}
```

Although it is practically impossible to completely isolate the modeling operators from the data structures they manipulate, access operators reduce the potential for making errors in developing the modeling operators in the first place and when the data structures are modified and updated later on. This utility is of even greater importance to programmers who write application packages using the model and who cannot be expected to know the details of its implementation. Furthermore, their investment in writing the application packages is protected from obsolescence if and when the model is updated (which occurs normally during the model's life span), because the access procedure names, function, and parameters will not be changed even when the details of their implementation do change.

☐ BIBLIOGRAPHY

Eastman, C. M., *Introduction to Computer-Aided Design,* Carnegie-Mellon University, Pittsburgh, PA, 1982.

5

HIGH-LEVEL POLYGON OPERATIONS

Once a primitive polygon has been created, it can be *expanded* to include many segments and vertices. This expansion occurs by adding *segment/vertex* pairs, while maintaining *closure, orientation,* and *non-self-intersection,* and by adding *holes.* Furthermore, the expanded polygon may be *split* in two, and two polygons may be *merged* into one.

These (reversible) processes involve high-level topological manipulations of the data structure. This chapter describes these issues, which form the second layer in the shape modeling hierarchy. We shall develop operators to SPLIT and MERGE segments and vertices of existing polygonal boundaries, to ADD and REMOVE holes, and to SPLIT and MERGE polygons.

□ CONSTRUCTING COMPLEX POLYGONS

In compliance with the definitions we developed in Chapter 3, expansion of the primitive polygon into a meaningful, well-formed shape that represents some physical artifact involves the addition of segment-vertex pairs, as depicted in Figure 5.1.

This operation and its inverse (which contracts a nonprimitive polygon back to the primitive polygon state) involve the topological manipulation of the data structure in a manner that complies with the well-formedness rules of closure, consistent orientation, and non-self-intersection.

The topological operators that expand and contract polygonal boundaries are implemented by four procedures: ADD_SEGMENT, REMOVE_SEGMENT, SPLIT_SEGMENT, and MERGE_SEGMENT. The first pair of operators adds and removes existing segments to and from a given polygon. The second pair of operators creates a new segment-vertex pair and links it to a given polygon as the successor of a given segment or removes (and deletes) a given segment-vertex pair and reconnects their predecessor and successor segments in the polygon to maintain closure. By repeating the expansion or contraction process,

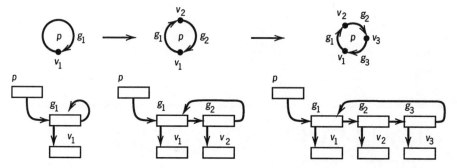

Figure 5.1. Expanding a primitive polygon by adding segment-vertex pairs.

complex polygons can be built, starting with a primitive polygon. Existing polygons can be shrunk back to the primitive polygon state for deletion purposes. Furthermore, existing segments can be moved from one polygon to another, a feat which is useful for splitting and merging whole polygons, as we shall see later in this chapter.

```
procedure add_segment (g1,g2 : gptr);
{Add segment g2 as successor of g1. g2 must already exist.}

begin
  g2^.gnext := g1^.gnext;
  g1^.gnext := g2;
  g2^.gpoly := g1^.gpoly
end; {add_segment procedure}


procedure remove_segment (g : gptr);
{Extract segment g from its current polygon, without deleting
 it, by connecting its predecessor segment with its successor.}

var  gpred : gptr;
     p     : pptr;

begin
  p := g^.gpoly;
  if p^.glist = g
    then p^.glist := g^.gnext;
  gpred := predecessor (g);
  gpred^.gnext := g^.gnext;
  g^.gpoly := nil; g^.gnext := nil
end; {remove_segment procedure}
```

```
procedure split_segment (g        : gptr;
                         var gnew : gptr;
                         var v    : vptr);
{Create new segment gnew and add it as the successor of g. The
 new segment references vertex v, and the same polygon as g.}

begin
  create_segment (gnew, v);
  add_segment (g,gnew)
end; {split_segment procedure}

procedure merge_segment (var g : gptr);
{Remove segment g , then delete g. G must not be the same as
 g^.gnext (i.e., it must not be the only segment in the
 polygon).}

begin
  remove_segment (g);
  delete_segment (g)
end; {merge_segment procedure}
```

□ ADDING AND REMOVING POLYGONS AND HOLES

The operators we have discussed so far deal with a single polygonal boundary only. The scope of our modeling interests includes, nevertheless, artifacts made of multiple polygons and polygons that contain holes. The modeling of artifacts made of multiple polygons is discussed at length in Part Four of this book, because it involves the association of polygons (and solids) in assemblies and other database groupings. Here we address only the linkage of polygons in simple lists.

The polygon data structure developed in Chapter 3 includes the provision to link one polygon record to another. This provision, in the form of the PNEXT field in the polygon record, can be used to construct lists of polygons as well as list of holes in a single polygon. Procedures ADD_POLYGON and REMOVE_POLYGON perform these simple operations.

```
procedure add_polygon (var p,plist : pptr);
{Add polygon p to the list of polygons headed by plist. P must
 not already be in plist.}

begin
  p^.pnext := plist;
  plist := p
end; {add_polygon procedure}
```

```
procedure remove_polygon (p : pptr; var plist : pptr);
{Remove polygon p from the list of polygons headed by plist.}

var  pl    : pptr;
     found : boolean;

begin
  if p = plist
    then plist := p^.pnext
    else begin {find predecessor of p in plist}
      pl := plist; found := false;
      while not found do
        if p = pl^.pnext
          then found := true
          else pl := pl^.pnext;
      pl^.pnext := p^.pnext
    end;
  p^.pnext := nil
end; {remove_polygon procedure}
```

The addition and removal of holes follows principles that are similar to those for adding and removing polygons, with the added adjustment of the PARENT and CHILD fields. It should be noted that when a polygon is made into a hole, or when a hole is made into a polygon, its *orientation must be reversed,* both topologically and geometrically, in order to comply with the right-hand rule. This reversal is performed by linking its segments to their former predecessors in the list, as demonstrated by procedure REVERSE_POLYGON.

```
procedure reverse_polygon (p : pptr);
{Reverse the orientation of the segments in polygon p.}

var  g1,g2,g3 : gptr;
     v1,v2    : vptr;

begin
  {reverse topology}
  g1 := p^.glist; g3 := g1^.gnext;
  repeat
    g2 := g3;
    g3 := g3^.gnext;
    g2^.gnext := g1;
    g1 := g2
  until g1 = p^.glist;
  p^.glist := predecessor (p^.glist);
```

```
{reverse geometry}
g1 := p^.glist;
repeat
  v1 := g1^.gvert; v2 := other_vertex (g1);
  compute_line (v1^.form, v2^.form, g1^.form);
  g1 := g1^.gnext
until g1 = p^.glist
end; {reverse_polygon procedure}

procedure add_hole (h,p : pptr);
{Add polygon h as a child (hole) of parent polygon p, and
 transform it into a hole polygon. Parent polygon must NOT be
 a hole itself!}

begin
  {add h to list of holes in p}
  add_polygon (h, p^.child);

  {make h hole polygon}
  reverse_polygon (h);
  h^.hole := true;
  h^.parent := p
end; {add_hole procedure}

procedure remove_hole (h : pptr);
{Remove hole polygon h from its parent polygon list of holes,
 and transform it to a non-hole polygon.}

begin
  {remove h from list of holes}
  remove_polygon (h,h^.parent^.child);

  {make h non-hole polygon}
  reverse_polygon (h);
  h^.hole := false;
  h^.child := nil
end; {remove_hole procedure}
```

□ DELETING POLYGONS

With the availability of operators to add and remove segments and operators to add and remove holes, we can now complete the task of deleting whole polygons, a task which is left over from Chapter 4. Polygon deletion is regarded a high-level modeling operation, beyond the powers of the operators discussed in Chapter 4, because before a polygon can be deleted it must be "shrunk" back to the primitive polygon state, and its holes (if it has any) must be removed and deleted as well.

Procedure DELETE_POLYGON performs this task. It is a *recursive* procedure, which first REMOVEs holes from their parent polygon, and thus turns them into nonhole polygonal boundaries. It then deletes each polygon separately, by applying REMOVE_SEGMENT iteratively to its segments until it reaches the primitive polygon state, when it is finally deleted.

```
procedure delete_polygon (var p : pptr);
{Delete polygon p and all its holes, recursively. The polygon
 being delete is never a hole!}

var  h : pptr;
     g : gptr;

begin
  {remove and delete holes in p, recursively}
  while p^.child <> nil do
    begin
      h := p^.child;
      remove_hole (h);    {turn hole h into a nonhole polygon}
      delete_polygon (h) {recursive call}
    end;

  {remove all segments of p but one}
  while p^.glist <> p^.glist^.gnext do
    begin
      g := p^.glist^.gnext;
      merge_segment (g)
    end;

  {delete last segment and dispose of p}
  delete_segment (p^.glist);
  dispose_polygon (p)
end; {delete_polygon procedure}
```

□ SPLITTING AND MERGING POLYGONS

Once polygons have been constructed, we may want to SPLIT them in two or to MERGE two polygons into one. These topological changes are performed by the SPLIT_POLYGON and MERGE_POLYGONS procedures, which operate on polygons that are geometrically coincident at one of their segments.

Given that the desired function of these operators is to *divide* or *combine* the segment lists of the operant polygons, they can be implemented by *removing* segments from one polygon and *adding* them to the other. This method, which operates on the existing segment records of the operant polygons, manipulates only their connecting pointers. Some new segment records may be added, or existing ones removed, to avoid duplications in the product polygon's segment list. The net effect is to *expand* one of the input polygons to encompass segments of the other polygon in the case of MERGE_POLYGONS, and to create and expand a new polygon, which will form the boundary of one of the split polygon's parts while *contracting* the input polygon to represent the other part, in the case of SPLIT_POLYGON.

The use of existing data structures and manipulating mostly their pointers makes this approach computationally efficient. Its efficiency is, however, somewhat compromised by the removal and addition of *each* segment, rather than a *list* of segments at a time. This redundancy is, nevertheless, tolerated here, because it allows us to implement the entire process by means of the operators we have discussed in Chapter 4 and earlier in this chapter. In contrast, manipulation of segment lists, which constitute neither a well-formed polygon nor individual segments, introduces nonstandard operators. Standardization and hierarchical layering are preferred to optimal efficiency, in light of the principles discussed in Chapter 1. Procedures SPLIT_POLYGON and MERGE_POLYGONS demonstrate the implementation of this method. Their step-by-step actions are depicted in Figures 5.2 and 5.3, respectively.

```
procedure split_polygon (var p1,p2 : pptr; g1,g2 : gptr);
{Split polygon p1 by removing its segments from g1 to the
predecessor of g2, and adding them to p2. Return polygon p2.
```

```
  p1                                p1              p2
+------+------>+               +----+        ---->+
¦          g1  ¦      ==>      ¦    ¦ gnew1 ¦ g1  ¦
¦   g2         ¦               ¦ g2 ¦ gnew2 ¦     ¦
+<-----+------+               +<----        +----+
```

```
This procedure works for all cases: when g1=g2, when
g2=g1^.gnext, and when they are not adjacent.}

var  gnew1,gnew2,g,pred1,pred2 : gptr;
     vnew1,vnew2               : vptr;

begin
   {create new polygon coincident with the vertex of g2}
   create_polygon (p2, gnew2, vnew2);

   {assign geometry to vnew2}
   vnew2^.form := g2^.gvert^.form;

   if g1 <> g2
     then begin
       {set traversal pointers}
       pred1 := predecessor (g1);
       pred2 := gnew2;
```

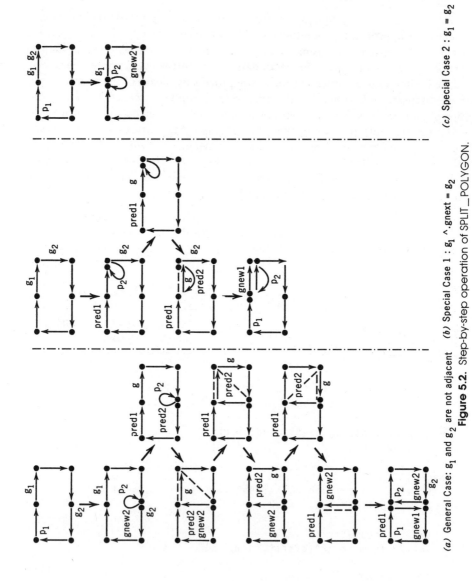

(a) General Case: g_1 and g_2 are not adjacent   (b) Special Case 1 : $g_1 \wedge .gnext = g_2$ (c) Special Case 2 : $g_1 = g_2$

Figure 5.2. Step-by-step operation of SPLIT_POLYGON.

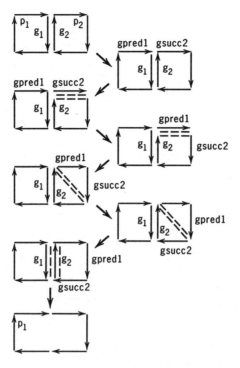

Figure 5.3. Step-by-step operation of MERGE _ POLYGONS.

```
while pred1^.gnext <> g2 do
   begin
      g := pred1^.gnext;
      remove_segment (g);       {from p1}
      add_segment (pred2, g); {to p2}
      pred2 := g
   end;

   {create new segment and vertex on p1}
   split_segment (pred1,gnew1,vnew1);

   {assign geometry to vnew1}
   vnew1^.form := g1^.gvert^.form;
   {set seg-list pointer on p1 to gnew1}
   p1^.glist := gnew1

   {update line equations of gnew1 and gnew2}
   end
end; {split_polygon procedure}
```

```
procedure merge_polygons (var p1,p2 : pptr; var g1,g2 : gptr);
{Merge polygons p1 and p2 into p1 along segments g1 and g2, by
removing all segments of p2 (except g2) and adding them to
p1, deleting g1 and p2. Note: g1 and g2 must belong to
different polygons. They should be geometrically congruent,
and in opposite orientations to each other.
```

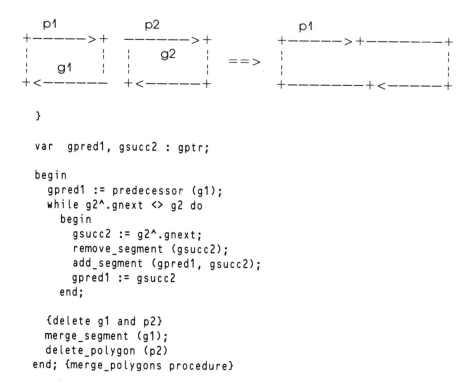

```
}

var  gpred1, gsucc2 : gptr;

begin
  gpred1 := predecessor (g1);
  while g2^.gnext <> g2 do
    begin
      gsucc2 := g2^.gnext;
      remove_segment (gsucc2);
      add_segment (gpred1, gsucc2);
      gpred1 := gsucc2
    end;

  {delete g1 and p2}
  merge_segment (g1);
  delete_polygon (p2)
end; {merge_polygons procedure}
```

☐ CREATING AND DELETING HOLES

Procedure MERGE_POLYGONS is applicable to all cases where the segments
along which the polygons are to be merged belong to *different* polygonal boundaries. A different operator must be used to merge a polygon along two segments
that belong to the same polygonal boundary, because such a merger *creates a
hole*. Likewise, procedure SPLIT_POLYGON can be applied only when its two
segments belong to a single polygonal boundary, and another operator must be
applied when the segments belong to different polygons, because such splitting
eliminates a hole. These cases are depicted in Figure 5.4.

The operators we use for this purpose are, accordingly, MAKE_HOLE and
KILL_HOLE. It is interesting to note that although the operation involved in

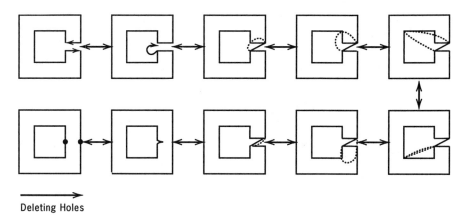

Deleting Holes

Figure 5.4. Creating and deleting holes.

making a hole is logically equivalent to MERGE_POLYGONS (except that the segments belong to a single polygonal boundary), the actual operator that is used is SPLIT_POLYGON. Likewise, in KILLing a hole we use MERGE_ POLYGON to "fuse" the two boundaries. Another characteristic of MAKE_HOLE and KILL_HOLE is the need to "grow" struts or remove them explicitly, because the operators SPLIT_POLYGON and MERGE_POLYGONS, which are used by MAKE_HOLE and KILL_HOLE, respectively, require that such segments be provided as their parameters. Note that the orientation of the newly created hole complies with the right-hand rule and does not have to be reversed.

```
procedure make_hole (var p : pptr; g1,g2 : gptr);
{Split off segments of polygon p between g1 and g2 to create a
  new polygon, which then becomes a hole of p:
```

```
+------------------>+       +------------------>+
¦ p                 ¦       ¦ p                 ¦
¦    +<-----+       ¦       ¦    +<------+      ¦
¦    ¦      ¦ g1    ¦       ¦    ¦ h     ¦      ¦
¦    ¦    +<----+   ¦       ¦    ¦       ¦      ¦
¦    ¦    +---->+   ¦  ==>  ¦    ¦       ¦      ¦
¦    ¦      ¦ g2    ¦       ¦    ¦       ¦      ¦
¦    +----->+       ¦       ¦    +------>+      ¦
¦                   ¦       ¦                   ¦
+<------------------+       +<------------------+
```

```
}

var  h : pptr;
```

```
    procedure kill_strut (var g : gptr);
    {Merge the two successors of g into g itself.}

    var gpred : gptr;

    begin
      gpred := predecessor(g);
      merge_segment (gpred);
      merge_segment (g)
    end; {kill_strut procedure}

begin {make_hole}
  split_polygon (p,h, g1,g2);

  {clean up "umbilical cord" on p and h}
  kill_strut (g1);
  kill_strut (g2);

  {test which polygon is the hole}
  if point_in_polygon (h^.glist^.gvert^.form, p)†
    then add_hole (h,p)
    else add_hole (p,h)
end; {make_hole procedure}

procedure kill_hole (p : pptr; var h : pptr; g1,g2 : gptr);
{Kill hole h in polygon p by connecting it to p with an
"umbilical cord" made of segments succeeding g1 and g2.
```

```
+------------->+            +------------->+
: p            :            : p            :
:   +<----+    : g1         :   +<-----+   : g1
:   : h    :   :            :   :      :   :
:   :      +   :            :   :    +<--+ :
:   : g2   :   +            :   :    +-->+ :
:   :      :   :            :   : g2  :    :
:   +---->+    :            :   +----->+   :
:             :   ==>       :              :
+<-----------+             +<------------+
```

```
}
```

```
    procedure make_strut (g : gptr);
    {Add two coincident segments (a strut) following g.}

    var   gnew1,gnew2 : gptr;
          vnew1,vnew2 : vptr;
```

†This is an adapted version of the same function, discussed in Chapter 2.

```
      begin
        split_segment (g,gnew1, vnew1);
        split_segment (g,gnew2, vnew2)
      end; {make_strut procedure}

  begin {kill_hole}
    {remove hole h from its parent polygon}
    remove_hole (h);
    reverse_polygon (h);

    {create "umbilical cord"}
    make_strut (g1);
    make_strut (g2);

    {merge polygon p with hole h}
    g1 := g1^.gnext; g2 := g2^.gnext;
    merge_polygons (p,h, g1,g2)
  end; {kill_hole procedure}
```

☐ COPYING POLYGONS

A useful application of the high-level polygon operators that we have discussed in this chapter is the *copying* of polygons, a traditional utilization of computing power in many drafting and CAD systems. This operator allows the designer to create an object once, then "stamp" it all over the design as if a rubber stamp were used. Procedure COPY_POLYGON demonstrates how this operator can be constructed from the high-level polygon operators.

```
procedure copy_polygon (p,parent : pptr; var pnew : pptr);
{Create and return a copy of polygon p.}

var  g,gnew,gtemp : gptr;
     vnew         : vptr;

begin
  create_polygon (pnew,gnew,vnew);
  g := p^.glist;
  vnew^.form := g^.gvert^.form;
  gnew^.form := g^.form;
  repeat
    g := g^.gnext;
    split_segment (gnew, gtemp, vnew);
    vnew^.form := g^.gvert^.form;
    gnew^.form := g^.form;
    gnew := gtemp
  until g = p^.glist;
```

```
      if p^.hole
        then begin
          pnew^.hole := true;
          pnew^.parent := parent;
          if p^.pnext <> nil
            then copy_polygon (p^.pnext, parent, pnew)
        end
      else if p^.child <> nil
          then begin
            parent := pnew;
            copy_polygon (p^.child, parent, pnew)
          end
end; {copy_polygon procedure}
```

6

PLANAR GEOMETRY OF POINTS AND LINES

We have now developed all the purely *topological* operators needed to create, modify, and delete polygons. However, to make these operators meaningful design tools, the topological elements they manipulate must be assigned *geometrical* attributes.

The geometrical attributes associated with polygons and their components are *points* and *lines*. In this chapter we shall see how points and lines can be represented computationally, how they can be operated on, and how they can be associated with the vertex and segment topologies, respectively.

□ THE REPRESENTATION OF POINTS

A *point* is a particular geometrical location in some frame of reference. A particularly convenient frame of reference, which we have been using so far, although informally, is the *Cartesian coordinate system.* In the two-dimensional Euclidean space (E2), this frame of reference consists of two perpendicular lines, called the *coordinate axes.* The horizontal axis is called the X axis, and the vertical one is called the Y axis. The point where the X axis intersects the Y axis divides each of them into two parts and is used as the starting point for marking the coordinates on each axis, hence it is called the *origin* of the coordinate system. The coordinates to the right of and above the origin are considered *positive;* those to the left and below the origin are considered *negative.* Any point in E2 can now be uniquely identified by using the Cartesian coordinate system as a frame of reference; that is, by its rectilinear distance from the X axis and from the Y axis, respectively (Figure 6.1).

A different method for referencing points in E2 uses an angular and a linear measure rather than two linear distances as in the Cartesian system. This so-called *polar coordinate system* requires, therefore, only one axis and a point on it which serves as the origin. Any point in E2 can be uniquely defined by using the

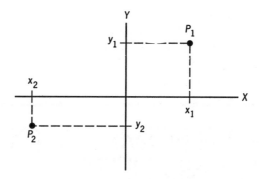

Figure 6.1. The Cartesian coordinate system.

polar coordinate system as a frame of reference. We measure both its distance from the origin and the anticlockwise angle that the line connecting it with the origin makes with the coordinate axis (Figure 6.2).

For the purposes of modeling shapes it is convenient, in most cases, to use the cartesian coordinate system, where points are identified by two linear distance values. We use polar coordinates when we deal with angular dimensions, such as in the case of circle, arcs, and rotational displacements.

□ OPERATING ON POINTS

The Distance Between Two Points

The distance between two points $<x1,y1>$ and $<x2,y2>$ can be easily calculated through the Pythagorean theorem:

$$d = \sqrt{(x1 - x2)^2 + (y1 - y2)^2}.$$

This function can be implemented easily in Pascal, as demonstrated by function POINT_DISTANCE.

```
function point_distance (pnt1,pnt2 : point) : real;
{Return linear distance between points pnt1 and pnt2.}

begin
  point_distance := sqrt(sqr(pnt1[x] - pnt2[x]) +
                         sqr(pnt1[y] - pnt2[y]))
end; {point_distance function}
```

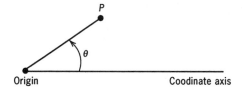

Figure 6.2. The polar coordinate system.

The Angle Formed by Three Points

If we use polar coordinates, the angle formed by three points can be easily calculated by considering the apex point of the angle as the origin and by subtracting the angles formed by each one of the lines connecting the other points with the origin and the coordinate axis (Figure 6.3).

Because we chose to use Cartesian coordinates, the angles must be calculated using the trigonometric function ARCTANGENT. The nature of the ARC-TANGENT function makes this calculation sensitive to the position of the points relative to the coordinate axes, and some special care must, therefore, be exercised in order to obtain meaningful results for all cases. This is demonstrated by functions THETA and ANGLE, which were first introduced in Chapter 2.

```
function theta (pi,pj : point) : real;
{Compute angle between the line segment defined by <pi,pj> and
 the positive x axis.}

const epsilon = 10e-6;
      radians = 0.0174532925;

var  t,dx,dy : real;

begin
  dx := pj[x] - pi[x];
  dy := pj[y] - pi[y];

  if abs(dx) < epsilon
    then t := 90*radians
    else t := arctan(dy/dx);
```

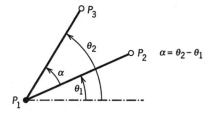

Figure 6.3. Calculating the angle formed by three points.

```
        if (dx < 0) or ((abs(dx) < epsilon) and (dy < 0))
          then theta := t + 180*radians
          else if dy < 0
            then theta := t + 360*radians
            else theta := t
    end; {theta function}

    function angle (p1,p2,p3 : point) : real;
    {Compute the angle from the line defined by points [p1,p2] to
     the line defined by points [p1,p3]. the lines intersect at p1.}

    const radians = 0.0174532925;

    var  a : real;

    begin
      a := (theta(p1,p3) - theta(p1,p2))/radians;

      if a > 180
        then angle := a - 360
        else if a < -180
          then angle := a + 360
          else angle := a
    end; {angle function}
```

☐ THE REPRESENTATION OF LINES

Lines cannot be as easily represented as points, because they are made of an infinite number of points. Therefore, instead of using a direct means to geometrically represent a line, we must use a *function* to describe it, which discriminates between points that belong to the line and points that do not. This function, which is known as the *line equation,* can be derived in many ways. For straight lines in E2, which are of interest to us in the current context, the function can be calculated using proportions: given two points in E2, $<x1,y1>$ and $<x2,y2>$, through which the line is known to pass, any other point $<x,y>$ in E2 that belongs to this line must satisfy the following equation, derived from the similarity of triangles (Figure 6.4):

$$\frac{y - y1}{x - x1} = \frac{y2 - y1}{x2 - x1} . \tag{6.1}$$

The proportion $(y2 - y1)/(x2 - x1)$ is a constant and is known as the *slope* of the line. It will be denoted by m in the following equations. Equation (6.1) can thus be rewritten as:

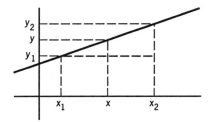

Figure 6.4. Deriving the explicit line equation.

$$\frac{y - y1}{x - x1} = m$$

or

$$y = mx + (y1 - mx1),$$

where $(y1 - mx1)$ is another constant, which we denote k and which represents the *intercept* of the line with the Y axis of the coordinate system (i.e., $y = y1 - mx1$ when $x = 0$). By substituting k in the equation, we derive the *explicit equation of straight lines*:

$$y = mx + k \tag{6.2}$$

Equation (6.2) has, nevertheless, one major drawback: it cannot represent vertical lines, such as $x = 5$ (Figure 6.5). The reason for this deficiency is the implicit division by $(x2 - x1)$ in Equation (6.2), which is a necessary step in its derivation.

If, instead of dividing by $(x2 - x1)$, we multiply both sides of Equation (6.1) by $(x - x1)(x2 - x1)$, we get a more general line equation:

$$(y - y1)(x2 - x1) = (x - x1)(y2 - y1) \tag{6.3}$$

Equation (6.3) is known as the *implicit equation of straight lines,* because evaluation of y for a given value of x requires the solution of a linear equation,

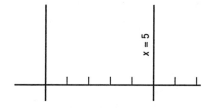

Figure 6.5. A vertical line defined by $x = 5$.

which essentially returns us to the explicit form given by Equation (6.2). When that step is taken, vertical lines again cannot be represented. Equation (6.3) itself, nevertheless, can represent vertical lines, provided we do not attempt to compute the value of y for a given value of x. We can, however, use Equation (6.3) to determine whether a given point is on the line or not, by simply substituting its x and y values and testing whether the two sides of the equation balance.

Equation (6.3) can be rearranged by eliminating the parentheses and by multiplying its terms, as follows:

$$x(y1 - y2) + y(x2 - x1) + (x1y2 - x2y1) = 0.$$

By denoting the constants in this equation, a, b, and c, which are known as the *parameters of the line*, we derive the general form the implicit line equation:

$$a = y1 - y2$$
$$b = x2 - x1$$
$$c = x1y2 - x2y1$$
$$ax + by + c = 0. \tag{6.4}$$

Note that the parameters a, b, and c are not unique: any constant multiple λ of them will satisfy Equation (6.4):

$$(\lambda a)x + (\lambda b)y + (\lambda c) = 0.$$

This property is significant because it demonstrates that the relationships (i.e., the ratios) between a, b, and c are of the essence, rather than their absolute values. It helps us in normalizing line equation parameters to eliminate computational round-off errors and in deriving alternative coordinates systems for lines and points, as described later in this chapter.

Equation (6.4) and the definition of the parameters a, b, and c can be directly implemented in a procedure to compute the implicit equation of a straight line in E2, given two points that are known to be on that line, as shown by procedure COMPUTE_LINE.

```
procedure compute_line (pnt1,pnt2 : point; var ln : line);
{Compute the parameters of the straight line equation which
 passes through points pnt1 and pnt2.}


begin
  ln[a] := pnt2[y] - pnt1[y];
  ln[b] := pnt1[x] - pnt2[x];
  ln[c] := pnt1[x]*pnt2[y] - pnt2[x]*pnt1[y]
end; {compute_line procedure}
```

The Normalized Line Equation

By using the definition of the parametric ratios directly, we can derive alternative equations for the line, with powerful properties. One such alternative, which is known as the *normalized equation of straight lines,* is derived by dividing all the parameters by one of them. If we select the divisor to be the parameter c, we obtain:

$$(a/c)x + (b/c)y + 1 = 0$$

If we now denote

$$u = a/c$$

and

$$v = b/c,$$

then the equation becomes:

$$ux + vy + 1 = 0. \tag{6.5}$$

The symmetrical properties of Equation (6.5) allow us to manipulate it in some special ways. For example, if u and v are held constant (i.e., a, b and c are constant), then x and y prescribe *all the points* along the line. However, if we hold x and y constant and allow u and v to vary, the equation now defines *all the lines* passing through the point $<x,y>$.

The significance of this alternative form of representation is that a line and a point are each defined by *two* parameters: the coordinates x and y for a point and the parameters u and v for a line. Furthermore, this derivation demonstrates the dual relationship that exists between points and lines: two points define a line, just as two intersecting lines define a point. In the following we shall continue to use the more conventional representation of lines through the parameters a, b, and c. The reader is advised, however, to remember that points and lines are interchangeable, just as vertices and segments were shown to be equally capable of representing polygons, as discussed in Chapter 3.

☐ OPERATING ON LINES

Distance of a Point From a Line

Given a point $<x,y>$ and a line defined by its parameters a, b, and c, we have seen that the line equation can help us determine if the point is on the line. The *distance* of the point from that line can be calculated in a similar manner, using the following formula:

$$d = \sqrt{\frac{(ax + by + c)^2}{(a^2 + b^2)}}$$

This formula can be easily programmed in Pascal, as depicted in function LINE_DISTANCE.

```
function line_distance (pnt : point; ln : line) : real;
{Return shortest distance between point pnt and line ln.}

begin
  if (sqr(ln[a]) + sqr(ln[b])) = 0
    then line_distance := 0
    else line_distance :=
      sqrt(sqr(ln[a]*pnt[x] + ln[b]*pnt[y] + ln[c])/
          (sqr(ln[a]) + sqr(ln[b])))
end; {line_distance function}
```

Line Segments

The general equation $ax + by + c = 0$ defines a line of infinite length. To define a *segment* of that line, two additional parameters are required, such as the x or the y coordinates of the two points that bound the segment. Given either one of the coordinates, we can determine the other by substitution in the line equation. Such a five-parameter definition is, however, redundant, because it includes one more variable than the alternative definition of the segment through its endpoints $<x1,y1>$ and $<x2,y2>$.

To determine whether a given point $<x,y>$ lies on the segment, a two-step algorithm must be used:

1. Determine if the point is on the line (by determining if its distance from the line is zero).
2. Determine if it is within the bounds defined by the endpoints.

The first part of this algorithm has been demonstrated earlier through function LINE_DISTANCE. Its second part is implemented in function IN_BOUNDS.

```
function in_bounds (pnt, pnt1,pnt2 : point) : boolean;
{Return true if point pnt is within the bounds of the segment
 joining points pnt1 and pnt2.}

begin
  in_bounds :=
      (((pnt[x] >= pnt1[x]) and (pnt[x] <= pnt2[x])) or
       ((pnt[x] >= pnt2[x]) and (pnt[x] <= pnt1[x])))
  and (((pnt[y] >= pnt1[y]) and (pnt[y] <= pnt2[y])) or
       ((pnt[y] >= pnt2[y]) and (pnt[y] <= pnt1[y])))
end; {in_bounds function}
```

The Intersection of Two Lines

The intersection of two lines can be determined by solving the system of simultaneous equations:

$$\begin{cases} a1x + b1y + c1 = 0 \\ a2x + b2y + c2 = 0. \end{cases}$$

This can be done in many ways, one of which is to multiply the first equation by $b2/b1$ and then subtract the second equation from the first one, which results in:

$$x = (b1c2 - b2c1)/det$$

$$y = (c1a2 - c2a1)/det,$$

where $det = (a1b2 - a2b1)$ is the determinant of

$$\begin{bmatrix} a1 & b1 \\ a2 & b2 \end{bmatrix}$$

This divisor, which is common to both x and y, is *zero* when the two lines are parallel. The computation of the point where two lines intersect is performed by procedure COMPUTE_POINT.

```
procedure compute_point (ln1,ln2 : line; var pnt : point);
{Compute the coordinates of the intersection point between lines
 ln1 and ln2. The lines must NOT be parallel!}

var  det : real;

begin
  {compute determinant}
  det := (ln1[a]*ln2[b] - ln2[a]*ln1[b]);

  pnt[x] := (ln1[b]*ln2[c] - ln1[c]*ln2[b])/det;
  pnt[y] := (ln1[c]*ln2[a] - ln1[a]*ln2[c])/det
end; {compute_point procedure}
```

When we are interested in the intersection of line segments rather than the lines, the LINE_INTERSECT function must be augmented to test whether the point of intersection is within the bounds of *both* segments (Figure 6.6).

The Angle Between Lines

The angle θ between two lines whose parameters are $<a1,b1,c1>$ and $<a2,b2,c2>$ can be computed through the following formula:

$$\cos\theta = \sqrt{\frac{a1a2 + b1b2}{(a1^2 + b1^2)(a2^2 + b2^2)}} \; .$$

The two lines are parallel if $a1b2 = a2b1$, and they are perpendicular if $a1a2 + b1b2 = 0$. For the purposes of modeling polygons, we will usually need to compute the angle between line segments, rather than between lines. The angle between line segments can be computed by function ANGLE, which was discussed earlier, using the end points of the segments as input. We shall, therefore, not present here a Pascal function to compute the angle between lines, which is unnecessarily complicated because Pascal does not have a built-in ARCCOS function.

☐ THE GEOMETRIC ATTRIBUTES OF VERTICES AND SEGMENTS

The geometric attributes of vertices are composed of *points,* which are sets of coordinate values in E2. They can be represented by the POINT data structure that was introduced in Chapter 3:

```
coords = (x,y,z,w);
point  = array [coords] of real;
```

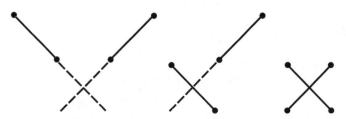

Figure 6.6. Determining the intersection of two line segments.

The **POINT** data structure can be easily associated with the **VERTEX** record, through its **FORM** field:

```
v^.form := pnt
```

The geometric attributes of segments are represented by the **LINE** data structure, which comprises the parameters of the implicit line equation to which the segment belongs. In this book, we address only straight lines, where the line equation $ax + by + c = 0$ can be used.

```
params = (a,b,c);
line   = array [params] of real;
```

The association of **LINE** geometry with the **SEGMENT** record is done through its **FORM** field:

```
g^.form := ln
```

Problems arise when the geometric attributes of segments and vertices must be matched, because they are not independent of each other; the geometric location (point) of each vertex is also the intersection of the lines underlying the two segments it bounds, and the line underlying each segment must pass through the geometric locations (points) of its two bounding vertices.

The methods for computing the parameters of a straight line equation, given two points through which it passes, and for computing the intersection of two straight lines, given their equations, were discussed earlier. We can use them to complete the geometric association of vertices and segments with points and lines, respectively, through procedures **PLACE_VERTEX** and **PLACE_SEGMENT**. These procedures compute and assign the geometric attributes of vertices and segments, given the geometrical attributes of one of the two data structures.

```
procedure place_vertex (v : vptr; g1,g2 : gptr);
{Compute and assign geometric location to vertex v, given the
 two segments g1 and g2 it bounds, along with their line
 equations.}

begin
   compute_point (g1^.form, g2^.form, pnt);
end; {place_vertex procedure}
```

```
procedure place_segment (g : gptr);
{Compute and assign geometric location to segment g, by
 computing the equation of the line passing through the two
 vertices that bound it.}

var  v1,v2 : vptr;

begin
  v1 := g^.gvert; v2 := other_vertex (g);
  compute_line (v1^.form, v2^.form, g^.form)
end; {place_segment procedure}
```

For simplicity and clarity, we will compute the line equations of segments from the points locating their bounding vertices, thereby assuming a vertex-based geometrical approach to the modeling of polygons. This approach is justified, because the ability of the designer to interact with the model, as we shall see in Chapter 30, is restricted to indicating points by locating the cursor on the screen of a graphics workstation.

The construction of polygons can now be completed by assigning geometry to their respective topological elements. We can turn our attention, therefore, to polygon operators that involve both topological and geometric attributes.

□ BIBLIOGRAPHY

Behnke, H., F. Bachmann, K. Fladt, and H. Kunle, eds., *Fundamentals of Mathematics*, MIT Press, Cambridge, MA, 1974.

7

INTER-POLYGON OPERATORS

Inter-Polygon operators represent the highest level of polygon modeling functionality. They construct new polygons by *cutting* and by *pasting* existing polygons and by combining pairs of existing polygons through the *set theoretic* operations of UNION, INTERSECTION, and DIFFERENCE.

☐ THE CONCEPT BEHIND INTER-POLYGON OPERATORS

The *Inter-Polygon* operators are powerful design tools: they allow the user to operate on polygons in an intuitively straight-forward manner, much like manipulating physical pieces of paper. The user works with whole polygons and, therefore, need not be concerned with individual vertices and segments, as depicted in Figure 7.1.

By complying with polygon well-formedness conditions, the Inter-Polygon operators produce polygons that can be used as operandi in subsequent applications of the same operators, thereby achieving any desired form complexity. Furthermore, by deferring the generation of the resulting forms to the computer, the designer may witness the emergence of new forms that he may not have thought of initially, as depicted in Figure 7.2.

The Inter-Polygon operators involve both topological and geometrical manipulation of the data structure and usually employ all the basic and high-level polygon operators we have discussed so far, as well as the geometrical operators. They are themselves hierarchically dependent. *Cut* and *paste* operators, which use the high level SPLIT_POLYGON and MERGE_POLYGONS operators, are used by the set theoretic operators to accomplish their tasks as depicted in Figure 7.3.

We shall, therefore, begin our discussion of inter-polygon operators by presenting the *cut* and *paste* polygon operators and later discuss the set theoretic ones.

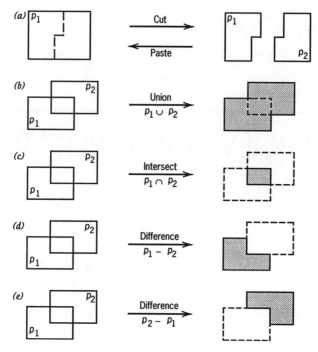

Figure 7.1. Inter-Polygon operators.

☐ CUT AND PASTE POLYGON OPERATORS

In Chapter 5 the operators SPLIT_POLYGON and MERGE_POLYGONS were discussed. These operators perform *topological* operations on polygon data structures. The CUT_POLYGON and PASTE_POLYGONS operators extend these high-level polygon operators by including *geometrical* information, thereby allowing the line of intersection, or the "seam," to follow a specific route, as depicted in Figure 7.3. To this end, the *cut* and *paste* operators require as input a *list of segments,* in addition to the polygons themselves. This list represents the route that will be followed in cutting the operant polygon or the seam along which two polygons will be pasted.

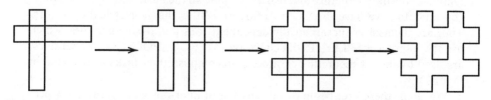

Figure 7.2. Repeated application of inter-polygon operators as a means to achieve high form complexity.

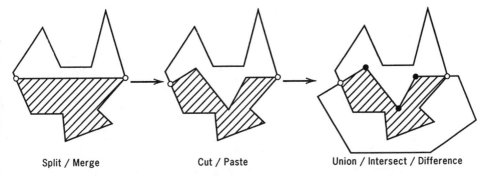

Split / Merge   Cut / Paste   Union / Intersect / Difference

Figure 7.3. Hierarchical dependence of inter-polygon operators.

In compliance with the modularity principles that were discussed in the Introduction, the *cut* and *paste* operators must use the *split* and *merge* operators to perform the topological manipulation of the polygon data structures. Simply splitting the polygon depicted in Figure 7.4 will, however, ignore the contour traced by the list of cut segments. Therefore, after the polygon has been split, each one of its resulting parts must be merged with a copy of the segment list, so it will assume the desired form. The list of segments, however, is not a polygon. Hence, the *cut* and *paste* operators must first convert this list into one or more polygons. This conversion is performed through the polygon operators discussed so far. After the segment list has been converted into polygons, the *split* and *merge* operators can be used on it as discussed in Chapter 5. The algorithm followed by the CUT_POLYGON procedure is depicted in Figure 7.4.

```
procedure cut_polygon (var p1,p2 : pptr;
                            g1,g2 : gptr;
                            glist,glast : gptr);
{Split polygon p1 into two polygons p1 and p2, from g1 to g2,
 along list of segments headed by glist and tailed by glast, by
 splitting p1 then making the list of segments into two polygons
 and merging them with the appropriate parts of p1. Note: one of
 the polygons made from glist must be reversed before it is
 merged!}

var   p11,p12,p21,p22 : pptr;
      gtemp1,gtemp2    : gptr;

function seg_list_polygon (glist,glast : gptr) : pptr;
{Create and return a polygon made from the list of segments
 glist through glast. Note: the polygon may self-intersect!}

var   pnew                 : pptr;
      g,gfirst,gnew,gtemp : gptr;
      v,vnew               : vptr;
```

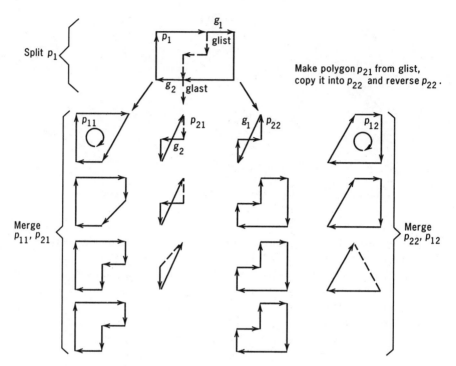

Figure 7.4. The CUT_POLYGON algorithm.

```
begin
  {create new lamina polygon from glist itself}
  create_polygon (pnew,gfirst,vnew);
  assign_point (vnew, glast^.gvert^.form);
  split_segment (gfirst,gnew,vnew);
  assign_point (vnew, glist^.gvert^.form);
  place_segment (gfirst);

  {traverse seg list and grow new polygon}
  g := glist^.gnext;
  while g <> glast do
    begin
      split_segment (gnew,gtemp,vnew);
      assign_point (vnew, g^.gvert^.form);
      place_segment (gnew);
      gnew := gtemp;
      g := g^.gnext;
    end;
  place_segment (gnew);

  seg_list_polygon := pnew
end; {seg_list_polygon function}
```

```
begin {cut_polygons}
  p11 := p1;
  split_polygon (p11,p12, g1,g2);

  p21 := seg_list_polygon (glist,glast);
  p22 := copy_polygon (p21);
  reverse_polygon (p22);

  gtemp1 := p11^.glist; gtemp2 := p21^.glist;
  merge_polygons (p11,p21, gtemp1,gtemp2);
  gtemp1 := p12^.glist; gtemp2 := p22^.glist;
  merge_polygons (p12,p22, gtemp1,gtemp2);

  p1 := p11;
  p2 := p12
end; {cut_polygon procedure}
```

Pasting two polygons along a segment list is, by comparison, a simple operation. It requires only deletion of the intermediate segments and merging of the polygons by the MERGE_POLYGONS operator discussed in Chapter 5. It is demonstrated here by procedure PASTE_POLYGONS.

```
procedure paste_polygons (var p1,p2 : pptr;
                          g11,g12,g21,g22 : gptr);
{Merge polygons p1 and p2 into polygon p1 along list of segments
 from g11 to g12.
```

```
                          g22                                g22
+-------->+             +-->+               +---------->+-->+
¦  p1     ¦ g11         ¦   ¦               ¦   p1          ¦
¦     +<--+     +---->+  ¦   ¦  -->  ¦               ¦
¦     ¦       g21 ¦     p2  ¦       ¦               ¦
+<--+       +<--------+       +<--+<--------+
  g12                                   g12
```

```
}

begin
  {delete internal segments}
  while g11^.gnext <> g12 do
    begin g := g11^.gnext; merge_segment (g) end;
  while g21^.gnext <> g22 do
    begin g := g21^.gnext; merge_segment (g) end;

  merge_polygons (p1,p2, g11,g21)
end; {paste_polygons procedure}
```

Now that we have discussed the *cut* and *paste* operators, we can turn to the much more complicated set theoretic operators, where the list of cutting segments is itself a polygon, as depicted in Figure 7.3.

□ SET THEORETIC POLYGON OPERATORS

The set theoretic Inter-Polygon operators (which are also known as the *Boolean operators*) are an adaptation of the general mathematical set operators of *union, intersection,* and *difference* to the domain of shapes. They provide one of the most powerful tools for the interactive manipulation of shapes and the means to generate shapes of high form complexity in an easy and natural way by direct addition and subtraction of areas.

While intuitively simple, the implementation of set theoretic polygon operators as sequential instruction sets makes them one of the most difficult algorithms in computational geometry. This complexity is further increased by the special attributes of boundaries, such as their orientations. These attributes place the algorithm more in the domain of manifold theory than of set theory. An algorithm that can successfully negotiate these complexities, along with all their special cases (in particular, the presence of coincidental segments), and which relies on the polygon operators discussed this far, is presented. It relies on principles borrowed from general mathematical set theory and Boolean algebra, which are elaborated upon in Appendix A.

The set theoretic Inter-Polygon operators combine a pair of operant polygons, $p1, p2$, such that the product is made in one of the following manners:

1. For UNION: From all the segments of $p1$ that are *outside $p2$* and all the segments of $p2$ that are *outside $p1$*
2. For INTERSECTION: From all the segments of $p1$ that are *inside $p2$* and all the segments of $p2$ that are *inside $p1$*
3. For DIFFERENCE: From all the segments of $p1$ that are *outside $p2$* and all the segments of $p2$ that are *inside $p1$*

Depending on such factors as polygon concavity, the presence of holes, and the relative nestedness of the operant polygons, this algorithm may produce one, none, or a list of polygons as its product, as depicted in Figure 7.5.

Determining the parts of the boundary of each polygon that participate in constructing the boundary of the product polygons is relatively simple when the operandi are disjoint or subjoint. If they are disjoint, their *union* produces new polygons whose boundaries are the boundaries of the two operandi. Their *intersection* is null because there are no points in the two-dimensional Euclidean space (E2) that are shared by both polygons. Their *difference* is $p1$. If one of the operandi is subjoint to the other, their *union* produces a new polygon whose boundary is equivalent to that of the outermost operant, whereas their *intersec-*

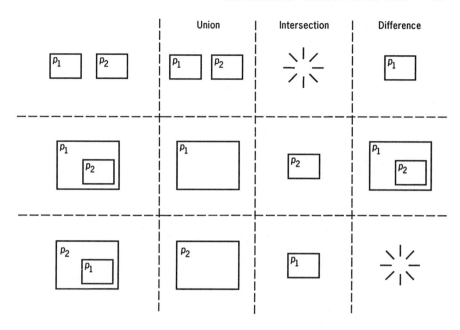

Figure 7.5. Applying the set theoretic operators to nonintersecting polygon boundaries.

tion produces a new polygon whose boundary is equivalent to that of the innermost of the two operandi. Their *difference* may result in a polygon with holes or nothing at all (Figure 7.5).

An implementation of this relatively simple form of the set operations algorithm is demonstrated by function NON_INTERSECTING_POLYGONS.

```
function non_intersecting_polygons (p1,p2 : pptr;
                                    set_op : integer) : pptr;
{Compute and return results of applying the set operation set_op
 to nonintersecting polygons p1 and p2.}

var  plist : pptr;

begin
  {determine relative inclusion of p1 and p2}
  if point_in_polygon (p1^.glist^.gvert^.form, p2)
    then case set_op of
      -1 : plist := p2; {union       }
       1 : plist := p1; {intersection}
       0 : plist := nil {difference  }
    end
```

```
     else if point_in_polygon (p2^.glist^.gvert^.form,p1)
        then case set_op of
           -1 : plist := p1; {union        }
            1 : plist := p2; {intersection}
            0 : begin           {difference }
                   plist := nil;
                   add_polygon (p1, plist);
                   add_hole (p2, p1)
                end
        end
     else case set_op of
        -1 : begin {union}
                plist := nil;
                add_polygon (p1, plist);
                add_polygon (p2, plist)
             end;
         1 : plist := nil; {intersection}
         0 : plist := p1   {difference }
     end;

  non_intersecting_polygons := plist
end; {non_intersecting_polygons function}
```

The generalization of this algorithm over polygons that are conjoint (i.e., that intersect), is more difficult. In that case it is necessary to *partition* the bounding segments of each operant polygon into ones that participate in the construction of the boundary of the product polygons and parts that do not. Such partitioning is accomplished by determining the *points of intersection* where the two boundaries cross each other. These points partition each boundary into subsets of segments, some of which are inside the other polygon and some which are outside it. Once these segment subsets have been identified, they must be *separated* from the rest of the boundary of each operant polygon, forming multiple polygon subsets. These polygon subsets, like the segment subsets they are made of, can be unambiguously classified as being inside or outside the other polygon. The appropriate polygons in each subset must be *joined* together into one or more well-formed boundaries, representing the product polygons, while the others must be deleted.

This sequence of operations is represented in the following algorithm, which is depicted in Figure 7.6 and implemented in function SET_OPERATION:

1. Compute the points of intersection between $p1$ and $p2$ and store them in the Intersection Point List.

2. If the Intersection Point List is empty ($p1$ and $p2$ do not intersect), apply function NON_INTERSECTING_POLYGONS to produce the list of product polygons.

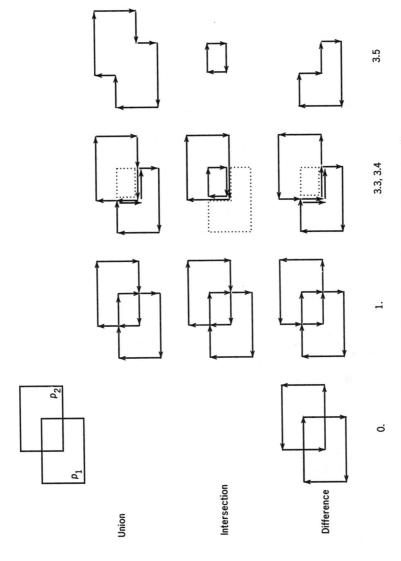

Figure 7.6. A graphic outline of the set theoretic algorithm.

3. If the Intersection Point List is not empty:

    3.0 If the desired set operation is DIFFERENCE, reverse polygon $p2$ and change the set operation to INTERSECTION.

    3.1 Pair the points of intersection into cut segments.

    3.2 Partition $p1$ at the cut segments.

    3.3 Delete the polygons resulting from partitioning $p1$, which will not partake in the product polygon. (For UNION—delete the parts of $p1$ that are inside $p2$; for INTERSECTION—delete the parts of $p1$ that are outside $p2$.)

    3.4 Depending on the desired set operation:

        3.4.1 For UNION—paste the polygons remaining from cutting $p1$ with $p2$.

        3.4.2 For INTERSECTION—delete $p2$.

    3.5 Collect the remaining polygons into a list of polygons that is the product of the set operation algorithm.

```
function set_operation (p1,p2 : pptr; set_op : integer) : pptr;
{Main body of the set operation procedure.}

var  ilist : iptr;

begin
  ilist := nil;
  intersect_polygons (p1,p2, set_op, ilist);

  if ilist = nil
    then plist := non_intersecting_polygons (p1,p2, set_op)
    else begin
      if set_op = 0 {difference}
        then begin
          reverse_polygon (p2);
          set_op := 1 {intersection}
        end;

      pair_intersections (ilist);
      partition_polygon (ilist, set_op);

      if set_op = -1 {union}
        then glue_polygons (ilist)
        else delete_polygon (p2);
      collect_polygons (ilist, plist)
    end;

  set_operation := plist
end; {set_operation function}
```

In the following sections we shall discuss each task and its subtasks.

Computing the List of Intersection Points

This first task lays the foundation for the entire set theoretic operation. In addition to topological manipulation of the data structure, this task performs the only geometric calculations needed for executing the algorithm and is, therefore, most sensitive to numerical errors. In this task, the boundary segments of polygon $p2$ are traversed, and each segment's intersections with all the segments of $p1$ are computed. These intersections signify the transition points where the boundary of $p2$ crosses the boundary of $p1$. The segments of both polygons are split at these intersections, unless a vertex already exists there. The vertices of intersection are link-listed in a data structure we shall call the INTERSECTION_POINT record, which is used throughout the operation. This record stores pointers to the two segments, one on each polygon, which emanate from the intersection point, and a flag that tells whether the segments represent outside-in (entry) or inside-out (exit) transition of their respective boundaries to or from the domain of E2 bounded by the other polygon. Outside-in transitions are considered POSITIVE; inside-out transitions are considered NEGATIVE. An additional pair of pointers in the INTERSECTION_POINT record will be used later to pair them into cut segments.

```
type iptr = ^intersection_point;
     intersection_point = record
        segment : array [1..2] of gptr;
        trans   : array [1..2] of integer;
        pair    : array [1..2] of iptr;
        inext   : iptr
     end;
```

The pairwise intersection test is performed for all contours of the two polygons to account for holes. It is, therefore, the most expensive part of the set theoretic algorithm. Because each segment of each polygon must be tested for intersection with each segment of the other polygon, this is an $O(mn)$ test (m and n being the numbers of segments in each of the two intersecting polygons, respectively). It is demonstrated here in procedure INTERSECT_POLYGONS and depicted in Figure 7.7. (A method for reducing this combinatorial complexity by performing "wholesale" testing of entire polygonal contours is discussed in Part Five of the book.)

```
procedure intersect_polygons (p1,p2 : pptr;
                              set_op : integer;
                              var ilist : iptr);
{Compute the intersections between all contours of p1 and p2,
 recursively.}

var  h2 : pptr;
```

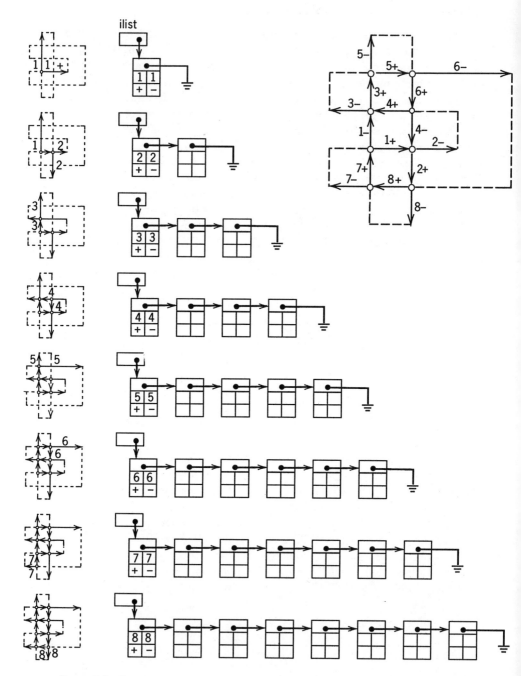

Figure 7.7. Step-by-step intersecting of polygons and building the intersection list.

```
procedure intersect_contours (c1,c2 : pptr;
                              set_op : integer;
                              var ilist : iptr);
{Compute points of intersection between contours c1 and c2.
 Split segments of c1 and c2 at the points of intersection by
 inserting new vertices and segments.}

var  g1,g2 : gptr;
     pnt   : point;

begin
  g1 := c1^.glist;
  repeat      {loop through segments of c1}
    g2 := c2^. glist;
    repeat    {loop through segments of c2}
      if test_intersection (g1,g2, set_op, pnt)
        then add_intersection_point (g1,g2,pnt,ilist);
      g2 := g2^.gnext
    until g2 = c2^.glist;  {end of c2 loop}
    g1 := g1^.gnext
  until g1 = c1^.glist     {end of c1 loop}
end; {intersect_contours procedure}

begin {intersect_polygons procedure}
  intersect_contours (p1,p2,set_op,ilist);
  h2 := p2^. child;
  while h2 <> nil do {loop through holes of p2}
    begin
      intersect_contours (p1,h2,set_op,ilist);
      h2 := h2^.pnext
    end;

  if p1^.hole {recurse through holes of p1}
    then p1 := p1^.pnext
    else p1 := p1^.child;

  if p1 <> nil
    then intersect_polygons (p1,p2,set_op,ilist)
end; {intersect_polygons procedure}
```

In the following sections we shall examine how each one of the steps leading to the construction of the intersection point list can be developed.

Computing the Point of Intersection. A clear and well-defined partitioning is crucial for carrying out the algorithm. It allows the classification of the regions into those that participate in the construction of the product polygon and those that do not. There exist, however, cases where intersecting the boundaries of the operant polygons may produce an ill-behaved list of intersection points that cannot be properly paired and that make the partitioning impossible. Such occurrences, which we refer to as *singularities,* are the result of intersecting two polygons, some or all of whose segments *coincide.* In such cases the transition from "inside" one polygon to its "outside" is accomplished along a *line segment* rather than a *point,* as in the well-behaved cases. Such line segments are neither "inside" nor "outside" either polygon, but rather "on" the boundary of both polygons. Thus they do not conform to the set theoretic basis of the algorithm and may render it inapplicable.

If the algorithm is to handle such boundary coincidences, then we must resolve the singularities; that is, associate the region of coincidence with either that part of the boundary of each operant polygon which will partake in forming the boundary of the product polygon or the one which will not. In pragmatic terms, it is necessary to deem that line segment as being inside the other polygon or outside it. The following set of rules accomplishes the desired unambiguous identification of transition points, relying on the discussion presented in Appendix A:

A segment g, that belongs to polygon $p1$, is considered intersecting the boundary of polygon $p2$ if its two vertices $v1$ and $v2$, [where $v1=g^\wedge$.gvert, and $v2=$ other_vertex(g)], meet one of the following conditions (which are depicted in Figure 7.8):

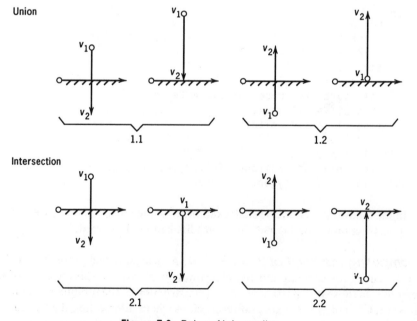

Figure 7.8. Rules of intersection.

1. For UNION (where the boundary of *p2* is considered part of the product polygons), when:

   1.1 *v1* is *outside* and *v2* is *inside or coincident* with *p2*.

   1.2 *v1* is *inside or coincident* with *p2*, and *v2* is *outside*.

2. For INTERSECTION (where the boundary of *p2* is not considered part of the product polygons), when:

   2.1 *v1* is *outside or coincident* with *p2*, and *v2* is *inside*.

   2.2 *v1* is *inside* and *v2* is *outside or coincident* with *p2*.

Figure 7.8 also demonstrates one of the major techniques used in geometric modeling, known as *complete enumeration*. The small number of possible segment-to-segment relationships allows us to examine all of them and thereby guarantees that the algorithm we devise to handle them is complete.

In addition to these rules, to avoid duplications every vertex must be considered only once. Therefore, either *v1* or *v2* should be considered intersecting, but not both (which would create duplications for succeeding segments that intersect *p2* at their joining vertex).

The task of identifying the point of intersection between two segments is carried out by function TEST_INTERSECTION, which returns true if two segments *g1* and *g2*, which belong to polygons *p1* and *p2*, respectively, intersect, and return their point of intersection.

```
function test_intersection (g1,g2 : gptr;
                            set_op : integer;
                            var pnt : point) : boolean;
{Return true if segments g1 and g2 intersect geometrically and
 topologically, and return the point of their intersection.}

var  pos1,pos2 : integer;

begin
  test_intersection := false; {initialize test result}
  if intersect (g1,g2, pnt)   {geometrical intersection}
    then begin
      pos1 := position (g1^.gvert,g2);
      pos2 := position (other_vertex (g1),g2);

      if ((pos1 = -1) and (pos2 = 1))
      or ((pos1 = 1) and (pos2 = -1))
      or ((pos1 = 0) and (pos2 = set_op))
      or ((pos2 = 0) and (pos1 = set_op))
        then test_intersection := true
    end
end; {test_intersection procedure}
```

The point of intersection between segments *g1* and *g2* is computed by means of procedure COMPUTE_POINT, which was introduced in Chapter 6. It is

adapted to handle bounded segments and parallel lines in Function
INTERSECT.

```
function intersect (g1,g2 : gptr; var pnt :  point) : boolean;
{Return true if segments g1 and g2 intersect, and return the
 point of their intersection.}

const epsilon = 10e-6; {an arbitrarily small number}
var    ln1,ln2 : line;

begin
  intersect := false;
  ln1 := g1^.form; ln2 := g2^.form;

  {verify that segments are not parallel}
  if abs (ln1[a]*ln2[b] - ln2[a]*ln1[b]) > epsilon
    then begin {test if segments intersect}
      compute_point (ln1,ln2, pnt);
      if (in_bounds (pnt, g1^.gvert^.form,
                          g1^.gnext^.gvert^.form)
      and in_bounds (pnt, g2^.gvert^.form,
                          g2^.gnext^.gvert^.form))
        then intersect := true
    end
end; {intersect function}
```

Determining the position of a vertex in relation to a segment is a simple matter of computing the *sign* of the area of the triangle formed by the vertex and the
segment. This test relies on the *orientation* of the segment that, according to the
right-hand rule, indicates which side of the segment faces the inside of the polygon and which one its outside. If the area is *positive,* the vertex is on the *right-
hand side* of the segment. If the area is *negative,* the vertex is on the *left-hand
side* of the segment, as depicted in Figure 7.9. If the area is *zero,* the vertex is
coincident with the segment. Function POSITION performs this computation.
Note that because we are dealing here with a vertex and a segment, we cannot
say that the vertex is "inside" or "outside" the polygon to which the segment
belongs.

```
function position (v : vptr; g : gptr) : integer;
{Compute the relationship of vertex v to segment g, using
 triangle area. Return 1 for positive, 0 for coincident, and
 -1 for negative relationships.}

const epsilon = 10e-6;
var    area    : real;
```

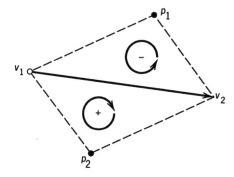

Figure 7.9. Computing the position of a point relative to a segment, using triangle area.

```
begin
  area := tri_area (v, g^.gvert, other_vertex (g));†
  if abs(area) < epsilon
    then position := 0
    else if area > 0
      then position := 1
      else position := -1
end; {position function}
```

Creating Intersection Records. Once an intersection point has been identified, two actions must be taken:

1. Segments $g1$ and $g2$ must be split by a new segment-vertex pair each, unless a vertex already exists at the point of their intersection.
2. A new intersection point record must be added to the intersection point list, recording the two intersecting segments and their relation to the other polygon (i.e., whether they represent outside-in or inside-out transitions relative to the boundary of the other polygon).

To determine whether a segment must be split or whether a vertex already exists at the point of intersection, we can use the POSITION function we used earlier. Although this geometric test is error-prone (due to numerical imprecision), the use of the same function on the same data in different cases ensures a degree of consistent accuracy. If a segment must be split, both topology and geometry must be updated. The determination of the need to split, and the split itself, are combined in function INTERSECTING_SEG.

†This is an adapted version of the same function, discussed in Chapter 2.

```
function intersecting_seg (g1,g2 : gptr) : gptr;
{Determine if one of the vertices of g1 coincides with g2, or if
 g1 must be split. If so, split it. Return pointer to the
 segment whose vertex is at the point of intersection.}

var  pos1,pos2 : integer;
     vnew       : vptr;
     gnew       : gptr;

begin
  pos1 := position (g1^.gvert,g2);
  pos2 := position (other_vertex (g1),g2);

  if [pos1,pos2] = [-1,1]
    then begin {split segment g1 at pnt}
      split_segment (g1,gnew,vnew);
      gnew^.form := g1^.form;
      vnew^.form := pnt
    end;

  if pos1 = 0
    then intersecting_seg := g1
    else intersecting_seg := g1^.gnext
end; {intersecting_seg function}
```

To determine whether the point of intersection is already on the intersection list, we must search the list and test if a record consisting of the two intersecting segments identified by INTERSECTING_SEG function already exists. This search is implemented here by the Boolean function IN_INTERSECTION_LIST.

```
function in_intersection_list (g1,g2 : gptr) : boolean;
{Return true if pair of segments g1 and g2 is in
 intersection_list.}

var  ip    : iptr;
     found : boolean;

begin
  ip := ilist;  found := false;
  while (ip <> nil) and not found do
    if (ip^.segment[1] = g1) and (ip^.segment[2] = g2)
      then found := true
      else ip := ip^.inext;

  in_intersection_list := found
end; {in_intersection_list function}
```

Determining the type of transition (entry or exit) represented by each segment again uses the POSITION function, which was used earlier on two occasions for consistency. Nevertheless, because the segments that were tested earlier may have been split by procedure INTERSECTING_SEG, the current application of the POSITION function may involve different segments. The transition flag test can be made part of the procedure that creates the intersection point record, as demonstrated by procedure ADD_INTERSECTION_POINT.

```
procedure add_intersection_point (g1,g2 : gptr;
                                  pnt : point;
                                  var ilist : iptr);
{Add to ilist a new entry made of g1 and g2, possibly after they
have been split and provided they are not already in ilist.
Determine the transition represented by g1 in relation to the
polygon of g2, and vice versa (1 = entry; -1 = exit). Note:
Segments intersect at their vertices. The transition flag of
g1 is the same as the position of other_vertex (g1). If it is
coincident (pos = 0) then test position of the preceding
vertex. The transition flag of g2 is the opposite of g1.}

var   int_point   : iptr;
      pos         : integer;
      iseg1,iseg2 : gptr;

begin
  iseg1 := intersecting_seg (g1,g2);
  iseg2 := intersecting_seg (g2,g1);

  if not in_intersection_list (iseg1,iseg2)
    then begin
      {compute relation of iseg1 to iseg2}
      pos := position (other_vertex (iseg1), iseg2);
      if pos = 0
        then pos := position (iseg1^.gvert, iseg2);

      new (int_point);
      with int_point^ do
        begin
          segment[1] := iseg1;
          segment[2] := iseg2;
          inext := ilist;
          trans[1] := pos
          trans[2] := -pos
        end;

      ilist := int_point
    end
end; {add_intersection_point procedure}
```

The results of this rather involved set of steps are (1) a pair of polygons whose boundaries have been partitioned at their points of intersection and (2) a list of intersection point records with additional information concerning the type of transition the records represent for each polygon. These results are depicted in Figure 7.7. We can now turn our attention to *pairing* the intersection points into cut segments.

Pairing Intersection Points

The records in the intersection list must be paired to create cut segments where pairs of intersection points represent matching outside-in and an inside-out transitions of one polygon's boundary to the domain of E2 occupied by the other polygon. The segments referenced by each of these paired intersection point records on each polygon form the parameters for the CUT_POLYGON operator which will be applied to partition the polygon along cut segments.

Each intersection point record is used twice, once for each polygon, because it represents an outside-in transition on one polygon and an inside-out transition on the other polygon. Thus, a pair of intersection points *IP*1, *IP*2, representing outside-in and inside-out transitions, respectively, on one polygon, is connected by a sequence of segments on the other polygon (from *IP*2 to *IP*1), which include no other intersection points.

The principles underlying the pairing of intersection points into cut segments are derived from polygon well-formedness. The *closure* property of well-formed polygons, combined with the careful identification of intersection points, which was discussed in the previous section, guarantees that intersection points are *paired;* that is, for every out-in transition there must exist an in-out transition. The *orientation* property of well-formed polygons means that given a point where the boundary of *p*1 *enters* *p*2, we can traverse the boundary of *p*1 to find a matching point where it *exits* *p*2. Furthermore, the list of segments of *p*1 that were traversed in this process of seeking the exit point comprises the *cut list* of segments, which will be used later to partition *p*1 into two parts, one inside *p*2, the other outside it.

These two principles, together with the list of intersection points constructed earlier, can be used to form an efficient algorithm to pair intersection points into cut segments (Figure 7.10):

To pair cut vertices for polygon *p*1:

1. Find an *exit* (negative) transition point on *p*1 by searching the intersection point list.
2. Traverse *p*2, starting at the segment of *p*2 referenced by the point identified in step 1, until you find another segment of *p*2 that is referenced by one of the points in the intersection list. The point that references this segment is the *entry* point on *p*1 which matches the exit point identified in step 1.
3. Repeat steps 1 and 2 until there are no more exit points of *p*1 left to be found in the intersection list.

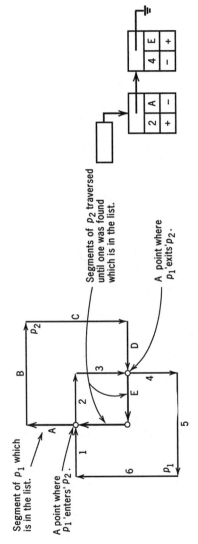

Figure 7.10. Pairing intersection points.

This algorithm is implemented here in procedure PAIR_INTERSECTIONS.

```
procedure pair_intersections (ilist : iptr);
{Pair intersection points for polygon p1.}

var  ip1,ip2 : iptr;
     opp_seg : gptr;
     found   : boolean;

begin
  ip1 := ilist;
  repeat
    {find negative transition (exit)}
    found := false;
    while (ip1 <> nil) and not found do
      if ip1^.trans[1] = -1
        then found := true
        else ip1 := ip1^.inext;

    if found
      then begin
        {find matching positive transition}
        opp_seg := ip1^.segment[2];
        found := false;
        repeat
          opp_seg := opp_seg^.gnext;
          ip2 := ilist;
          while (ip2 <> nil) and not found do
            if ip2^.segment[2] = opp_seg
              then found := true
              else ip2 := ip2^.inext;
        until found;

        ip1^.pair[1] := ip2;
        ip2^.pair[1] := ip1;

        {search for next pair of cut vertices}
        ip1 := ip1^.inext
      end
  until ip1 = nil
end; {pair_intersections procedure}
```

Figure 7.11 depicts the paired intersection point list of a complex case of inter-secting polygons.

Partitioning Polygon *p1*

Once the intersection points have been paired, polygon $p1$ must be partitioned (possibly more than once) into parts that are either completely inside $p2$ or completely outside it. This process, which is implemented in procedure PARTI-TION_POLYGON, generates multiple polygons (whose number depends on the number of paired intersection points). By calling CUT_POLYGON such that its parameters correspond to the respective cut segments (identified through the paired intersection points), the results of the partitioning process (polygons $p11$, $p12$) correspond to an outside and an inside polygon each, respectively. This designation, nevertheless, is *local* to each cut segment and may change as the polygons are split again, as depicted in Figure 7.12. The end result, however, matches the overall inclusion scheme because the cut segments are not independent of each other; they were generated by proper intersections of well-formed polygonal boundaries.

```
procedure partition_polygon (ilist : iptr; set_op : integer);
{Cut polygon p1 along paired intersection points.}


var   ip1,ip2                  : iptr;
      g11,g12,g21,g22, gpred12 : gptr;
      p1,p2                     : pptr;
      found                     : boolean;


begin
  ip1 := ilist;
  repeat
    {find positive intersection point on p1}
    found := false;
    while (ip1 <> nil) and not found do
      if ip1^.trans[1] = +1
        then found := true
        else ip1 := ip1^.inext;


    if found
      then begin
        ip2 := ip1^.pair[1];


        g11 := ip1^.segment[1]; g12 := ip2^.segment[1];
        g21 := ip1^.segment[2]; g22 := ip2^.segment[2];
        gpred12 := predecessor (g12);
```

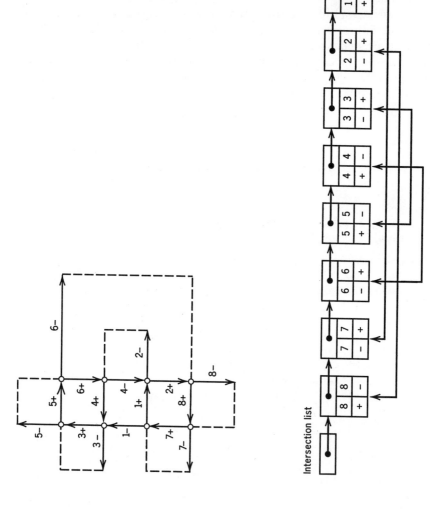

Figure 7.11. Paired intersection points in a case of complex polygon intersection.

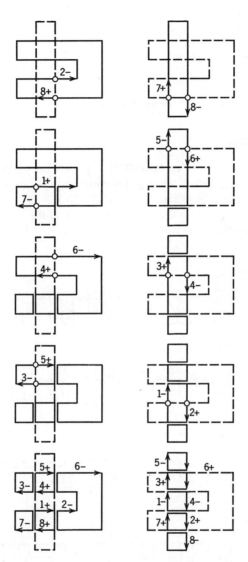

Figure 7.12. Dynamic designation of polygons' relative positions during the splitting process.

```
        p1 := g1^.gpoly;
        cut_polygon (p1,p2, g11,g12, g21,g22);

        if set_op = -1 {union}
           then ip2^.segment[1] := gpred12^.gnext;

        ip1 := ip1^.inext
      end
   until ip1 = nil
 end; {partition_polygon procedure}
```

Gluing Polygons

To conclude the set theoretic operation, the remaining polygons must be "glued" to form the product polygon (possibly more than one). This process relies on PASTE_POLYGONS and on MAKE_HOLE as well as on the cut list. MAKE_HOLE is used when the two segments, identified by the intersection point list, belong to the same polygon (Figure 7.13).

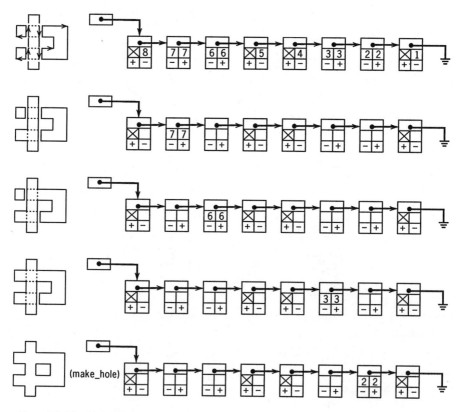

Figure 7.13. Gluing the remaining polygons in the case of a UNION set operation.

```
procedure glue_polygons (ilist : iptr);
{Merge remaining polygons with p2. Note: using i = 1 pairs of
 cut vertices. This procedure is only called if set_op = union
 (-1).}


var   ip1,ip2          : iptr;
      g11,g12,g21,g22  : gptr;
      p1,p2            : pptr;
      found            : boolean;

begin
  ip1 := ilist;
  repeat
    {find negative (outside) intersection point}
    found := false;
    while (ip1 <> nil) and not found do
      if ip1^.trans[1] = -1
        then found := true
        else ip1 := ip1^.inext;

    if found
      then begin
        ip2 := ip1^.pair[1];

        g11 := ip1^.segment[1]; g21 := ip2^.segment[1];
        g12 := ip1^.segment[2]; g22 := ip2^.segment[2];

        p1 := g11^.gpoly;
        p2 := g21^.gpoly;

        if p1 <> p2
          then paste_polygons (p1,p2, g11,g12,g21,g22)
          else make_hole(p1,g11,g21);

        ip1 := ip1^.inext
      end
  until ip1 = nil
end; {glue_polygons procedure}
```

Collecting Disjoint Polygons into a List

In the case of an INTERSECTION set operation, the result of the steps discussed above may be a list of disjoint polygons. They must be collected into a *list* that is returned by function SET_OPERATION as its product. This final step is implemented in procedure COLLECT_POLYGONS.

```
procedure collect_polygons (ilist : iptr; var plist : pptr);
{Traverse ilist and collect non-hole polygons into plist.}

var  ip : iptr;
     p  : pptr;

begin
  ip := ilist;
  while ip <> nil do
    begin
      if ip^.segment[1] <> nil
        then begin
          p := ip^.segment[1]^.gpoly;
          if not p^.hole
            then add_polygon (p, plist)
        end;
    ip := ip^.inext
  end
end; {collect_polygons procedure}
```

As evident from this discussion, Inter-Polygon operations, in particular the set theoretic ones, are complex and intricate. They must handle many interrelated operations, both topological and geometric, which are closely knit: The way we approach one operation affects other ones. This interrelationship between the components of the set theoretic Inter-Polygon operators requires, therefore, that they be regarded as a single modeling transaction in the polygon operators abstraction hierarchy. Of course there are many different ways to implement them, some better in certain respects than others. The approach presented here was chosen because of its relative presentational conciseness, completeness, and reliance on the previously discussed polygon operators. It does not represent the most efficient way, computationally, to implement Inter-Polygon operators. The reader is encouraged to explore other, more efficient solutions.

☐ BIBLIOGRAPHY

Eastman, C. M., and C. Yessios, "An Efficient Algorithm for Finding the Union, Intersection, and Difference of Spatial Domains," Institute of Physical Planning, Technical Report 31, Carnegie-Mellon University, Pittsburgh, PA, September 1972.

Sutherland, I. E., and G. W. Hodgman, "Reentrant Polygon Clipping," *Communications of the ACM,* **17**(1):32–42, January 1974.

Weiler, K., "Polygon Comparison Using a Graph Representation," *Proceedings of ACM SIGGRAPH 80,* 1980, pp. 10–18.

8

EXERCISE 1: POLYGON MODELING

For computers to be useful design tools, we must provide them with a computational model of the artifact or the environment being designed. This model can be implemented as an abstract data type, which consists of a data structure and operators that manipulate it. In Part One, we developed and presented a hybrid, segment-vertex-based model. In this exercise, you are asked to design and implement a *vertex-based* model, which will be capable of representing and manipulating polygons.

Your first task in this exercise is to design a vertex-based data structure to represent polygons, which will be concise and self-consistent. Your second task is to write the low- and high-level topological and geometric operators needed to manipulate the data structure you design, in a manner that complies with the polygon well-formedness rules we discussed in Chapter 2. Your third task is to make use of the data structure and the operators you designed, in implementing two specific applications: Chamfering and Break-segment.

☐ POLYGON DATA STRUCTURE

A polygon, as defined in Chapter 2, can be represented by its boundaries. Each boundary can be considered a circuit of n points connected by n straight line segments. The points are called vertices, and the connecting lines are called segments.

Two types of data are involved in making a polygon data structure: topology and geometry. The topology determines which vertices are adjacent to which segments, and the geometry determines the location of both vertices and segments.

109

There are also three well-formedness conditions that must be satisfied if the data structure is to represent polygons:

1. Each vertex must be adjacent to exactly two segments (and vice versa).
2. Adjacent segments must intersect at a vertex; nonadjacent segments must not intersect at all.
3. Segments must be consistently directed.

The first condition guarantees that the shape will be closed and will have no "dangling" vertices or segments. The second condition guarantees that the area bounded by the shape is continuous. The third condition guarantees that the polygon has a well-defined inside and outside.

While the data structure itself cannot guarantee that segments do not self-intersect, it can (and should) guarantee that each vertex is adjacent to exactly two sides and that the polygon has a consistent orientation. The non-self-intersection condition should be guaranteed by the operators.

There are several different ways in which a polygon data structure can be set up. Because of the duality of the polygon definition, it can be represented by means of its vertices, by means of its segments, or by both. In this exercise, you are asked to design a vertex-based data structure. Note that segments, while not explicitly represented by this data structure, exist nonetheless and must be manipulated by the operators.

□ POLYGON OPERATORS

Your second task in this exercise is to write operators to manipulate the polygon data structure, both topologically and geometrically. The basic topological operators for a vertex-based polygon data structure create and destroy vertices, as depicted in Figure 8.1, are items 1 through 4 below. In addition to these topological operators, there is also one geometrical operator, item 5.

1. INIT_POLY creates a minimal polygon made of one vertex. The vertex must be connected to itself, because it serves as both end points for the implicitly represented segment.
2. DELETE_POLY deletes a minimal polygon, including its vertex.
3. SPLIT_SEGMENT adds a new vertex and thereby a new implicit segment.
4. MERGE_SEGMENT deletes an existing vertex, along with its implicit segment.
5. PUT_VERTEX assigns an ⟨x, y⟩ location to a given vertex.

You should design and implement these operators in such a way that the well-formedness of the polygon will be maintained at all times.

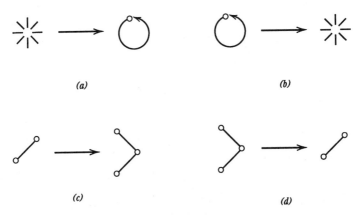

Figure 8.1. Basic topological polygon operators: (a) INIT_POLY, (b) DELETE_POLY, (c) SPLIT_SEGMENT, and (d) MERGE_SEGMENT.

In order to test them out, you will have to provide some auxiliary operators and provide the necessary user interface to the system. These are:

1. MAKE_POLY, which reads user-defined cursor locations and creates a corresponding polygon (using INIT_POLY, SPLIT_SEGMENT and PUT_VERTEX).
2. KILL_POLY, which performs successive MERGE_SEGMENTs on a user-picked polygon until a minimal polygon is reached, then performs a DELETE_POLY.
3. PICK_VERTEX, which reads a cursor location and returns a pointer to the vertex of the polygon which is closest to it.
4. PICK_SEGMENT, which reads a cursor location and returns a pointer to the segment of the polygon which is closest to it.
5. MOVE_VERTEX, which reads a cursor location and assigns it to a given vertex by means of PUT_VERTEX.

The first two operators will allow users to create and delete arbitrary polygons. The third through the fifth allow users to modify a polygon by adding and deleting vertices and segments and by moving vertices to new locations.

☐ APPLICATIONS

Your third task in this exercise is to apply your polygon model in two specific applications that perform Chamfering and Break-segment operations (Figure 8.2). These operators are useful for many design operations. Chamfering is used to trim away corners of existing polygons, simply by pointing at the corner (or,

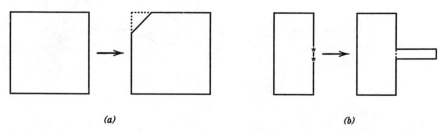

(a)   (b)

Figure 8.2. Applications of high-level polygon operations: (a) Chamfering; (b) Break-segment.

rather, the vertex). Break-segment is used in creating architectural floor plans by "growing" new walls from existing ones. Both operators can be implemented as combinations of the operators you have designed in the first two parts of this exercise.

PART TWO

3D CONSTRUCTION

9

THE PROPERTIES OF SOLIDS

Solids form a family of three-dimensional shapes that have the property of enclosing volume. In addition, their form is independent of their location and orientation in space. In contrast, nonsolid shapes include such forms as wire frames, which enclose no volume, and liquids, whose shapes depend on the containers that hold them. Solidity (the property of having an invariant, volumetric shape) is the most important attribute of many physical objects, because it literally causes them to "materialize" in the three-dimensional space and provides a frame of reference to which other attributes, such as material and color, may be assigned.

Computers, however, can deal only with symbolically represented entities. Therefore, they cannot deal directly with solids; solids must be represented by means of symbol structures. There are different ways in which symbol structures for representing solids can be constructed. In this part of the book, we shall study some of them and devise measures to evaluate their properties.

□ THE DEFINITION OF SOLIDS

The most general formal definition of a solid is *a compact set of contiguous points in three-dimensional space.* Points that belong to the solid can be distinguished from other points in the same space that are not part of the solid. This property, which we call *solidity,* is the most important characteristic of the three-dimensional shapes we shall deal with. The other important property of a solid is *compactness.* The set of points that form the solid, although infinitely large, occupies only a finite amount of space and, therefore, can be "wrapped" by a boundary of a finite size. The property of *contiguity,* which was mentioned in the definition, ensures that a path will exist between any two points that are part of the solid. This path is made exclusively of points that are themselves part of the solid. The property of contiguity excludes solids made of multiple disjoint parts, but does not exclude *cavities,* which are equivalent to holes in polygons.

It is impossible, of course, to represent in the computer all the points that make up the three-dimensional point set of a solid. Instead, we must devise a more economical symbolic representation, which will uniquely and unambiguously correspond to the theoretical point set. As was the case with polygons, the particular symbol structure we shall use to represent solids must posses certain properties, which include:

1. **Well formedness:** The symbol structure should represent only "no-nonsense" objects, unlike the one depicted in Figure 9.1. Otherwise, the artifacts and environments it represents may not be physically realizable. Well-formedness thus guarantees uniqueness and unambiguity: a one-to-one correspondence between the physical object and its symbolic representation.

2. **Completeness:** The symbolic representation should provide the necessary data for computing all the formative properties of the object it describes, such as its volume and center of inertia. This property is particularly important when the model must support an open-ended range of applications, many of which are not known in advance.

3. **Generality:** The model should be capable of representing a wide variety of forms and all the forms that can be derived by manipulating the forms it can represent. A model that can represent only curved forms, for example, cannot be used in architecture, and one that can represent only planar-faced polyhedra cannot be used in the automotive and aerospace industries. If certain operations applied to representable forms result in nonrepresentable forms, then the modeler is poor indeed.

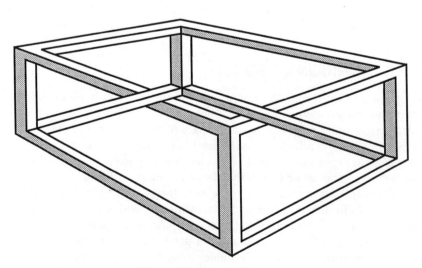

Figure 9.1. Ill-formed shape.

4. **Efficiency:** The amount of information required to store models in the computer's memory and to transmit them over data links must be minimal. To allow for timely manipulation of shape information and to guarantee the well-formedness of that information, relatively few redundant data items should be maintained.

How can we devise a representation scheme that will have all these desired properties? Are there different methods of representation that fulfill all the requirements? If so, which ones are better than others? To answer these questions, we shall first briefly review the generic classes of shape representation methods, then focus on one method that appears to be more suitable than others for the purposes of modeling solids.

□ METHODS OF REPRESENTATION

The symbolic representation of physical solids in the memory of computers is a problem that has been studied by many researchers for more than two decades. These studies have not only resulted in a host of methods and techniques for the representation of solids, but have also established a rigorous theory that underlies such representations.

Spatial Occupancy Enumeration

Early attempts to represent solids used the point-set concept in a rather literal way: The entire Euclidean space was represented by means of a 3-dimensional array of cells (called "voxels"), which were usually cubes of a fixed size set in a fixed spatial grid. The object itself was defined as the subset of adjacent cells within the universal grid that were partially or fully occupied by the object. This method, which is known as *spatial occupancy enumeration*, has the advantages of easy spatial addressing (accessing a given point in space) and ensuring spatial uniqueness (the avoidance of two objects occupying the same space at the same time). It lacks, however, object coherence, in that there is no explicit relationship between the spatial units that make up the object. This method is also extremely expensive in terms of storage space. It is highly redundant, because any cell is likely to have the same state of occupancy as the cells adjacent to it (i.e., contain "matter" or not). Only at the boundaries of the shape is this not so. Furthermore, to achieve a smooth surface representation, the size of the individual cells of the grid must be small. However, halving the size of individual cells increases their number eightfold (2^3).

To overcome the problem of storing n^3 cells for each solid, thereby achieving a resolution of $1/n$, a structuring technique called *octree subdivision* can be used. According to this method, a cube representing the entire spatial array is recursively subdivided into eight octants until the content of each cell is homogeneous (i.e., it contains either "matter" of "void") or until minimal-size cubes are reached. The solid is thus represented by a structure containing cells of different sizes (Figure 9.2).

The low resolution offered by spatial occupancy enumeration makes it inadequate for the purpose of modeling engineered objects and environments. It has, nevertheless, found use for other purposes, such as tomography, where the degree of acceptable resolution is low in comparison and where data collection techniques provide fuzzy information to begin with (e.g., X rays and nuclear magnetic resonance—NMR).

Constructive Solid Geometry (CSG)

A different approach, which yielded one of the two currently most important solid representation schemes, is based on representing solid objects as Boolean combinations (union, intersection, and difference) of a limited set of primitive components. A modeling system that uses this method organizes a complex solid as a binary tree: nonterminal nodes represent operators that may be either linear transforms (rotation and translation) or Boolean operations. The terminal nodes contain primitive solids or transformed instances of those. These primitive solids include cubes, cylinders, wedges, and other shapes. Each subtree represents an object that is the combined result of applying the operators stored in the nonterminal nodes to the primitives stored in the leaf nodes (Figure 9.3).

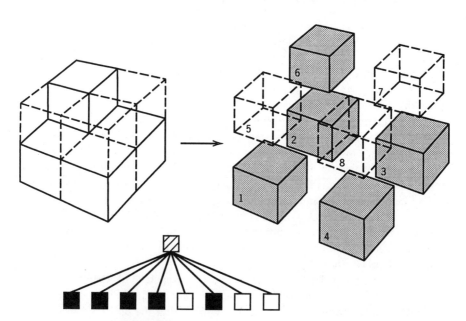

Figure 9.2. Octree representation of a solid.

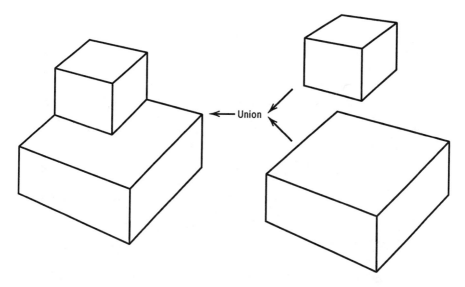

Figure 9.3. A constructive solid geometry (CSG) representation of a solid.

The generality of the Constructive Solid Geometry (CSG) representation method is determined by its set of primitives and by the operators that combine them. Some implementations include, in addition to Boolean operations, also generalized sweep operations, which can "extrude" polygons into prismatic solids. The well-formedness of solids represented as CSG trees is guaranteed if the set of primitives is well-formed and closed under the available operators. However, while providing an extremely compact representation, CSG-represented solids are inefficient sources of geometric data for applications that require explicit information about the composite shape or its boundary.

Boundary Representation (B-rep)

A representation method that is less concise than the CSG model, but one that provides explicit access to the boundary elements of a polyhedral shape, can be constructed by representing explicitly only those points of the set forming the solid where the transition between solid and void occurs. The set of explicitly represented points comprises an abstract entity known as the *bounding surface* of the solid. It partitions the universal point set into two (or more) disjoint domains, exactly one of which is bounded and contains those points that are internal to the solid. The boundary representation model facilitates compact storage and high object resolution. The shapes represented by it are, however, much more difficult to manipulate than those represented by means of the CSG model and are, in particular, inefficient for spatial addressing. It is an algorithmically difficult operation to determine whether a given point is inside or outside the shape.

The bounding surface is typically subdivided at its geometrical curvature discontinuities into *faces*. Each face is bounded by a circuit (called a *ring*) of edges, which are connected pairwise-sequentially by vertices (Figure 9.4). In this respect, faces are equivalent to *polygons* of the type discussed in Part One. Faces abide by all the conditions associated with polygons and can be manipulated by the same operators if certain extensions are provided. The boundary of a solid may consist of multiple disjoint *shells*, as in the case of a solid that contains cavities, such as a pressure vessel. The role of cavities in solids is equivalent to the role of holes in polygons.

This so-called *polyhedral representation* consists of two classes of information: *geometry*, which includes the physical dimensions and location in space of each component (face, edge, vertex), and *topology*, which describes the relationships between the components. Both geometrical and topological information are necessary to completely describe a shape; each having its own conceptual and practical significance. Specifically, topology maintains the coherence of the shape representation, and geometry materializes and fixes the shape in three-dimensional Euclidean space.

The boundary representation method was chosen for the purposes of this book because of its advantages and because it continues the line of reasoning developed by representing polygons through their boundaries. We shall see that solids can actually be built from polygons, thus reinforcing the principles of modularity and abstraction that are at the core of geometric modeling.

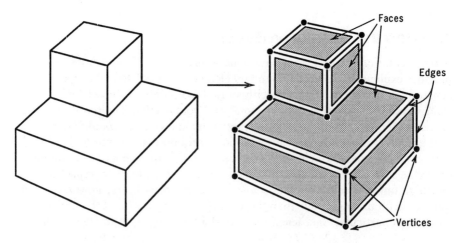

Figure 9.4. A boundary representation (B-rep) of a solid.

□ WELL-FORMEDNESS

The boundary of a solid has some unique characteristics that distinguish it from purely mathematical set-theoretic point sets, as discussed in Appendix A, and place it in the domain of *manifolds*. In particular, these characteristics support coherent object representation and allow determination of well-formedness through localized tests that are particularly suitable for computer manipulation.

From a mathematical point of view, it is not immediately apparent that a surface can represent fully and unambiguously the solid it bounds. Stated more formally, in general a subset of E^n does not uniquely represent E^n itself. It is necessary, therefore, to establish the conditions under which such simplification is permitted. These conditions are part of the general well-formedness conditions we have discussed in Chapter 1, which any shape representation method must satisfy.

Derived from general topology and homology theory, well-formedness conditions can be stated as *semantic integrity constraints*. This statement allows well-formedness conditions to be related to a particular solid representation method, such as the boundary representation, and provides a basis for making assertions about the validity of the model at various stages of its manipulation by examining only its boundary.

The application of semantic integrity constraints to the boundary of a solid relies on the ability to *triangulate* any E2 manifold embedded in E3; that is, subdivide the boundary into multiple areas (called 2-simplices), each bounded by three edges (called 1-simplices) and the vertices that bound them (called 0-simplices).† Such subdivision results in each vertex being surrounded by a set of triangles, each pair of which are adjacent at an edge. The edges of these triangles opposite the vertex form a polygon, which is known as the *link* of the vertex (Figure 9.5).

The constraints that guarantee the well-formedness of the bounding surface of a solid can now be formulated as follows:

1. The link of every vertex of a triangulated surface must be complete (i.e., must be a well-formed, though not necessarily planar, polygon).
2. The triangles of a triangulated surface must be consistently orientable.

Compliance with the first condition guarantees that the triangulated surface is *closed* and *connected*. Closedness implies that the surface has no ends. Connectedness implies that there exists a path from one triangle to any other triangle on the same surface, which can be traversed by crossing shared edges. When the surface is not closed or is disconnected, its triangulation fails to produce a proper link for each vertex, as shown for some cases in Figure 9.6. Because the link constraint is concerned only with adjacency relationships between the com-

---

†More formally, a triangulation is defined as a *homomorphism from E^n to a (finite) set of simplical complexes that are subsets of E^n*. In our case, $n = 3$, and the simplices are of dimensions 2 (faces), 1 (edges), and 0 (vertices).

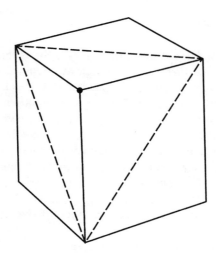

Figure 9.5. The link of a vertex in a triangulated surface.

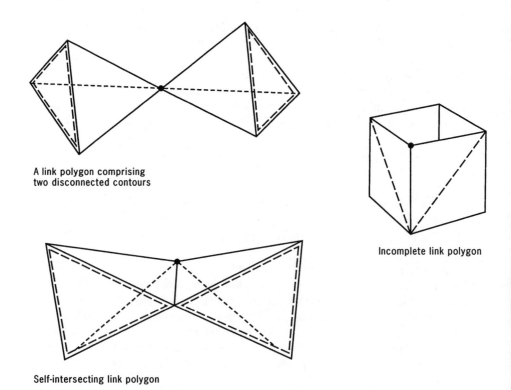

A link polygon comprising
two disconnected contours

Incomplete link polygon

Self-intersecting link polygon

Figure 9.6. Ill-formedness detectable by the link condition.

ponents of the bounding surface, it is a *topological* property and can therefore be verified by means of local tests.

Orientability is a property that allows differentiation between one topological structure and its mirror image, detects self-intersections, and guarantees that any pair of adjacent faces is geometrically consistent. In addition, orientability guarantees that the topological structure of a solid is consistent with it geometric structure. Orientability, therefore, is both a *topological* and a *geometrical* property of shapes.

Topologically consistent orientation can be verified by means of Möbius' law:

A closed surface is consistently oriented if by traversing its triangles (resulting from an arbitrary triangulation) in a clockwise direction, each edge is traversed exactly *twice* and in *opposite* directions (Figure 9.7).

Möbius' law is instrumental, for example, in detecting the ill-formedness of shapes such as the Klein bottle, which is depicted in Figure 4 in the Introduction.

Geometrically consistent orientation guarantees that any pair of adjacent points (that are not part of the boundary itself and are not separated by it) belong to the same domain of E3, as partitioned by the boundary. Geometrically consistent orientation can be verified by testing whether the normals to any adjacent pair of regions on the bounding surface point to the same domain of space, as partitioned by the boundary (i.e., both point "inside" the shape, or both point "outside" it). Such consistency is important particularly for operations that rely on the ability to identify the containment relationship between points in E3 and the shape, such as the spatial set operators that are discussed in Chapter 16.

The consistency between topological orientation, as defined by Möbius' law, and the geometric orientation, as defined by consistent orientation of surface normals, can be verified by two tests:

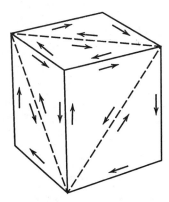

Figure 9.7. Möbius' Law verifies consistent orientation of a triangulated surface.

1. Consistent compliance with a convention such as the right-hand rule
2. Non-self intersection.

The *right-hand rule convention,* similar to the one discussed in Chapter 2, can best be illustrated by considering a planar-faced, triangulated shape. When traversing the three vertices of any face in a clockwise direction, the normal to the plane they define is pointing outward.

Non-self intersection is a test that requires global shape data for its verification. It ensures that the geometric surfaces associated with pairs of topologically adjacent faces intersect only along lines that correspond to topologically common edges and that surfaces associated with topologically nonadjacent faces do not intersect at all (or intersect outside their parts that form the boundary of the solid).

Triangulation, though convenient for illustrating the concepts of closedness and orientability, is not a necessary condition. It can be relaxed by considering the appropriate subsets of edges as links that bound the faces surrounding a vertex. In this case, the orientability criteria must be applied to these edges rather than to the triangles. Conceptually, this transition from triangles to faces can occur by combining pairs of curvature-continuous triangles into one face.

The assurance of topologically verifiable well-formedness constraints can be embedded completely within the operators that construct and modify the shape model. Such are the link constraints and the topological orientability constraints that are testable by Möbius' law. Many solid modeling systems that are based on the boundary representation method use a particular set of operators for this purpose, known as the *Euler operators*. These operators are based on the numerical relationships between the elements of a polyhedral shape that were discovered by the eighteenth century Swiss mathematician Leonhard Euler and are known as Euler's law:

$$F - E + V = 2$$

where F denotes faces, E denotes edges, and V denotes vertices.[†]

Geometrical well-formedness conditions, in particular those requiring global shape data, are difficult to ensure or even to verify. Consider, for example, a shape that consists of three shells (i.e., three distinct bounding surfaces), such as a pressure vessel (Figure 9.8). Its shells must be oriented (geometrically) relative to each other in a consistent way, in addition to each complying independently with the link and non-self intersection constraints. In particular, two adjacent shells (i.e., ones that are not separated by an intervening shell) must either be *disjoint,* in which case each shell is in the domain of space that is outside the other shell, or be *subjoint,* in which case each shell is in the domain of space that

---

[†]Euler's law can be expressed in more general terms as

$$F - E + V = H + 2*(1 - G)$$

where H is the number of holes in all the faces, and G is the genus of the shape. Euler's law is discussed more extensively in Chapter 11.

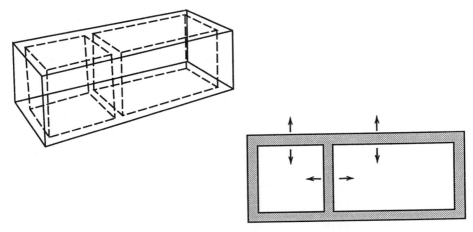

Figure 9.8. Verifying well-formedness conditions in a multiple-shelled shape.

is inside the other shell. It is possible, however, to invert one of the shells in Figure 9.8 such that it will violate the orientability constraint without affecting the topological well-formedness relations between its constituent parts. Verification of compliance with such well-formedness constraints requires computationally expensive algorithms and, therefore, is often not tested in existing solid modeling systems that are based on the boundary representation method.

□ CONSTRUCTING SOLIDS

To construct a spatial array representation of a shape, all that is needed is an ordered enumeration of all the cells in the array that are occupied by the object. Boundary representations are more difficult to construct. One method to do so is called *primitive instancing*. It is the simplest and most common way to define a new shape as a linear transformation of an existing shape. The transformed shape is often known as an "instance" of the original and may consist of a translation and rotation or may include scaling and shear (change in size and proportions). It is based on the notion of *object families*. The family is characterized by a generic primitive, such as a hexahedron or a cylinder, and each member of the family is distinguishable by a few parameters. For example, a family of hexahedrons may contain several items, such as a brick, a door, and a room. Their topological structure is the same, they only vary in their geometry, the variances classified as length (l), width (w), and height (h) (Figure 9.9).

The primitive, generic solids must, however, be constructed from more basic elements. There are three major techniques to construct them:

1. **Construct** them piece by piece from faces, edges, and vertices according to some syntactical rules.
2. **Sweep** them from a characteristic contour.

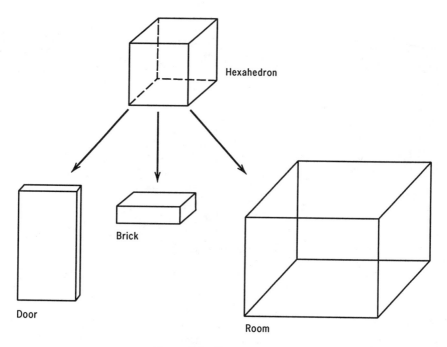

Figure 9.9. Shape families.

3. **Combine** primitive shapes into more complex ones by means of spatial set operators.

Constructing Shapes From Primitive Elements

Constructing solids from their elementary components of faces, edges, and vertices is the most general, yet cumbersome way of generating solid shape representations. The basic components serve as atomic units of a solid construction "language" and are combined into shapes according to some syntactical rules.

The Euler operators are a convenient tool for constructing shapes from their atomic elements while maintaining internal consistency within the data structure (Figure 9.10).

Obviously, constructing a shape from scratch by means of the Euler operators is a complex and tedious operation. However, it allows virtually unlimited freedom in defining shapes and is, therefore, often used as the base for all other solid generation operators.

Sweeping

The basic notion embodied in sweeping schemes is very simple: A polygon moving through space may sweep a solid whose shape depends on the contour of the polygon and its trajectory. Consider a polygon A lying in a plane and a line segment B perpendicular to the plane of A and having an end point on the plane

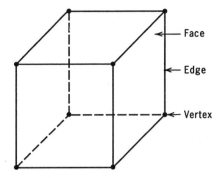

Figure 9.10. Generating solids by constructing them from primitive components.

(Figure 9.11a). A solid is swept by a translation perpendicular to the axis of B and along that axis. Rotational sweeping schemes may be defined in a similar manner: The polygon is swept around some axis rather than along a perpendicular line (Figure 9.11b).

Sweeping is also known as *extrusion,* and shapes generated by this method are sometimes referred to as "two-and-a-half" dimensional objects rather than three-dimensional objects, because their cross section is invariant. The trajec-

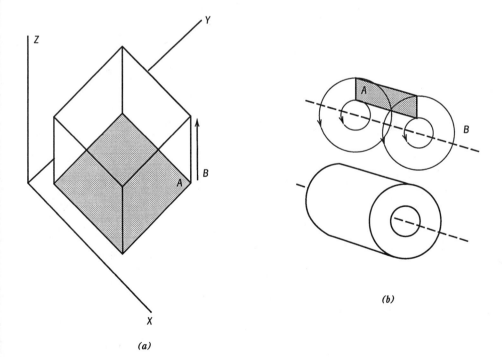

(a)

(b)

Figure 9.11. Generating solids by means of sweeping.

tory need not be a straight line, and the polygon may undergo deformations as it travels through space.

The domain of objects representable by sweeping schemes is limited to objects with translational or rotational symmetry. They are, however, very convenient to interface, and are, therefore, typically part of many solid modeling systems.

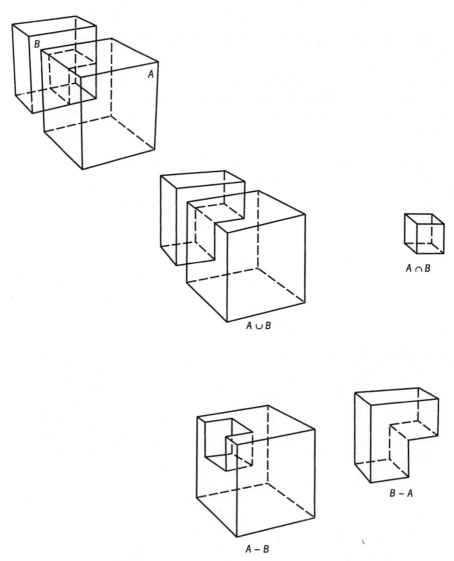

Figure 9.12. Generating solids by means of spatial set operators.

Shape Operations

To increase the set of definable shapes without having to construct each new shape from scratch, a set of operators, known as the *spatial set operators* or simply as the *shape operators*, can be used. Like the set operators discussed in Chapter 7 for combining polygons, solid shape operators are adaptations of the mathematical set operators of union, intersection, and difference, as applied to shapes (Figure 9.12).

Shape operators are an extremely powerful modeling tool. Their power lies in their iterative applicability, which allows easy definition of particularly complex shapes. Iterative applicability is made possible by preserving the well-formed-ness of both operandi and product shapes, thus providing a consistency of representation for both.

While intuitively easy to understand, shape operators are difficult to implement due to complications arising from special cases, such as coincident faces. In principle, shape operators are complete, in that given a suitable set of primitive shapes, they can be used to construct *any* representable shape. Still, shape operations are not always the right tool for shape generation. They are based on computationally expensive algorithms, and the sole use of simple primitives and operators may lead to a spuriously complicated and nonintuitive definition of quite simple and everyday parts.

☐ BIBLIOGRAPHY

Baer, A., C. Eastman, and M. Henrion, "Geometric Modeling: A Survey," *Computer-Aided Design* **11**(5):253–272, September 1979.

Eastman, C. M., and K. Preiss, "A Review of Solid Shape Modeling Based on Integrity Verification," *Computer-Aided Design*, **16**(2):66–80, March 1984.

Giblin, P. J., *Graphs, Surfaces, and Homology.* Chapman and Hall, New York, 1977.

Kalay, Y. E., "Determining the Spatial Containment of a Point in General Polyhedra," *Computer Graphics and Image Processing* **19**:303–334, 1982.

Kalay, Y. E., "Vertically Integrated Geometric Modeling Based on the Hybrid Edge Model," Technical Report, Computer-Aided Design and Graphics Laboratory, State University of New York at Buffalo, June 1987.

Lakatos, I., *Proofs and Refutations,* Cambridge University Press, New York, 1976.

Mantyla, M., *An Introduction to Solid Modeling,* Computer Science Press, Rockville, MD, 1988.

Requicha, A. A. G., "Representations for Rigid Solids: Theory, Methods, and Systems," *Computing Surveys* **12**(4):437–464, December 1980.

Samet, H., "The Quadtree and Related Hierarchical Data Structures," *ACM Computing Surveys,* No. 16, pp. 187–260, 1984.

Yessios, C., "The Computability of Void Architectural Modeling," *Computability of Design,* Y. E. Kalay, ed. Wiley-Interscience, New York, 1987.

10

THE REPRESENTATION OF SOLIDS

In this chapter we discuss edge-based data structures that can be used to implement the boundary representation scheme. Three such data structures are presented and compared: the Winged Edge model, the Split Edge model, and the Hybrid Edge model. The Hybrid Edge model is chosen for supporting the operators discussed in the following chapters.

□ A CANONICAL MODEL OF THE BOUNDARY REPRESENTATION

Combining the elementary components of the boundary (faces, edges, and vertices) into well-formed manifolds is the first step in generating models of boundary-represented solids. The basic components serve as atomic units of a solid construction "language" and are represented by the data structure. They are combined into manifolds according to some syntactical rules, represented by the operators that manipulate the data structure. The Euler operators, introduced in Chapter 9, provide not only the syntax of such construction rules, but also their semantics; they help maintain the consistency of the model as it develops toward a well-formed manifold.

The use of Euler operators for constructing boundary representation models of solids is predicated on tailoring a particular data structure, which explicitly represents all the boundary elements and the relationships between them, to a particular subset of the Euler operators that manipulate it. However, representation of all the boundary elements and all their relationships is neither necessary nor desirable, because verbosity and redundancy will make the data structure difficult to manipulate and may introduce inconsistencies. Existing modeling systems use, therefore, only subsets of all the theoretically possible relationships between the elements of the boundary. The different choices of such subsets account for the variances between different boundary representation models.

What constitutes a "sufficient" subset of elements and rules largely depends on the intended uses of the model, its domain of representable solids, and the operators to manipulate them. For example, an implementation that handles only planar polyhedra may consist of a data structure that represents explicitly only circular linked lists of vertices. The interpretation of this topologically vertex-based structure implies that pairs of adjacent vertices correspond to edges, while an entire circular list corresponds to a face. While concise and easy to manipulate, such an implementation raises difficult consistency and addressability problems. Because edges are not explicitly represented, it is difficult, for example, to associate with them nontopological attributes, such as graphics display flags for visibility control (so edges are not displayed twice) and information about the adjacency of faces (which is needed for implementing the spatial set operators). Most existing systems use, therefore, a richer data structure, which is based topologically on edges rather than on vertices.

Before some such data structures are discussed, it is useful to formalize the vocabulary that will be employed. In this context it is important to distinguish between the *topological* attribute of the boundary elements and their *geometrical* ones. The geometrical elements are:

Space, considered in its usual Euclidean notion as E3, an infinite set of points contiguous in three dimensions of X, Y, and Z.

Surface, a subset E2 of E3, the loci of a set of points contiguous in two dimensions.

Line, a subset E1 of E3, the loci of a set of points contiguous in one dimension.

Point, a subset E0 of E3, a particular location in space defined by three values x, y, and z.

The topological elements are:

Shell (bounding surface), the set of points that partition the universal set of points into several domains, exactly one of which is bounded and known as the *interior* of the shape.

Face, a region within the boundary bounded by edges, associated geometrically with a curvature-continuous part of the bounding surface.

Edge, one of the two components of the perimeter bounding a face or its holes, associated geometrically with a two-axis curvature discontinuity of the boundary.

Vertex, the other component of the perimeter bounding a face or its holes, associated geometrically with a three-axis curvature discontinuity of the boundary.

The Edge-Based Data Structure

The multiplicity of formative elements requires that some type of "glue" be provided to connect them into one integrated structure. This "glue" must not only connect the entities, but must also provide proper traversal *directionality* information. This information is used by a variety of operators, which include determination of "inside-outness" of the boundary-represented solid.

The "glue" used by most polyhedral solid modeling systems comes in the form of *edges*. In such edge-based data structures, each edge record includes many of its connections to other topological entities (faces, other edges, and vertices), as depicted in Figure 10.1. This data structure ensures topological well-formedness by complying with the link constraint discussed in Chapter 9 and allows the association of attributes with the edges (as well as with other boundary elements). It cannot, however, guarantee geometrical well-formedness in terms of consistent orientability and non-self-intersection or the consistency between topological and geometric orientations. These must be ensured by other means.

The structure depicted by Figure 10.1 shows how edges can form the centerpiece of the model because of their extensive connections. Each edge is connected in three ways:

1. To each of the two faces it is adjacent to
2. To the two endpoint vertices that bound it
3. To the four edges (two in each face) it is connected to

Because edges connect all the boundary elements, few additional connections are theoretically needed. However, for manipulation purposes, it is convenient to add links between faces and edge rings (holes) and between solids and faces.

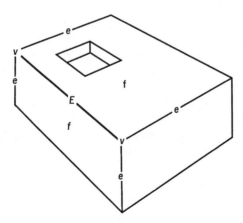

Figure 10.1. The canonical edge-based topology structure.

It is important not to confuse the edge-based topological structure with the particular geometric hierarchy with which the shape is associated. It is still possible to assign geometric information to any one of the topological boundary elements and to compute it for those elements not explicitly associated with geometry. For example, a line representing the geometry of an edge may be implied by its two end points, represented by the vertices of that edge, or it may be represented explicitly by means of an equation associated with the edge record itself. Although explicit representation speeds up operations that require edge-geometric information, such as graphical display, it slows down operations that modify the shape by making it necessary to update this additional information. The dual representation of each boundary element (topological and geometrical) further complicates the maintenance of well-formedness of boundary-represented shapes, because it requires not only that each representation be well-formed by itself, but also that it is consistent with the other representation.

☐ EDGE-BASED BOUNDARY MODELS

The centrality of edges as carriers of topological information, combined with their computational conciseness, has led to their almost universal acceptance as the basis for boundary-represented solids and as the medium through which semantic integrity constraints can be exercised and tested. Three edge-based models have been developed to date: the Winged Edge model (Baumgart, 1972), the Split Edge model (Eastman, 1982), and the Hybrid Edge model (Kalay, 1988). (See the Bibliography at the end of this chapter.)

The Winged Edge Model

Baumgart was the first to take advantage of edge-topological information for the purpose of developing a model capable of representing the bounding surface of arbitrary polyhedra. Through its bounding edges, each face of the polyhedron can identify all its immediate neighboring faces without using additional data structures. Baumgart augmented the edge record with directional information in the form of pointers to succeeding and preceding edges on each of the two faces it connects. His structure, depicted in Figure 10.2, resembles a butterfly, hence the name *Winged Edge*.

Baumgart was also the first to develop a set of operators to manipulate this complex data structure in a manner that guarantees topological well-formedness. He named this set *Euler operators* because they comply with Euler's extended law, which are discussed in Chapter 11.

```
direction = (pred, succ);
edge      = record
              esolid : sptr;
              enext  : array [1..2, direction] of ^edge;
              eface  : array [1..2] of ^face;
              evert  : array [1..2] of ^vertex
            end;
```

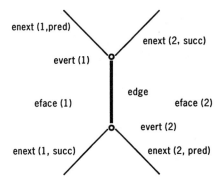

Figure 10.2. The Winged Edge model.

The Split Edge Model

The bundling of the two roles assumed by edges in one record (their role in bounding faces and their role in connecting adjacent faces) is, nevertheless, also the most significant (computational) drawback of the Winged Edge model, in all its derivations. This deficiency is apparent, in particular, when all the edges of one face have to be "visited" through a face-traversal procedure. Such traversal is often required by geometric or graphics operations applied to the model. Face traversal is, by definition, a *unidirectional* operation, due to the orientability of the bounding surface. However, in the Winged Edge model, each edge is used for bounding *two* faces; therefore, it participates in two face traversals. These traversals are opposite to each other, according to Möbius' law. Thus, each edge can be traversed in two opposite directions, depending on the particular face being operated on. It is necessary, therefore, to check and determine the direction in which individual edges must be traversed *at each traversal step,* a process that considerably increases traversal cost.

To solve this deficiency, Eastman has developed the Split Edge model, where the two roles of edges have been separated. This separation is achieved by "splitting" each Winged Edge into two halves, one for each of the two adjacent faces, hence the name *Split Edge.* Connectivity is maintained by adding an explicit pointer in each edge record that references the opposite "half," as depicted in Figure 10.3. While this model doubles the number of edge records, it significantly reduces traversal cost of individual faces.

```
edge = record
          esolid : sptr;
          enext  : ^edge;
          eface  : ^face;
          evert  : ^vertex;
          eopp   : ^edge
       end;
```

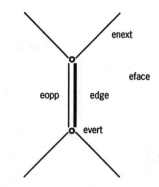

Figure 10.3. The Split Edge model.

The Hybrid Edge Model

Both the Winged Edge and Split Edge models (and their many derivatives) have been devised explicitly for the purpose of representing and manipulating solids. Hence, they take advantage of and deal effectively with the dual role of edges (as directed boundaries and as connectors of faces), thereby solving the difficult computational problems associated with the modeling of boundary-represented polyhedral solids. They are designed for representing edges that link adjacent faces. It is this specialized design that makes both models inadequate when considered candidates for implementing a more general model, capable of representing solids, individual polygons, and even line segments. The reason for this deficiency, in part, lies in the uniformity of the requirements that are met by edges of solids; they *always* bound pairs of adjacent faces and are *always* traversed bidirectionally. However, the directionality and adjacency requirements of polygons and lines are different.

More specifically, when they bind faces of a boundary-represented solid, edges are bidirectional entities (Figure 10.4a). Each edge is part of two faces, each of which abides by Möbius' law, as discussed in Chapter 9. However, when edges represent the boundary of individual polygons, as discussed in Part One, they are unidirectional (Figure 10.4b). When edges are used to represent the connectivity of line segments that do not bound polygons, edges are non-directional. Furthermore, polygons and lines have no adjacency requirements; therefore, any data structure and operators specific to maintaining adjacency relationships will be wasted if the same edge model which is used for representing solids is also used for representing polygons and lines. Moreover, lines do not bound areas, as polygons or faces of solids do. A line may, therefore, consist of an unequal number of segments and points (e.g., a single segment is bounded by two points). This inequality makes the use of the Split Edge model for representing lines impossible and the use of the Winged Edge model for that purpose inefficient.

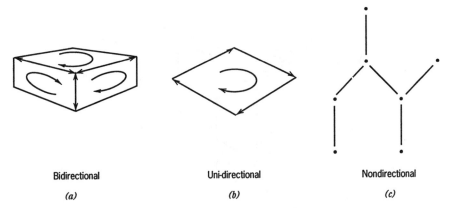

Bidirectional   Uni-directional   Nondirectional

(a)   *(b)*   *(c)*

Figure 10.4. Directionality of edges for different modeling purposes.

A solution to the problem of representing edges that can serve different modeling purposes can be achieved by separating the *connectivity* role of edges from their role as carriers of *directionality* information. The solution can be conceptually considered a combination of the advantages of the Winged Edge and the Split Edge models, as depicted in Figure 10.5, hence the name *Hybrid Edge*.

This combination is achieved by using *three* records to represent each edge: two segment records, of the type used in Part One, and one (new) edge record. The segment records contain the same directional information as do the Split Edge records (and the polygons of Part One), without referencing their "opposite" edge record. Instead, it is the new *edge* record that provides the connection between a pair of segment records to form one unit, yet it provides no directional information.

```
eptr= ^edge;
sptr= ^solid;
edge= record
         esolid : sptr; {backpointer to solid}
         enext  : eptr; {next edge record}
         eseg   : array [1..2] of gptr {pair of segment pointers}
      end;
```

Consequently, segment records (without the edge record) can be used to represent the boundaries of polygons without redundancy. Pairs of segments, one from each polygon, can be combined through an edge record to represent the edges of a solid. This way, the directional information of polygons and solids can be maintained at the segment level, while adjacency information is carried at the edge level. For example, polygons (whether individual ones or ones that represent faces of a solid) can be traversed easily by traversing successive segment records. To identify adjacent polygons, one need only follow the back-pointer

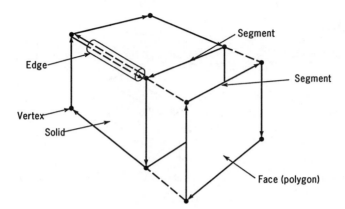

Figure 10.5. The Hybrid Edge model.

from the segment of one polygon to its parent edge (if one exists) and then find the other segment of that edge.

Because Hybrid Edge records can be linked without the encumbrance of directionality, they are also suitable for representing the components of lines without any specific order. In this case, the capacity of segment records for carrying directional information is not used.

□ THE HYBRID EDGE MODEL OF SOLIDS

The Hybrid Edge-based data structure for representing solids is composed of, for the most part, the same data structure that was used for representing polygons (introduced in Chapter 3). The only additions are an EDGE record and a SOLID record:

```
eptr = ^edge;
sptr = ^solid;

edge = record
        esolid : sptr; {backpointer to solid}
        enext  : eptr; {next edge record}
        eseg   : array [1..2] of gptr {pair of segment pointers}
      end;

solid = record
        elist : eptr; {nil-end list of edges}
        plist : pptr; {nil-end list of polygons}
        snext : sptr; {nil-end list of solids}
        case cavity : boolean of
          false : (child : sptr);
          true  : (parent : sptr)
      end;
```

The SOLID record contains references to two lists: a list of edges (ELIST) and a list of polygons (PLIST). The representation of a solid thus consists of vertices, edges (which are made of pairs of segments), and polygons. We shall, however, consider the polygons that form the boundary of a solid as *faces* for the sake of consistency with conventions (including Euler's law).

To facilitate the manipulation of the Hybrid Edge data structure, two back-pointers (pointers from a lower level entity to a higher level entity) are added to the data structure presented in Chapter 4: one from segments to edges in the SEGMENT record; the other from polygons to solids in the POLYGON record. These additions do not affect any of the segment and polygon operators developed so far (except INIT_SEGMENT and INIT_POLYGON), because the added pointers were not used at the polygon level. The data structure for representing solids using these records is depicted in Figure 10.6.

```
segment = record
            form  : line;
            gpoly : pptr;
            gedge : eptr; {back-pointer to edge}
            gnext : gptr;
            gvert : vptr
          end;

polygon = record
            form   : plane;
            pnext  : pptr;
            psolid : sptr; {back-pointer to solid}
            glist  : gptr;
            case hole : boolean of
              false : (child : pptr);
              true  : (parent : pptr)
          end;
```

The Representation of Cavities

Similar to holes in polygons, solids can have cavities. The representation of a solid's exterior boundary is, nevertheless, identical to the representation of the boundary of a cavity. Therefore, the same record can be used for representing both. The only difference is in that solids can have cavities, but cavities cannot have cavities. This difference is reflected in the variant part of the SOLID record. If the Boolean field selector CAVITY is FALSE, the record represents an exterior boundary and may have a list of cavities. If it is TRUE, then the record represents a cavity. In that case, a pointer to its "parent" solid is provided.

Geometry

To complete the model, the topological information must be associated with geometrical information. As with topological data structures, hierarchy and generality are prime considerations in developing the geometrical data structure.

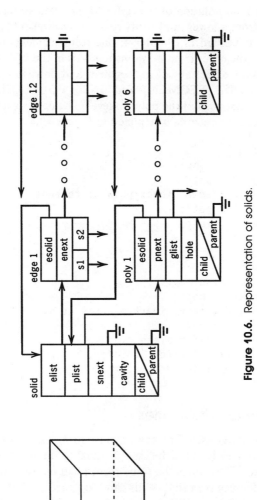

Figure 10.6. Representation of solids.

The geometrical hierarchy follows closely the topological hierarchy, with one major difference: It describes the relative position of each formative entity within the geometrical space in which it is embedded, rather than the entity itself. A point, for example, is geometrically described by three coordinate values that define its location in the Euclidean 3 space (E3). Similarly, a line is described by a line equation.

The multiplicity of geometrical information needed to completely (and generally) define a formative entity may lead to inconsistencies, such as when the points bounding a line segment do not lie on the line itself. It must, therefore, be managed in compliance with a set of well-formedness rules, similar to the topological structures. Furthermore, it is desirable to limit the number of distinct geometrical structures to the required and sufficient minimum.

Part One discussed the topological entities that are associated with geometrical attributes: segments and vertices, which are associated with line and point geometries, respectively. Polygons, although of major interest in Part One, were not associated with a geometrical attribute (a surface) because they were assumed to lie in the plane. However, for the complete geometrical description of all the topological entities that form the boundary of a solid, surface geometries must also be included and must be associated with polygons.

Geometrical information is cyclically equivalent, as depicted in Figure 10.7. Line equations can be computed from pairs of points or the intersection of two planes. Point locations can be computed from intersections of two lines or three planes. Plane equations can be computed from three points or two lines. Nevertheless, to reduce redundancy and to enhance the integrity of the model, we shall compute segment geometries from their end-point geometries and surface information from three noncollinear vertices of their polygonal boundaries. For the sake of simplicity, we shall deal here only with straight lines and with planes. This pseudo-hierarchical approach to geometrical computation is preferable to a more verbose approach, because it lends itself to conciseness and generality, the two prime objectives stated earlier. It also allows several entities to share geometrical attributes in different combinations without redundancy. For example, edges are geometrically defined by their segment geometries. The geometrical surface associated with a polygon is also defined by the same points, thereby eliminating duplicity.

The responsibility for making and for maintaining the geometrical representation of shapes, like the their topological representation, is vested in a set of geometrical operators. These operators are also responsible for ensuring the geometrical well-formedness of the model. They include operators to assign primitive geometrical attributes (i.e., point locations) and to compute line and surface equations, as well as to compute and manipulate combinations of these attributes by way of their interpolation, intersection, and extrapolation. These operators are discussed in Chapter 13.

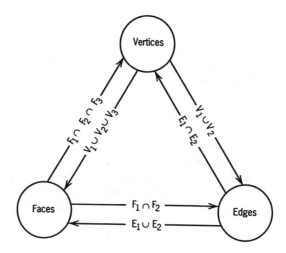

Figure 10.7. Cyclic equivalence of geometric entities in planar polyhedra.

☐ BIBLIOGRAPHY

Baumgart, B., "Winged Edge Polyhedron Representation," Technical Report CS-320, Stanford Artificial Intelligence Laboratory, Palo Alto, CA, October 1972.

Eastman, C. M., "Introduction to Computer-Aided Design," Course Notes, Carnegie-Mellon University, 1982.

Jackins, C. I., and S. L. Taminoto, "Octree and Their Use in Representing 3D Objects," *Computer Graphics and Image Processing,* **14**:249–270, 1980.

Kalay, Y. E., "The Hybrid Edge: A Topological Data Structure for Vertically Integrated Geometric Modeling," Technical Report, Computer-Aided Design and Graphic Laboratory, State University of New York at Buffalo, June 1988.

Requicha, A. A. G., "Representations for Rigid Solids: Theory and Systems," *Computing Surveys* **12**(4):437–464, December 1980.

Requicha, A. A. G., and R. Tilove, "Mathematical Foundation of Constructive Solid Geometry: General Topology of Regular Closed Sets," Technical Report 27, Production Automation Project, University of Rochester, March 1978.

Samet, H., "The Quadtree and Related Hierarchical Data Structures," *ACM Computing Surveys* **16**:187–260, 1984.

Weiler, K., "Edge-Based Data Structures for Solid Modeling in Curved-Surface Environments," *IEEE Computer Graphics and Applications,* **5**(1):21–40, January 1985.

11

BASIC SOLID OPERATIONS

Basic solid operators, as they apply to the boundary representation model, are also called *Euler operators*. They create, modify, and destroy the edge-based data structure records and the links between them. The main virtue of the Euler operators is maintenance of well-formedness of the model throughout its manipulation. This chapter discusses the concept underlying the Euler operators and presents a particular implementation for manipulating the Hybrid Edge model.

□ THE EULER OPERATORS

The basic concept underlying the operators that manipulate solid boundary models, and which we call Euler operators, is the maintenance of well-formedness while creating, deleting, and modifying the data structure.

The Euler operators derive their name from Euler's law, which describes the numerical relationships between faces, edges, and vertices of a polyhedral solid:

$$F - E + V = 2$$

They can be implemented in two ways:

1. By operators that *add* new elements to a given boundary (starting with a primitive solid)
2. By operators that *subdivide* elements of a given boundary (starting with a primitive solid)

In this chapter we first consider the additive method to demonstrate the concept embedded in the Euler operators. In Chapter 12, we develop a particular set of Euler operators, using the Hybrid Edge representation, which uses subdivision to expand solid boundaries and is, therefore, more consistent with the approach used in Part One for manipulating polygons.

The first step in implementing solid modeling operators, similar to the first step in implementing polygon modeling operators, is the definition and the creation of a "primitive" shape. A primitive solid, according to Euler's law, comprises a single face and a single vertex. The face can be visualized as a balloon and the single vertex as its opening (Figure 11.1). This set is minimal, because it comprises the smallest combination of boundary elements that satisfy Euler's law:

$$1F - 0E + 1V = 2.$$

An operator that creates this minimal solid can be easily implemented, as we shall see later in this chapter. For the purposes of this introduction, we shall call it MSFV (Make Solid Face Vertex).

The minimal shape can be extended in two ways, both satisfying Euler's law, as depicted in Figure 11.2:

1. A new edge can be added, such that it is bounded by a new vertex:

$$1F - 1E + 2V = 2.$$

2. A new edge can be added, such that it closes on itself, making a new face:

$$2F - 1E + 1V = 2.$$

These two operators are known in the literature as MEV (Makes Edge Vertex) and MEF (Makes Edge Face). They are applicable not only to a minimal solid, but to *any* well-formed solid data structure. Therefore, they can be used iteratively to construct any desired combination of the three parameters F, E, and V, such that they comply with Euler's law while fulfilling the well-formedness conditions.

The simple form of Euler's law that MSFV, MEV, and MEF are based on excludes some classes of meaningful shapes, such as shapes that contain holes.

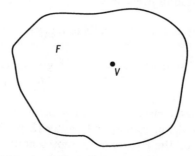

Figure 11.1. A minimal solid, according to Euler's law.

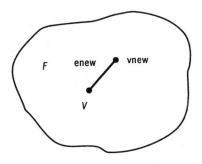 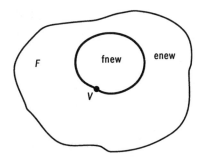

(a) Makes Edge Vertex   *(b)* Makes Edge Face

Figure 11.2. Two ways of adding an edge to a solid.

To allow for such shapes, we must base these operators on the extended form of Euler's law:

$$F - E + V = H + 2*(S - G),$$

where H is the overall number of holes within faces of the shape, S the number of shells, and G the genus.† For example, a doughnut-like shape has the following number of elements (Figure 11.3a):

$$10F - 24E + 16V = 2H + 2*(1S - 1G),$$

and a pressure vessel (Figure 11.3b) is represented as:

$$12F - 24E + 16V = 0H + 2*(2S - 0G).$$

†The *genus* of a solid is the number of holes that pierce it completely through. Such holes are not merely depressions in a face, like the bowl of a cup, but are rather passageways like the one formed by the handle of the cup. A sphere, for example, has no such holes, therefore its genus is zero. A doughnut, on the other hand, like the cup, has one such hole; therefore, its genus (like the cup's) is one. A pretzel has three such holes; therefore, its genus is three.

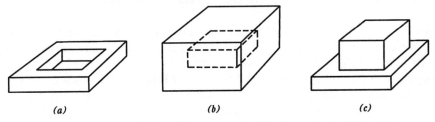

(a)   *(b)*   *(c)*

Figure 11.3. Solids that must be represented by the extended Euler law.

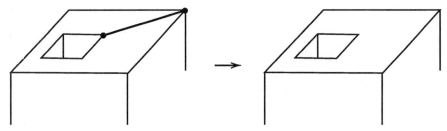

Figure 11.4. Making a hole, using KEMH.

Given the extended Euler law, operators that deal explicitly with holes, multiple shells, and genuses must be provided. One such operator creates a hole by deleting the edges that connect it to the circuit of edges bounding the face. A hole, according to this method, is first "grown" out of an existing face perimeter of edges, then the "umbilical cord" that connects it to the perimeter is deleted. An operator that implements this method is called KEMH (Kill Edge Make Hole), and is depicted in Figure 11.4.

The basic set of four Euler operators that were presented above (MSFV, MEV, MEF, and KEMH) must be complemented by a set of operators that "undo" what the first set does. These operators are:

> KSFV (Kill Solid Face Vertex)
> KEV (Kill Edge Vertex)
> KEF (Kill Edge Face)
> MEKH (Make Edge Kill Hole)

The eight basic Euler operators are depicted in Figure 11.5. An example of using them to create a tetrahedron is presented in Figure 11.6.

The Euler operators can be implemented in various ways. In the following sections we present a particular implementation, which is based on the Hybrid Edge boundary representation model and which uses the polygon operators discussed in Part One.

☐ HIERARCHY OF SOLID MODELING OPERATORS

Operators for creating, modifying, and deleting boundary-represented solids, like the operators for modeling polygons, can be structured hierarchically. Their particular typology depends on the data structure chosen for representing the solid. In this part of the book we use the Hybrid Edge model, which comprises vertices, segments, edges, polygons, and solids. Each operant is manipulated by a set of specific operators, which are structured in a hierarchy of layers. Four distinct layers can be readily identified:

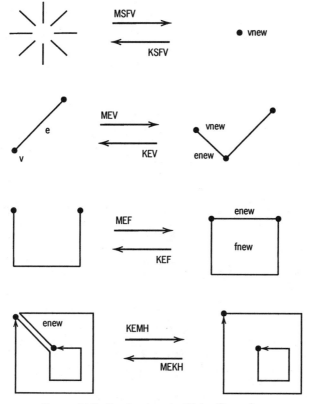

Figure 11.5. The basic set of Euler Operators.

1. Topological operators that initialize, create, delete, and dispose of the operandi
2. Topological operators that modify existing solids by adding and deleting topological components
3. Geometrical operators that place the components in the three-dimensional Euclidean space
4. Operators that create new shapes by cutting and pasting existing shapes and that combine existing shapes into new ones by means of the Boolean operators of union, intersection, and difference.

In developing the operators for manipulating solids, it is useful to lay them out in a tabular form that summarizes and classifies them, as depicted in Figure 11.7. Figure 11.7, which is an extension of the table presented in Figure 4.2, also shows that not all operators are applicable to all operandi, due to differences in their structure and purpose.

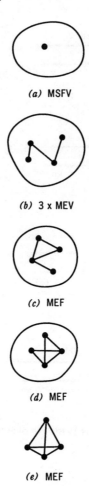

(a) MSFV

(b) 3 x MEV

(c) MEF

(d) MEF

(e) MEF

Figure 11.6. Constructing a tetrahedron using the Euler operators.

	vertex	segment	polygon	edge	solid
1. init/dispose	X	X	X	X	X
create/delete		X	X	X	X
access		X	X	X	
2. split/merge		X	X	X	X
add/remove		X	X	X	X
4. place	X	X			
5. cut/paste			X		X
union/intersect			X		X

Figure 11.7. Classes of solid and polygon operators.

Developing all these modeling operators individually will lead to proliferate and redundant efforts. Instead, we shall draw upon the similarities between the operations and build hierarchical tools that can be applied, in various combinations, to different aggregate elements of polygons and solids. The guiding principle in developing this hierarchy is *abstraction*: higher level operators are written in terms of lower level ones, such that they need not be concerned with specific implementation details. Lower level operators perform well-defined, specific tasks and are not concerned with the reasons for their invocation or how the results of their actions are used. For example, *create* operators are responsible only for allocating memory and initializing particular operandi, such as vertex, segment, polygon, edge, and solid records. *Add* operators take existing records and attach them to given structures in a manner consistent with Euler's law, such as adding a segment to a polygon while maintaining closure and non-self-intersection. *Cut* and *paste* operators, on the other hand, govern both creation and addition of operandi, such that they make particular higher level structures. The *cut* and *paste* operators are not concerned, however, with the particulars of creating or adding individual records to the structures they make.

We have already developed all the operators we need for manipulating vertices, segments, and polygons in Part One. We shall concentrate here only on the development of operators that manipulate edges and solids.

☐ BASIC SOLID OPERATORS

The lowest level solid modeling operators, which we call *basic* or *primitive* solid operators, comprise procedures and functions that initialize, create, delete, and dispose of boundary elements (vertices, segments, polygons, edges, and solids). These operators manipulate the data structures directly.

To minimize the number of required operators and to assign them the responsibility for maintaining at least some of the well-formedness conditions, we will require that they abide by Euler's law. We have seen earlier that, according to this law, the simplest of all possible solids is made of one solid, a single face, and a single vertex. It is our desire, however, to use the Hybrid Edge model so we can make use of the polygon and segment operators developed in Part One. To do so, we must represent *faces* as *polygons*. The simplest polygon, according to Chapter 4, is made of *one segment* and *one vertex*. Segments, in the Hybrid Edge model, must come in pairs, each of which is connected by an edge. The simplest solid in the Hybrid Edge model, therefore, consists of *two* primitive polygons, each of which is bounded by one segment and one vertex. The two segments are connected by an edge, as depicted in Figure 11.8.

The operators that create the primitive solid must, therefore, not only create the records it comprises (in this case, a solid, an edge, and two polygons, each made of a segment and a vertex), but also link them so that the well-formedness conditions discussed in Chapters 9 and 10 will be maintained. The following procedures perform these functions. Like the polygon operators discussed in

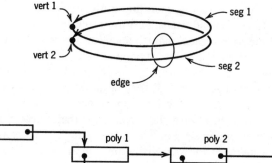

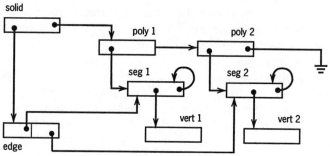

Figure 11.8. The primitive solid.

Chapter 4, they have been separated into operators that INITialize the records that represent solids and edges, and operators that CREATE data structures from combinations of these records.

```
procedure init_edge (var e : eptr);
{Allocate edge record and initialize its fields.}

begin
  new (e);
  with e^ do
    begin
      esolid := nil;
      enext:= nil;
      eseg[1] := nil;
      eseg[2] := nil
    end
end;   {init_edge procedure}
```

```
procedure init_solid (var s : sptr);
{Allocate solid record and initialize its fields.}


begin
  new (s);
  with s^ do
    begin
      snext := nil;
      elist := nil;
      plist := nil;
      cavity := false;
      child := nil
    end
end; {init_solid procedure}




procedure create_edge (var e : eptr; var g1,g2 : gptr);
{Create new edge record and link it to two segment records. If
 the two segment records are NIL, create new segment records.}


var  v1,v2 : vptr;


begin
  init_edge (e);
  if g1 = nil then create_segment (g1,v1);
  if g2 = nil then create_segment (g2,v2);

  e^.eseg[1] := g1; g1^.gedge := e;
  e^.eseg[2] := g2; g2^.gedge := e
end; {create_edge procedure}


procedure create_solid (var s : sptr);
{Create a primitive solid which consists of two polygons and one
 edge. Create the polygon and edge records as well.}


var   p1,p2 : pptr;
      g1,g2 : gptr;
      v1,v2 : vptr;
      e     : eptr;
```

```
begin
  init_solid (s);
  create_polygon (p1,g1,v1);
  create_polygon (p2,g2,v2);
  create_edge (e,g1,g2);

  {connect polygons and edge to solid}
  s^.plist := p1; p1^.pnext := p2;
  s^.elist := e
end; {create_solid procedure}
```

These INITialize and CREATE operators are complemented by a set of operators that DELETE and DISPOSE of the data structures and the records of which
they are made.

```
procedure dispose_edge (var e : eptr);
{Dispose of edge record and set e to nil.}

begin
  dispose(e);
  e := nil
end; {dispose_edge procedure}


procedure dispose_solid (var s : sptr);
{Dispose of solid record and set s to nil.}

begin
  dispose (s);
  s := nil
end; {dispose_solid procedure}


procedure delete_edge (var e : eptr);
{Merge the two segments of edge e then delete it.}

begin
  merge_segment (e^.eseg[1]);
  merge_segment (e^.eseg[2]);
  dispose_edge (e)
end; {delete_edge procedure}
```

(Note: The deletion of a solid is not a low-level operation, because it involves deletion of all its cavities and the boundary elements that bound them. It will be introduced in Chapter 12, together with the operators that construct more complex solids and cavities.)

□ ACCESS OPERATORS

For many operations, it will be necessary to access edges from the segments that compose them. It will also be necessary to access faces that are adjacent across a common edge, and access all the vertices that coincide at a point. Some data structure access operators that facilitate such accesses and demonstrate the power of the Hybrid Edge model to provide adjacency relationship information are listed here.

```
function get_edge (g : gptr) : eptr;
{Return the edge that references the given segment g.}

begin
  get_edge := g^.gedge
end; {get_edge function}


function other_segment (g : gptr) : gptr;
{Return other segment connected to g by the same edge.}

var   e : eptr;

begin
  e := get_edge (g);
  if e^.eseg[1] = g
    then other_segment := e^.eseg[2]
    else other_segment := e^.eseg[1]
end; {other_segment function}


function other_face (g : gptr) : pptr;
{Return polygon representing the other face adjacent to the
 polygon to which segment g belongs, across the edge that
 references segment g.}

var   e : eptr;
```

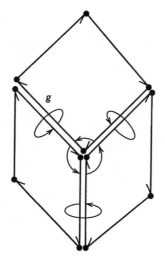

Figure 11.9. Traversing all vertices coincident at a point.

```
begin
  e := get_edge (g);
  if e^.eseg[1] = g
    then other_face :=      e^.eseg[2]^.gpoly
    else other_face := e^.eseg[1]^.gpoly
end; {other_face function}
```

In the Hybrid Edge model that was presented in Chapter 10, vertices are dupli-
cated; each vertex belongs to one and only one polygon (face). This redundancy,
which is convenient for topological manipulation purposes, requires that *all* vertices coincident at a geometrical point be traversed when a *geometrical* operation
is applied to the solid (e.g., transformation). The traversal of all vertices is facilitated by function NEXT_VERTEX, which is depicted in Figure 11.9.

```
function next_vertex (var g : gptr) : vptr;
{Return the vertex of the segment on an adjacent polygon that
 coincides with the vertex of g at a point. Also sets g to
 point at the segment that references this vertex.}

begin
  g := other_segment (g); {paired seg. on adj. polygon}
  g := g^.gnext;             {successor seg. on adj. poly}
  next_vertex := g^.gvert {vertex of succ. segment}
end; {next_vertex function}
```

☐ BIBLIOGRAPHY

Eastman, C. M., and K. Weiler, "Geometric Modeling Using the Euler Operators," Institute of Physical Planning, Technical Report 78, Carnegie-Mellon University, Pittsburgh, PA, February 1979.

Mantyla, M., and R. Sulonen, "GWB: A Solid Modeler with Euler Operators," *IEEE Computer Graphics and Applications* 2(7):17–31, September 1982.

Wilson, P. R., "Euler Formulas and Geometric Modeling," *IEEE Computer Graphics and Applications*, 5(8):24–36, August 1985.

12

HIGH-LEVEL SOLID OPERATIONS

Once a primitive solid has been created, it can be *expanded* to include multiple faces, edges, and vertices. This expansion, as discussed in Chapter 11, occurs by using the Euler operators, which add and remove boundary elements while maintaining well-formedness. Through the addition of holes and cavities, and through splitting and merging boundaries, an even more complex solid can be constructed.

These (reversible) processes involves high-level topological manipulations of the Hybrid Edge data structure. In this chapter we address these issues, which form the second layer in the solid modeling hierarchy. We will develop operators to SPLIT and MERGE edges, to ADD and REMOVE cavities, and to SPLIT and MERGE faces. Most of these operators are high-level adaptations of the operators developed for the manipulation of segments and polygons. The primary difference between them and the operators presented here is propagation of changes applied to one boundary element over its neighbors, across mutual edges.

□ CONSTRUCTING COMPLEX SOLIDS

Expansion of the primitive solid into a meaningful, well-formed shape involves the addition of faces, edges, and vertices in compliance with Euler's law. The principal Euler operators that perform such expansion (and their inverses) were discussed in Chapter 11. Their implementation in particular procedures and functions that operate on the Hybrid Edge data structure is discussed here.

The Euler operators that expand and contract solid boundaries comprise two pairs of procedures:

1. MEV and KEV, which create new edges by splitting existing ones (together with their segments) in two and delete (kill) edges by merging their segments, respectively

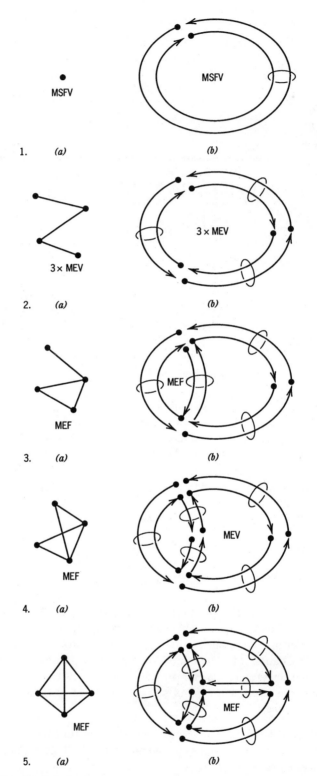

Figure 12.1. Constructing the topology of a tetrahedron (a) by adding boundary elements and (b) by subdividing boundary elements.

2. MEF and KEF, which in addition to splitting edges, also split a face (a polygon) and, in addition to merging edges, also merge a face (a polygon), respectively.

To implement these two pairs of operators for the Hybrid Edge data structure, we shall make full use of the representation of faces as polygons and of the extensive polygon operators we developed in Part One of the book. The use of high-level polygon operators to implement high-level solid operators requires that the latter be approached somewhat differently than by the Euler operators discussed in Chapter 11. Those were *additive* operators, which created new elements from scratch and linked them properly to the rest of the boundary. The particular implementation of the Euler operators we use here *subdivides* existing boundary elements to create new ones. The method employed is similar to the polygon operators discussed in Chapter 5, where new boundary elements were generated by splitting and merging segments. Not only is this approach consistent with the methods we have employed so far, but it also enhances the integrity of the model and reduces the potential for creating ill-formed structures. To demonstrate the difference between these two methods of implementation, consider how a tetrahedron can be constructed by each, as depicted in Figure 12.1.

Splitting and Merging Edges

The first pair (MEV and KEV) are implemented here by the procedures SPLIT_ EDGE and MERGE_EDGE, which are augmented by the two auxiliary procedures ADD_EDGE and REMOVE_EDGE, which are responsible for linking edges to the edge-list in the solid record. They make use of the SPLIT_ SEGMENT and MERGE_SEGMENT high-level polygon operators, as well as the low-level solid operators CREATE_EDGE and DELETE_EDGE.

```
procedure add_edge (e : eptr; s : sptr);
{Add edge e to list of edges in solid s.}

begin
  e^.enext := s^.elist;
  s^.elist := e;
  e^.esolid := s
end; {add_edge procedure}

procedure remove_edge (e : eptr);
{Remove edge e from the solid it belongs to. E must not be the
 only edge in the solid.}

var  epred : eptr;
     s     : sptr;
```

```
begin
  s := e^.esolid;
  if s^.elist = e
    then s^.elist := e^.enext
    else begin
      epred := s^.elist;
      while epred^.enext <> e do epred := epred^.enext;
      epred^.enext := e^.enext
    end;
  e^.esolid := nil;
  e^.enext := nil
end; {remove_edge procedure}

procedure split_edge (e : eptr;
                      var enew : eptr;
                      var vnew1,vnew2 : vptr);
{Create new edge enew by splitting both segments of e. Add enew
 as the successor of e. Return new edge and the new vertices.
```

```
seg1                          seg1           gnew1
+--------------->            +------->+--------->
        e          ==>              enew
<---------------+            <-------+<------+
       seg2                  gnew2       seg2
```

```
}

var  gnew1,gnew2, seg1,seg2 : gptr;

begin
  seg1 := e^.eseg[1]; split_segment (seg1, gnew1, vnew1);
  seg2 := e^.eseg[2]; split_segment (seg2, gnew2, vnew2);
  e^.eseg[2] := gnew2;
  create_edge (enew, gnew1,seg2);
  add_edge (enew, e^.esolid)
end; {split_edge procedure}

procedure merge_edge (var e : eptr);
{Delete edge e by merging its segments. E must not be the only
 edge in the solid.}

begin
  remove_edge (e);
  delete_edge (e)
end; {merge_edge procedure}
```

Splitting and Merging Faces

The second type of edge-making and edge-killing Euler operators (MEF and KEF) involve *faces* as well as the edges themselves. These operators *split* and *merge* faces when new edges are created or deleted, respectively. Because faces, in the Hybrid Edge data structure, are represented as polygons, MEF and KEF can be implemented as adaptations of the SPLIT_POLYGON and MERGE_POLYGON operators, with the additional provision that the splitted segments are "bundled" in a new edge, which is added to the solid, or the "bundling" edge is removed and deleted from the solid. Procedures SPLIT_FACE and MERGE_FACE implement the Euler operators MEF and KEF for the Hybrid Edge data structure. They use procedure SPLIT_POLYGON and procedure MERGE_POLYGON to accomplish their tasks; therefore, their structure is surprisingly simple. Some assistance to the implementation of SPLIT_FACE is provided by the particular implementation of SPLIT_POLYGON, where the newly created segments are adjacent to each other and coincide with the line of splitting, making their "bundling" into an edge straight-forward. The SPLIT_FACE and MERGE_FACE operators are aided by two auxiliary procedures, ADD_FACE and REMOVE_FACE, which are responsible for linking faces to the face-list in the solid record.

```
procedure add_face (f : pptr; s : sptr);
{Add face f to list of faces in solid s.}

begin
  f^.pnext := s^.plist;
  s^.plist := f;
  f^.psolid := s
end; {add_face procedure}

procedure remove_face (f : pptr);
{Remove face f from the solid it belongs to. F must not be the
 only face in the solid.}

var  fpred : pptr;
     s     : sptr;

begin
  s := f^.psolid;
  if s^.plist = f
    then s^.plist := f^.fnext
    else begin
      fpred := s^.plist;
      while fpred^.pnext <> f do fpred := fpred^.pnext;
      fpred^.pnext := f^.pnext
    end;
  f^.psolid := nil;
  f^.pnext := nil
end; {remove_face procedure}
```

```
procedure split_face (var f : pptr;
                          g1,g2 : gptr;
                          var fnew : pptr;
                          var enew : eptr);
{Make a new edge enew and a new face fnew by splitting the
 polygon representing face f from its segments g1 to g2. Add
 fnew and enew to the solid that f belongs to.}

begin
  split_polygon (f,fnew, g1,g2);
  create_edge (enew, f^.glist, fnew^.glist);
  add_edge (enew, f^.psolid);
  add_face (fnew, f^.psolid)
end; {split_face procedure}

procedure merge_face (var f1,f2 : pptr; var e : eptr);
{Merge faces f1 and f2 along edge e by merging the polygons that
 represent them and by removing and deleting edge e. Face f2
 is removed from the face-list in the solid it belongs to,
 and is deleted. Note: merge_polygons, which is used by this
 procedure, already merges the joint segments; therefore,
 dispose_edge is called rather than delete_edge.}

begin
  merge_polygons (f1,f2, e^.eseg[1], e^.eseg[2]);
  remove_edge (e);
  dispose_edge (e)
end; {merge_face procedure}
```

☐ ADDING AND REMOVING CAVITIES

The operators we have discussed concern singular solid boundaries. The scope of
our modeling interests include, nevertheless, artifacts made of solids that have
cavities. The Hybrid Edge data structure, which we developed in Chapter 10,
provides for linking one solid boundary to another. This provision, in the form of
the SNEXT field in the SOLID record, can be used to construct solids that contain cavities. Procedures ADD_CAVITY and REMOVE_CAVITY implement
these operations. They are aided by the procedures ADD_SOLID and
REMOVE_SOLID, which take care of linking solid boundaries in lists.

```
procedure add_solid (var s, slist : sptr);
{Add solid s to the list of solids headed by slist.}

begin
  s^.snext := slist;
  slist := s
end; {add_solid procedure}
```

```
procedure remove_solid (var s,slist : sptr);
{Remove solid s from the list of solids headed by slist.}

var  spred : sptr;

begin
  if s = slist
    then slist := s^.snext
    else begin
      spred := slist;
      while spred^.snext <> s do spred := spred^.snext;
      spred^.snext := s^.snext
    end;
  s^.snext := nil
end; {remove_solid procedure}
```

The addition and removal of cavities follows principles similar to those for the addition and removal of holes in polygons. Similarly, when a solid boundary is made into a cavity, or when a cavity is made into an external solid boundary, its *orientation* must be reversed, both topologically and geometrically, in order to comply with the well-formedness rules. The reversal of solid boundaries is similar to the reversal of polygonal boundaries and is performed by linking the segments of all polygons to their former predecessors in their respective lists. Procedure REVERSE_SOLID performs this task. It operates on one solid boundary at a time, because there exists only one external solid boundary that could become the cavity of another boundary and because cavities can contain no cavities of their own.

```
procedure reverse_solid (s : sptr);
{Reverse the orientation of the polygons (including their holes)
 in plist of solid s.}

var  p : pptr;

begin
  p := s^.plist;
  while p <> nil do
    begin
      reverse_polygon (p);
      p := p^.pnext
    end
end; {reverse_solid procedure}
```

```
procedure add_cavity (c,s : sptr);
{Add solid c as a child (cavity) of parent solid s and transform
 it into a cavity boundary. Parent solid must NOT be a cavity
 itself!}

begin
  {add c to list of cavities in s}
  add_solid (c, s^.child);

  {make c a cavity solid}
  reverse_solid (c);
  c^.cavity := true;
  c^.parent := s
end; {add_cavity procedure}

procedure remove_cavity (c : sptr);
{Remove cavity c from its parent solid list of cavities and
 transform it to a non-cavity solid.}

begin
  {remove c from list of cavities}
  remove_solid (c,c^.parent^.child);

  {make c a non-cavity solid}
  reverse_solid (c);
  c^.cavity := false;
  c^.child := nil
end; {remove_cavity procedure}
```

□ DELETING SOLIDS

With the availability of operators to remove faces and edges and operators to remove cavities, we can now return to the unfinished task of deleting whole solids, a task that remains from Chapter 11. The deletion of solids is regarded a high-level modeling operation, beyond the powers of the operators discussed in Chapter 11. Before a solid can be deleted, all its cavities (if it has any), faces, and edges must be removed and deleted.

Procedure DELETE_SOLID performs this task. It is a recursive procedure, which first removes cavities from their parent solid and turns them into noncavity solid boundaries. It then deletes each solid separately by removing and deleting all its faces and edges.

```
procedure delete_solid (var s : sptr);
{Delete solid s and all its cavities, recursively. The solid
 being deleted is never a cavity!}

var   c : sptr;
      p : pptr;
      e : eptr;
```

```
begin
  {remove and delete cavities in s, recursively}
  while s^.child <> nil do
    begin
      c := s^.child;
      remove_cavity (c); {this turns c into a non-cavity solid}
      delete_solid (c)    {recursive call}
    end;

  {remove and delete all the faces of s}
  while s^.plist <> nil do
    begin
      f := s^.plist;
      remove_face (f);
      delete_polygon (f)
    end;

  {remove and delete all edges of s}
  while s^.elist <> nil do
    begin
      e := s^.elist;
      remove_edge (e);
      dispose_edge (e)
    end
end; {delete_solid procedure}
```

☐ COPYING SOLIDS

A useful application of the high-level solid operators discussed in this chapter is the *copying* of a solid, which is a typical utilization of computing power in many CAD systems. This operator allows the designer to create an object once, then replicate it in the design. The copying of solids is considerably more difficult than the copying of individual polygons because of the cross linkage between the edges and the segments. Edges link particular segment pairs, each one from a different polygon. Because records must exist before they can be linked by pointers, edges cannot be fully constructed before all the polygons have been copied. However, once the polygons have been copied, all cross-reference information is lost. Therefore, a method for identifying the segments that are linked by individual edges must be devised and used. The method employed here uses the following algorithm:

1. Make a new solid record.
2. Copy all edges of the old solid and link them to the new one. Make the edge-to-segment pointers reference the segments of the *old* solid.

3. Make a copy of each polygon and link it to the new solid. While copying each segment of an old polygon, *find* the new edge that references it and adjust the pointers to reference the copy of the segment.

Function COPY_SOLID demonstrates how this involved operation can be constructed from the high-level solid and polygon operators.

```
function copy_solid (s : sptr) : sptr;
{Create and return a copy of solid s.}

var  snew            : sptr;
     p,pnew          : pptr;
     g,gnew,gtemp    : gptr;
     vnew            : vptr;
     e,enew          : eptr;
     index           : integer;
     stop            : boolean;

  function find_edge (s : sptr; g : gptr; i : integer) : eptr;
  {Find and return the edge of solid s which references segment
   g, and the index of the pointer (1 or 2)}

  var  e    : eptr;
       stop : boolean;

  begin
    e := s^.elist;
    repeat
      if (e^.eseg[1] = g) or (e^.eseg[2] = g)
        then begin
          find_edge := e;
          if e^.eseg[1] = g then i := 1 else i := 2;
          stop := true;
        end
      e := e^.enext
    until stop or e = nil
  end; {find_edge function}

begin {copy_solid}
  create_solid (snew);

  {copy all edges of s, point them at old segments}
  e := s^.elist;
  while e <> nil do
    begin
      init_edge (enew);
      enew^.eseg[1] := e^.eseg[1];
      enew^.eseg[2] := e^.eseg[2];
      add_edge (enew, snew);
      e := e^.enext
    end;
```

```
{copy all polygons. Adjust segment pointers of edges}
p := s^.plist;
while p <> nil do
  begin
    create_polygon (pnew,gnew,vnew);
    add_face (pnew,snew);

    g := p^.glist; stop := false;
    repeat
      {find new edge which points at old segment g and adjust
       pointers}
      enew := find_edge (snew, g, index);
      enew^.eseg[index] := gnew; gnew^.gedge := enew;

      {assign geometry to new segment and vertex}
      vnew^.form := g^.gvert^.form;
      gnew^.form := g^.form;

      {continue the traversal of p}
      g := g^.gnext;
      if g = p^.glist
        then stop := true
        else begin {create new segment}
          split_segment (gnew,gtemp,vnew);
          gnew := gtemp
        end
    until stop;
    p := p^.pnext
  end;

  copy_solid := snew
end; {copy_solid function}
```

This rather inefficient algorithm demonstrates some of the complexities associated with the modeling of solids. It could be improved if the edges were put in a temporary edge list, and when the edge-to-segment pointers of the edges have been adjusted, they could be removed from the temporary list and added to the new solid.

□ CONSTRUCTING COMPLEX SOLIDS

Solids, like polygons, can take many forms. It is impossible to find a method, or even a closed set of methods, that will generate all of them. General modeling tools are developed to provide the designer with the ability to generate any desired form. Some classes of solids, nevertheless, have been found to be more prevalent than others. Not only are they used on their own, but they often form

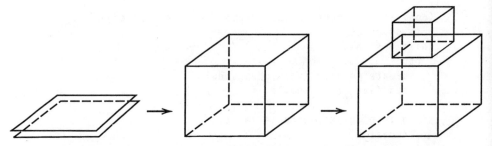

Figure 12.2. Extruding from a lamina solid and from the face of an existing solid.

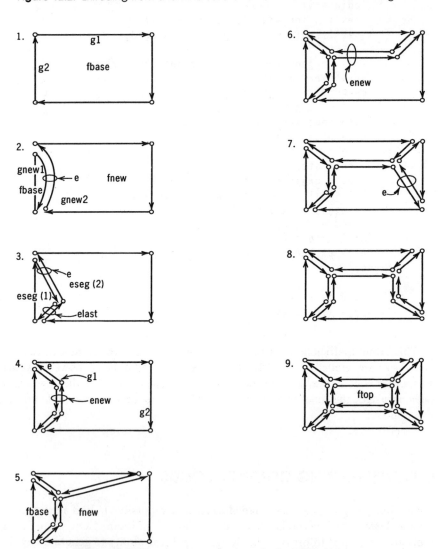

Figure 12.3. Step-by-step extrusion of a four-sided base.

the basis for developing more complex forms. These classes include *extruded solids,* which are also known as "two-and-a-half-D" shapes.

As members of the more general class of swept volumes, *forms of extrusion* are characterized by an invariant cross section. They are prismatic shapes, generated metaphorically by moving the given cross section, which is often a simple polygon, along some trajectory perpendicular to the plane of the polygon, as depicted in Figure 9.11. More generally, swept solids also include *forms of revolution,* where the generating polygon is moved around some axis of revolution. Other variations on this concept include forms where the shape of the generating polygon changes as it moves in space or is revolved as it moves, and forms where the trajectory is not straight or is made of multiple connected sections.

The utility of the high-level polygon operators can be demonstrated in their ability to construct this important class of forms. In the following, a generalized topological extrusion procedure is given, which is made only of the operators discussed so far. This procedure can be used to both generate extruded solids from scratch and to extrude additions to existing solids.

The base of the extruded solid is a *face of an existing solid.* This may be a lamina solid (i.e., a solid made of two congruent faces and whose volume is zero) or the face of an existing solid, as depicted in Figure 12.2.

The extrusion process comprises a series of calls to procedures SPLIT_ EDGE and SPLIT_FACE. New locations of the vertices generated by splitting the edges (and which comprise the top of the extruded solid) are assigned by the geometrical procedures discussed in Chapter 6, and are not detailed here. The topological extrusion of a four-sided base is depicted in Figure 12.3.

```
procedure extrude_base (fbase : fptr; var ftop : fptr);
{Generate extruded topology of the base face fbase in the same
 solid that fbase belongs to. Return pointer to the top face
 ftop, to simplify the later assignment of geometry.}

var   e,enew,elast : eptr;
      g1,g2        : gptr;
      vnew1,vnew2  : vptr;
      stop         : boolean;

begin
   g1 := fbase^.glist; g2 := g1^.gnext;
   split_face (fbase, g1,g2, f, e);
   split_edge (e, elast, vnew);

   stop := false;
   repeat
     split_edge (e, enew, vnew1, vnew2);

     g1 := e^.eseg[2]; g2 := g1^.gnext^.gnext;
```

```
    if g2^.gedge = elast
      then begin g2 := g2^.gnext; stop := true end;

    split_face (f, g1,g2, ftop, e)
  until stop
end; {extrude_base procedure}
```

13

THE GEOMETRY OF SOLIDS

The geometrical attributes associated with solids and their components are *points, lines,* and *surfaces.* In this chapter we shall see how these elements are represented computationally in three-dimensional space, how they are operated on, and how they are associated with the respective topological elements.

☐ THREE-DIMENSIONAL FRAMES OF REFERENCE

Geometry, as discussed in Chapter 6, represents particular locations in some frame of reference. The frame of reference we have been using throughout this book is the *Cartesian coordinate system.* In two-dimensional Euclidean (E2) space, this frame of reference consists of two coordinate axes, X and Y, that intersect at a point called the *origin* of the coordinate system. The coordinates to the right and above the origin are considered positive, whereas those to the left and below the origin are considered negative. This two-dimensional Cartesian coordinate system can be extended into a *three-dimensional* coordinate system by adding a third axis (called the Z axis), perpendicular to the plane formed by the X and Y axes. Together, this three-axis frame of reference allows for the unique identification of any point in the three-dimensional Euclidean (E3) space, by its rectilinear distances from the planes formed by pairs of axes (XY, XZ, and YZ).

There are two ways in which the third axis can be added to the first two. If the plane formed by X and Y is considered horizontal, then the Z axis can be added such that its positive half is *above* the plane (Figure 13.1a), or it can be added such that its positive half is *below* the plane (Figure 13.1b). The first defines what is known as a *right-handed* coordinate system, and the second defines what is known as a *left-handed* coordinate system.

It is a matter of convention which coordinate system is chosen as the frame of reference for the purposes of solid modeling. Typically, solids are *modeled* in a

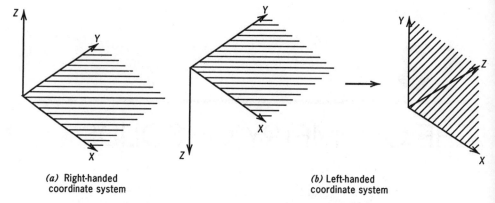

(a) Right-handed
coordinate system

(b) Left-handed
coordinate system

Figure 13.1. The Cartesian coordinate system in E3.

right-handed coordinate system and are *viewed* in a left-handed coordinate system. The right-handed coordinate system is convenient for modeling, because the Z axis seems to "grow out" of the horizontal plane formed by the X and Y axes, thus representing "height." The left-handed coordinate system is more convenient for viewing purposes, because the X and Y coordinates are defined in the plane of the screen, and the Z axis points away from the observer ("into" the screen).

☐ THE REPRESENTATION OF PLANES

Planes (and other surfaces) are the primary geometric elements in E3. A plane in E3, similar to a line in E2, is a surface characterized by a constant slope in two nonparallel directions. This property means that three noncollinear points determine a plane. We can tell whether any other point in E3 lies in the plane determined by the first three by comparing the ratios of coordinate differences. If all the ratios are the same (i.e., they are linear multiples of each other), then the point lies in the plane; otherwise it does not:

$$\frac{x - x1}{y - y1} = \frac{x2 - x1}{y2 - y1} = \frac{x3 - x1}{y3 - y1}$$

$$\frac{x - x1}{z - z1} = \frac{x2 - x1}{z2 - z1} = \frac{x3 - x1}{z3 - z1}$$

$$\frac{y - y1}{z - z1} = \frac{y2 - y1}{z2 - z1} = \frac{y3 - y1}{z3 - y1}$$

This property may be expressed more concisely in matrix form. The condition of linear dependency is satisfied when the determinant of the matrix is zero:

$$\begin{bmatrix} (x - x1) & (y - y1) & (z - z1) \\ (x2 - x1) & (y2 - y1) & (z2 - z1) \\ (x3 - x1) & (y3 - y1) & (z3 - z1) \end{bmatrix} = 0.$$

After extracting the unknowns x, y, z, and rearranging the terms, we can name A, B, C, D the multiplied combinations of the known quantities $x1, y1, z1$, $x2, y2, z2$, and $x3, y3, z3$. These parameters define the *equation of a plane*, which takes the form:

$$Ax + By + Cz + D = 0,$$

where

$$A = \begin{bmatrix} 1 & y1 & z1 \\ 1 & y2 & z1 \\ 1 & y3 & z3 \end{bmatrix} \quad B = \begin{bmatrix} x1 & 1 & z1 \\ x2 & 1 & z2 \\ x3 & 1 & z3 \end{bmatrix} \quad C = \begin{bmatrix} x1 & y1 & 1 \\ x2 & y2 & 1 \\ x3 & y3 & 1 \end{bmatrix} \quad D = \begin{bmatrix} x1 & y1 & z1 \\ x2 & y2 & z2 \\ x3 & y3 & z3 \end{bmatrix}.$$

We can expand the determinants and compute the coefficients explicitly:

$$A = y1(z2 - z3) + y2(z3 - z1) + y3(z1 - z2)$$
$$B = z1(x2 - x3) + z2(x3 - x1) + z3(x1 - x2)$$
$$C = x1(y2 - y3) + x2(y3 - y1) + x3(y1 - y2)$$
$$D = - x1(y2z3 - y3z2) - x2(y3z1 - y1z3) - x3(y1z2 - y2z1).$$

The derivation of the parameters for computational purposes is performed by procedure COMPUTE_PLANE. It uses the following data structure to represent the geometry of a plane:

```
type  params = (a,b,c,d);
      plane  = array [params] of real;

procedure compute_plane (pnt1,pnt2,pnt3 : point;
                         var pln : plane);
{Compute the parameters a,b,c,d of a plane equation determined
 by the three points pnt1,pnt2,pnt3, using the determinant
 method.}
var  x1,x2,x3,y1,y2,y3,z1,z2,z3 : real;
```

```
begin
  x1 := pnt1[x]; y1 := pnt1[y]; z1 := pnt1[z];
  x2 := pnt2[x]; y2 := pnt2[y]; z2 := pnt2[z];
  x3 := pnt3[x]; y3 := pnt3[y]; z3 := pnt3[z];


  pln[a] := (y2 - y1)*(z3 - z1) - (y3 - y1)*(z2 - z1);
  pln[b] := (x3 - x1)*(z2 - z1) - (x2 - x1)*(z3 - z1);
  pln[c] := (x2 - x1)*(y3 - y1) - (x3 - x1)*(y2 - y1);
  pln[d] := -pln[a]*x1 + pln[b]*y1 + pln[c]*z1
end; {compute_plane procedure}
```

The planes we use are the geometric attributes of the faces (polygons) of a solid. They can, therefore, be computed from the geometrical attributes of the vertices of these faces (their points). To compute a plane equation from points, however, the points must not be collinear (i.e., they must not be part of one line in E3). This condition can be stated as the following constraint:

The area of the triangle formed by the points is not zero.

For computational purposes, we can verify that the areas of the images of this triangle as projected onto the major planes XY, XZ, and YZ are not all zero, as implemented by function COLLINEAR.

```
function collinear (pnt1,pnt2,pnt3 : point) : boolean;
{Return true if points pnt1, pnt2, and pnt3 are collinear, else
 false. Method: compute the area of the three triangles formed
 by the projections of the points on the major planes. If the
 area of all three triangles is zero-the points are collinear.}

const epsilon = 10e-6;
var   x1,x2,x3,y1,y2,y3,z1,z2,z3, a1,a2,a3 : real;


begin
  x1 := pnt1[x]; y1 := pnt1[y]; z1 := pnt1[z];
  x2 := pnt2[x]; y2 := pnt2[y]; z2 := pnt2[z];
  x3 := pnt3[x]; y3 := pnt3[y]; z3 := pnt3[z];


  a1 := (x1 - x3)*(y2 - y3) + (x2 - x3)*(y3 - y1);
  a2 := (y1 - y3)*(z2 - z3) + (y2 - y3)*(z3 - z1);
  a3 := (z1 - z3)*(x2 - x3) + (z2 - z3)*(x3 - x1);

  collinear := (abs(a1) < epsilon) and
               (abs(a2) < epsilon) and
               (abs(a3) < epsilon)
end; {collinear function}
```

☐ OPERATING ON PLANES

The Orientation of a Plane

The orientation of a plane in E3 is defined by the direction of the *normal vector* to the plane, emanating from the origin of the coordinate system and defined by the coordinates A, B, C, which are also the parameters of the plane itself (Figure 13.2).

Orientation is an important characteristic of planes used in solid modeling because the planes underlie the faces of solids. As such, the orientation is used to discriminate between the "inside" of a solid and its "outside," as defined by its bounding surface. A polyhedral solid is made of many faces, each with its own underlying plane (Figure 13.3). It is important, therefore, that the orientation of all the planes be consistent (i.e., that the region of E3 identified by one plane as being "inside" the solid is not identified by another plane as being "outside" it).

The orientation of a plane, which is computed from three points, is determined by the direction formed by the points, with respect to the origin. If this direction is anticlockwise, as viewed from the origin, the sense of the normal to the plane they form is *away* from the origin. If the direction they form is counterclockwise, as viewed from the origin, the sense of the normal to the plane formed by them is *toward* the origin. We can use this property to verify that the polygons underlying the faces of the solid comply with the orientation well-formedness constraint, which was discussed in Chapter 9, both *topologically* and *geometrically*. If the vertices of all faces (polygons) form *anticlockwise* directions when viewed from *inside* the solid (i.e., the normals to all planes they form are directed

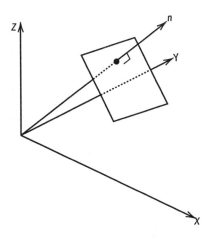

Figure 13.2. The normal vector to a plane.

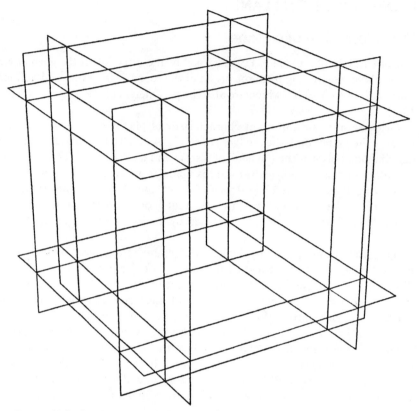

Figure 13.3. The planes underlying the faces of a hexahedron (a cube).

away from the solid), they are consistently oriented. This property also means that the normals point toward the *outside* the region of E3, as partitioned by the boundary of the solid. All the polygons that form the faces of a solid must be tested (or constructed) in this manner. If a polygon is found to be oriented in the wrong direction (i.e., the normal to the plane formed by its vertices is inconsistent with the outward orientation rule), then it must be reversed. It is important to note here that *concave* polygons have vertex sequences that form plane equations whose normals are opposite to the desired orientation, although the polygon as a whole is well-oriented (Figure 13.4). The points chosen for computing the plane equation, therefore, must be from the *convex* part of the polygon, rather than its concave part (if any), as well as be noncollinear.

Figure 13.4. A concave polygon has vertex sequences that form plane orientations opposite to the orientation of the polygon as a whole.

The Distance Between a Point and a Plane

A useful geometric utility, as we shall see later in the this chapter, is provided by knowing the *distance* between a point and a plane, particularly if the *sign* of this distance indicates which side of the plane the point is on, where "side" is the orientation of the plane as determined by its normal (i.e., "above" is the side of the plane where the normal is positive, and "below" is the side of the plane where the normal is negative). The distance between a point and a plane can be computed in a manner similar to the one we used in Chapter 6 to compute the distance between a point and a line in the plane. It can be determined by substituting the coordinates of the point in the plane equation and normalizing the result by dividing it by the cosine correction factor. This process is implemented by function POINT_PLANE_DISTANCE.

```
function point_plane_distance (pnt : point; pln : plane) : real;
{Compute and return the signed (positive or negative) distance
 of point pnt from plane pln, by substituting the point
 coordinates in the plane equation and dividing by the cosine
 correction factor.}

const epsilon = 10e-6;
var   dis,fac : real;

begin
   dis := pnt[x]*pln[a] + pnt[y]*pln[b] + pnt[z]*pln[c] - pln[d];
   fac := sqrt(sqr(pln[a]) + sqr(pln[b]) + sqr(pln[c]));
   if (abs(dis) < epsilon) or (abs(fac) < epsilon)
     then point_plane_distance := 0.0
     else point_plane_distance := dis/fac
end; {point_plane_distance function}
```

The Intersection Between a Line Segment and a Plane

Given the operator to compute the signed distance between a point and a plane, we can develop a simple operator that will compute the *point of intersection* between a line segment, given by its two end points and a plane. This operator is based entirely on the distances of the end points from the plane and on the fact that the point of intersection divides the line segment proportionally to these distances, as shown schematically in Figure 13.5. It is computationally considerably more efficient and numerically more stable than using an analytical method for computing the point of intersection by solving a system of linear equations made of the equations of the plane and the line.

This process is implemented by procedure LINE_PLANE_INTERSECT, which assumes that the line segment does intersect the plane. The input to this function consists of the signed distance of each point from the plane and the equation of the plane itself.

```
procedure line_plane_intersect (dis1,dis2 : real;
                                pln : plane;
                                var p_int : point);
{Compute the point of intersection between the line segment
 bounded by two points, whose distances from the plane are dis1
 and dis2, and the plane pln. Note: Assume such an intersection
 exists (i.e., both points are not on the same side of the plane
 or both coincident with the plane).}

const epsilon = 10e-6;
var   p,r     : real;
      i       : coords;
```

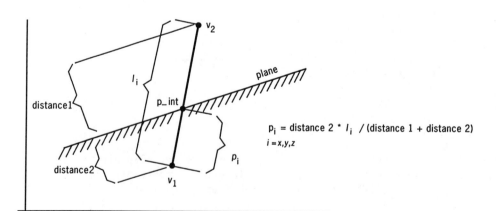

Figure 13.5. Determining the intersection point between a line segment and a plane on the basis of proportions.

```
begin
  if abs(dis1) < epsilon
    then p_int := pnt1
    else if abs(dis2) < epsilon
      then p_int := pnt2
      else begin
        p := abs(dis2)/(abs(dis1) + abs(dis2));
        for i := x to z do
          begin
            r := p*abs(pnt1[i] - pnt2[i]);
            if pnt1[i] < pnt2[i]
              then p_int[i] := pnt1[i] + r
              else p_int[i] := pnt1[i] - r
          end
      end
end; {line_plane_intersect procedure}
```

☐ THE INTERSECTION BETWEEN A POLYGON AND A PLANE

Line-plane intersections are one of the most important and most frequently used geometric operators in solid modeling. In particular, they are used to find the lines of intersection between a polygon and a plane. Such lines of intersection are needed to compute the intersection between solids, as discussed in Chapter 14, and between polygons (for such purposes as hidden line removal).

The difference between line-plane intersections and polygon-plane intersections is due not only to the iterative use of the first by the second, but more important, to the need to resolve singularities. *Singularities* are special cases that arise when a line segment is coincident to the plane at one or both its end points. In such cases, two successive line segments of a polygon will produce *two* points of intersection that are geometrically congruent. This redundancy is not only wasteful, but may significantly and unnecessarily complicate subsequent topological and geometrical operations.

It is desirable, therefore, to resolve singularities at the line-plane intersection level. This resolution is based on the observation that a point of proper intersection between the boundary of a polygon and a plane represents a *transition* of the polygonal boundary from one side of the plane to its opposite side. Therefore, two consecutive line segments, joined at a vertex which is coincident to the plane, either represent a single point of transition (Figure 13.6a) or no transition at all (Figure 13.6d). Figure 13.6 enumerates all the possible relationships between a pair of consecutive segments a plane.

It is evident from this enumeration that certain cases represent no singularity problems (e.g., Figures 13.6e, f, k, and l). The others can be resolved if we consider the *direction* of the transition (from one side of the plane to its other side) as well as its existence. If we are interested in *above-below* transitions, then vertex 2 in Figure 13.6c will not be considered a point of intersection, but vertex 2 in

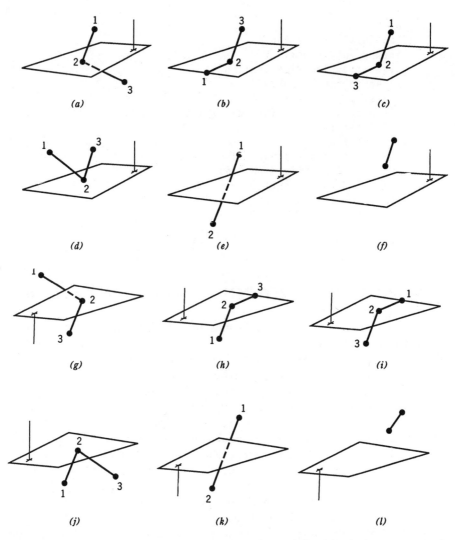

Figure 13.6. Complete enumeration of the possible relationships between segment pairs and a plane.

Figure 13.6i will. If, on the other hand, we are interested in *below-above* transitions, than vertex 2 in Figure 13.6b will be considered a transition, but vertex 2 in Figure 13.6h will not. Either way, vertex 2 in Figures 13.6d and 13.6j will not be considered intersections, because no below-above or above-below transitions occur.

The directionality of the transition can be included as a parameter in the polygon-plane intersection algorithm, which will use it as a discrimination factor for determining whether a point of singularity represents an intersection or it does not. This determination can be summarized as follows:

A segment is considered intersecting the plane in one of the following cases:

1. If its two end points are on opposite sides of the plane
2. If its *first* end point is coincident with the plane, and the other is on the side of the plane that corresponds to the direction of transition we are interested in (i.e., "below" if we are interested in an above-below transition, and "above" if we are interested in a below-above transition).

Because we deal with well-formed solids, the orientations of the planes correspond to the outside-inside relations of the void and the solid with respect to the boundary of the solid. "Above," therefore, is considered "outside" the solid, and "below" is considered "inside."

Procedure POLYGON_PLANE_INTERSECT implements these rules and observations for the purpose of computing the intersection between a given polygon and a plane. It returns an unsorted list of intersection points. The determination whether the segment intersects the plane or not is simplified by using the symmetry between the two sides of the plane. In procedure POLYGON_PLANE_INTERSECT, we classify points that are inside the solid (i.e., "below" the plane) as *positive* points ($+1$) and points that are outside the solid (i.e., "above" the plane) as *negative* points (-1). The direction of transition is also given in the same terms (-1 for an inside-out and $+1$ for an outside-in transition). We then construct a SET of integers -1 to 1, which consists of these classifications. An intersection exists if the cardinality (the number of elements in the set) is more than one (i.e., both points are not on the same side of the plane) and if the integer denoting the direction of the transition is a member of this set. For simplicity and clarity, we use an array of points to store the points of intersection:

```
type   i_list = array [1..100] of point;

procedure polygon_plane_intersect (p : pptr;
                                    pln : plane;
                                    dir : integer;
                                    var i : integer;
                                    var p_int_list : i_list);
{Compute and return unsorted list of intersection points between
 polygon p and plane pln. The variable i tells how many points
 were found.}

var   g             : gptr;
      dis1,dis2     : real;
      position_set  : set of (-1..1);
```

```
      function cardinality : integer;
      {Compute and return number of elements in position_set.}

      var  r    : -1..1;
           count : integer;

      begin
         count := 0;
         for r := -1 to 1 do
           if r in position_set then count := count + 1;
         cardinality := count
      end; {cardinality function}

      function side (dis : real) : integer;
      {Return 1 if dis > 1, -1 if dis < 0, 0 if dis = 0.}

      const epsilon = 10e-6;

      begin
        if abs(dis) < epsilon
          then side := 0
          else if dis > 0 then side := 1 else side := -1
      end; {side function}

begin  {polygon_plane_intersect}
  g := p^.glist; i := 0;
  dis1 := point_plane_distance (g^.gvert^.form, pln);

  repeat
    g := g^.gnext;
    dis2 := point_plane_distance (g^.gvert^.form, pln);

    position_set := [side(dis1), side(dis2)];

    if (cardinality > 1) and (dir in position_set)
      then begin
        line_plane_intersect (dis1,dis2, pln, p_int)
        i := i + 1;
        p_int_list[i] := p_int
      end;

    dis1 := dis2
  until g = p^.glist
end; {polygon_plane_intersect procedure}
```

☐ ASSIGNING GEOMETRIC ATTRIBUTES TO POLYGONS

The geometric attributes of polygons, as mentioned earlier, comprise plane equations, which are represented by their parameters A, B, C, and D. The plane can be represented by the PLANE data structure and computed from three non-collinear, convex vertices of the polygon, as implemented in procedure COMPUTE_POLY_PLANE.

```
type  plane = array [params] of real;


procedure place_polygon (p : pptr);
{Compute the plane of polygon p from three of its non-collinear
 vertices. Assume three non-collinear vertices exist.}


var  g        : gptr;
     v1,v2,v3 : vptr;


begin
   g := p^.glist; v1 := g^.gvert;
   g := g^.gnext; v2 := g^.gvert;
   repeat
      g := g^.gnext; v3 := g^.gvert
   until not collinear (v1^.form, v2^.form, v3^.form);


   compute_plane (v1^.form, v2^.form, v3^.form, p^.form)
end; {place_polygon procedure}
```

When the vertices of the polygon are relocated in space, its plane equation must be recomputed. Because we restricted our discussion to planes, it is also important to verify that all the points lie in one plane, otherwise the face must be split into multiple triangular faces, each of which is planar (Figure 13.7).

To determine if the points of a polygon are coplanar, we can compute their distances from the plane formed by three of the points, as implemented by function COPLANAR. It returns TRUE if all the points are within range epsilon of the plane.

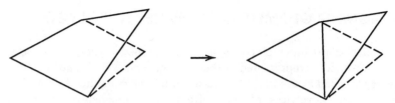

Figure 13.7. Triangulating a nonplanar face.

```
function coplanar (p : pptr) : boolean;
{Return true if all vertices of polygon p are in the plane
 formed by three of its non-collinear vertices.}

const epsilon = 10e-6;

var  g        : gptr;
     inplane  : boolean;
     dis      : real;

begin
  inplane := true;
  g := p^.glist;
  repeat
    dis := point_plane_distance (g^.vert^.form, p^.form);
    if abs(dis) > epsilon
      then inplane := false
    g := g^.gnext
  until not inplane or (g = p^.glist);
  coplanar := inplane
end; {coplanar function}
```

There are many more operations that are applicable and useful for the geometrical manipulation of solids in E3. They include nonplanar geometries and such calculations as the line formed by two intersecting planes. The reader is encouraged to explore them and is referred to the bibliography at the end of this chapter for further reading.

□ BIBLIOGRAPHY

Blinn, J. F., "Platonic Solids," *IEEE Computer Graphics and Applications,* **7**(11):62–66, November 1987.

Bowyer, A., and J. Woodwark, *A Programmer's Geometry,* Butterworth, London UK, 1983.

Faux, I. D., and M. J. Pratt, *Computational Geometry for Design and Manufacture,* Wiley, New York, 1979.

Hearn, D., and M. P. Baker, *Computer Graphics,* Prentice-Hall Inc., Englewood Cliffs, NJ, 1986.

Kalay, Y. E., "Modeling Polyhedral Solids Bounded by Multi-Curved Parametric Surfaces," *Computer Aided Design* 15(3):141–146, May 1983.

Lee, Y. T., and A. A. G. Requicha, "Algorithms for Computing the Volume and Other Integral Properties of Solids II: A Family of Algorithms Based on Representation Conversion and Cellular Approximation," *Communications of the ACM,* 25(9):635–650, September 1982.

Rogers, D. F., and J. A. Adams, *Mathematical Elements for Computer Graphics,* McGraw-Hill, New York, 1976.

Selby, P. H., *Analytic Geometry,* Harcourt, Brace, Jovanovich, New York, 1986.

Shamos, I. M., and F. Preparata, *Computational Geometry,* Springer Verlag, New York, 1985.

14

SPATIAL SET OPERATORS

Spatial set operators, which are also known as *shape operators*, are powerful computational tools. They facilitate interactive generation of complex forms in an easy and natural way that resembles sculpting in clay; that is, by direct addition and subtraction of volumes. From a mathematical point of view, the spatial set operators are an extension to the set-theoretic operators of *union*, *intersection*, and *difference*, as they are applied to spatial sets of points, as discussed in Appendix A.

While intuitively simple, the implementation of spatial set operators for boundary represented solids makes them one of the most difficult algorithms in computational geometry. This complexity is further increased by the special properties of surfaces, such as orientation, which places the algorithm in the domain of manifold theory more than in set theory.

In this chapter we shall discuss an algorithm that successfully negotiates these complexities, together with all their special cases (in particular, the presence of coincidental surfaces). This algorithm is based on the Hybrid Edge method of representing solids.

□ INTER-SOLID OPERATORS

The utility of hierarchical structuring is revealed when inter-solid operators, which make use of high-level solid and polygon operators, are considered. Such operators include splitting a solid by a plane (e.g., for the purpose of generating sections), splitting a solid along a polygon inscribed on its bounding surface, or combining solids to create more complex forms (Figure 14.1).

Given that solids are represented by structured collections of polygons, their splitting by a plane, by a polygon, or by another solid can be implemented by high-level polygon and solid operators of the kind discussed in Chapters 5 and 12, if certain extensions are added. For example, a solid can be split by a plane using the following algorithm:

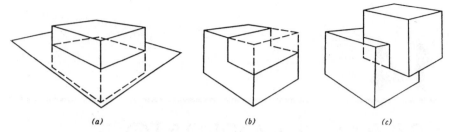

Figure 14.1. Splitting a solid by (a) a plane, (b) a polygon, and (c) another solid.

1. Split each one of the solid's faces, which are intersected by the splitting plane, along pairs of points identified by procedure **POLYGON_PLANE_INTERSECT** (presented in Chapter 13).
2. Mark A all the faces of the solid on one side of the splitting plane and B the ones on the other side of the splitting plane.
3. Merge all the faces identified as A or B, depending on the desired orientation of the section, along their joining edges that are not coincident with the splitting plane into one polygon.

The resulting shape is a well-formed solid made of faces A or B alone and a single merged face of the opposite characterization, which geometrically coincides with the splitting plane. Obviously, implementation of this algorithm requires testing, sorting, and structuring details not elaborated here. Rather than elaborate this algorithm, we shall present in this chapter an algorithm that performs the *spatial set operations*, which include the other two types of solid splitting operations.

The spatial set operators are one of the most powerful, yet intuitively simple, tools that solid modeling systems provide to designers of physical artifacts. A derivative of the mathematical set theoretic operators of union, intersection, and difference, the spatial set operators provide designers with the means to combine pairs of well-formed solids into new solids that are the respective product of the operation. By preserving the well-formedness of the operant solids, these operators allow reuse of the products as operandi in subsequent applications, thereby increasing the form complexity of the shapes attainable by the modeling system beyond that which is possible to attain by other means (Figure 14.2).

While intuitively easy to understand and use, the implementation of the spatial set operators for boundary-represented solids is an algorithmically difficult task: it involves a tight interaction between topological and geometrical operations and, therefore, provides the ultimate test-bed for the performance of any geometric modeler. A geometric modeling system that supports iterative application of spatial set operators without exceptions is necessarily well-formed, general, and complete (its efficiency, nevertheless, is largely a matter of implementation).

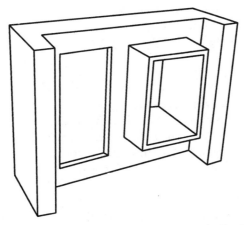

Figure 14.2. Spatial set operations increase the form complexity of solids attainable by a solid modeling system.

Due to the sequential nature of computation, the spatial set operators must be decomposed into a large number of more primitive operators that are themselves complicated by special cases (such as the case of coincident faces). Therefore, many modeling systems that employ spatial set operators have placed restrictions on their use and sometimes employ multiple different subsets of these operators to accomplish specific tasks, thereby requiring the user to consciously discriminate between different shape configurations (e.g., shapes that touch on a face but do not penetrate each other).

In this chapter we present a general algorithm for implementing the spatial set operators for the Hybrid Edge boundary method of representation. It is based on the polygon operators and the low and high level solid operators discussed earlier. The final product of the algorithm is a well-formed solid, whose boundary is made of the appropriate parts of the bounding surfaces of the two operandi and which is reusable as an operant in subsequent applications of the algorithm. The algorithm guarantees the integrity of the product solid data structure, by preserving the initial well-formedness of the operant solids and by resolving the consequences of all possible geometric relationships. The general principles that underlie spatial set operations in two and three dimensions and topics from topology, homology, and manifold theory relevant to the algorithm, are discussed in Appendix A.

☐ THE BOUNDARY OF A COMBINED SOLID

The general algorithm for computing the spatial set product of two operant shapes is based on *partitioning* the bounding surface of each operant shape at its intersection into two (or more) disjoint parts, each of which is exclusively inside the other shape or outside it. Once so partitioned, the parts of each operant that will not partake in the product shape are *identified and deleted*. The remaining parts are *"glued"* along the line of intersection to form the unified boundary of the product shape.†

Before an algorithm for accomplishing this task can be developed, the rules regarding the composition of the boundary of the product solid must be established. These rules will help us determine *where* the boundaries must be partitioned and *which* parts must be deleted. Appendix A derives the underlying principles for combining the boundaries of shapes directly from set-theoretic principles and from the manifold-theoretical properties of the boundary itself. These principles can be summarized as follows:

1. The boundary of the product shape resulting from a spatial *union* operation on two operant shapes consists of the noncoincident parts of the boundary of each operant *that are outside the domain of E3 occupied by the other shape.*

2. The boundary of the product shape resulting from a spatial *intersection* operation on two operant shapes consists of the noncoincident parts of the boundary of each operant *that are inside the domain of E3 occupied by the other shape.*

3. In addition to one of the above, those parts of the boundary of *one of the operandi that coincide with the boundary of the other operant and that are oriented toward the domain of E3 that is outside the other shape* also partake in forming the boundary of the product shape (both for union and for intersection).

4. The *difference* between two shapes can be regarded as an *intersection* after the subtracted shape's boundary has been *inverted*.

The implementation of rule 3 does not depend on which of the operandi is chosen; therefore, either one of them can be chosen as the shape whose coincident boundary elements will participate in the product shape.

The first step in the spatial set operation algorithm consists of computing the line of intersection between the boundaries of the two operant solids. The boundary of each operant must, by definition, be partitioned into subsets of two types of elements: those that are inside the other shape and those that are outside it. Because both boundaries are well-formed, for each outside-in penetration of one boundary into the domain of E3 bounded by the other solid there must also be an inside-out exit from that domain and into the domain of E3, which is outside the other solid. It follows, therefore, that the line of intersection dividing the boundary of each operant into subsets of inner and outer elements, with respect to the boundary of the other solid, comprises one or more *well-formed*

---

†Operating on two shapes may produce a product that is made of multiple disjoint or subjoint shells. Higher level shape management routines must sort these shells into separate shapes.

polygons inscribed on the bounding surface of each operant shape. This line is, therefore, a closed *ring* (or rings), as depicted in Figure 14.3.

Once this ring has been computed (as discussed in the next section), the faces and edges of each operant that straddles across it, and are thus partly inside and partly outside the other solid, must be *split* into multiple parts along the line of intersection. The computation of the loci of intersection is a geometric operation that can be performed by procedure POLYGON_PLANE_INTERSECT, which was presented in Chapter 13. The splitting of the faces is a topological operation that can be performed by procedure SPLIT_FACE, which was presented in Chapter 12.

Singularities may arise due to faces and edges that are *coincident* with the bounding surface of the other solid. They must be resolved such that each face and edge is uniquely and unambiguously identified as being either inside or outside the other shape. The resolution is based on the previously defined composition of the boundary of the product solid, which can be restated in the form of the following rules:

A union B:

1. All the parts of the boundary of *A* that are *outside B*, and all the parts of the boundary of *A* that are coincident with the boundary of *B* and are oriented in the *same* direction as the boundary of *B* (that is, toward its outside)
2. All the parts of the boundary of *B* that are *outside A*

A intersection B:

1. All the parts of the boundary of *A* that are *inside B*, and all the parts of the boundary of *A* that are coincident with the boundary of *B* and are oriented in the *same* direction as the boundary of *B* (that is, toward its outside)
2. All the parts of the boundary of *B* that are *inside A*.

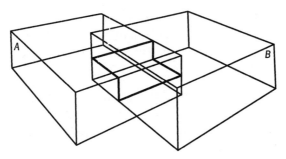

Figure 14.3. Closedness of the ring of intersection.

The product of *A difference B*, as stated earlier, is produced in the same manner as the product of *A intersection B*, after *B* has been inverted. The ring of intersection can thus be redefined as:

The loci of transition of the boundary elements of each operant shape from the domain of E3 outside the other operant to the domain of E3 that is inside it, considering both the relative position of the elements and the particular shape operation

These rules have been incorporated into procedure POLYGON_PLANE_INTERSECT, which was presented in Chapter 13, and whose arguments include the parameter DIR that indicates the desired relative orientation of segments to be considered intersecting the plane.

□ THE GENERAL SHAPE OPERATIONS ALGORITHM

The general spatial set operations algorithm, which will be called here the *shape operations algorithm*, comprises three major operations, each consisting of multiple suboperations (Figure 14.4). These are:

1. Identifying the rings of intersection between the two shapes and partitioning their bounding surfaces accordingly
2. Merging the faces that will not be part of the product shape into a single face
3. Joining the remaining faces of each operant at the line of intersection into one new boundary.

In the following, each one of the three major operations constituting the shape operations algorithm is discussed in detail for shapes bounded by planar surfaces and represented by the Hybrid Edge data structure.

Computing the Ring of Intersection

In general, the edges forming the ring of intersection (denoted here as *cut edges*) can be computed one at a time by determining the line of intersection between pairs of faces, one from each shape. This *O(mn)* operation (*m* and *n* are the numbers of the faces in each operant shape, respectively) consists of two steps:

1. Determining the *geometric* location where a pair of faces intersect
2. Updating the *topology* of each shape by inserting new edges and vertices at the intersection, thereby (possibly) splitting the faces.

The line along which a pair of faces intersect can, in most cases, be determined by simple geometric operations (in the planar case), as discussed in Chap-

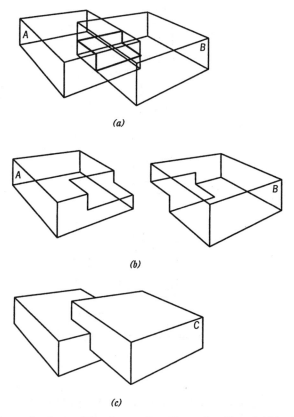

Figure 14.4. The major steps of the shape operations algorithm: (a) identify the rings of intersection; (b) merge faces that will not partake in making the product shape; and (c) "glue" the remaining parts into one boundary.

ter 13. However, the determination of the geometric line of intersection serves no purpose in itself. Rather, it is used for establishing the loci of the *topological partitioning* of each face into parts that are either inside or outside the other shape. It is, therefore, important to apply the geometric intersection operators discriminately. In other words, it is desirable to partition faces only to the necessary minimum number of parts, rather than multiple redundant ones that will have to be rejoined later. The purpose of the following discussion is thus to explore how the global rules described earlier can be implemented in the most efficient way through local discrimination tests.

The line along which each face is intersected can be computed by determining the points where its edges intersect the plane embedding the other face. Relying on planarity conditions, these points define an unbounded line that lies in both planes. This line must, however, be (1) trimmed and bounded in segments that lie within the region of the plane bounded by the corresponding face and (2) overlapped by the segment that lies in the region of the other plane that is bounded by its corresponding face (Figure 14.5).

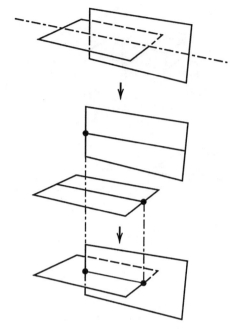

Figure 14.5. Computing the geometric intersection between two faces.

The points where each face intersects the plane underlying another face can be computed by procedure POLYGON_PLANE_INTERSECT. They must be sorted into pairs and matched with the pairs of intersection points where the other face intersects the plane underlying the first one. The sorting and matching can be done by a merge-sort algorithm, of the type commonly used in many programming practices. Once sorted and merged, overlapping segments may be identified.

Once the geometric intersection has been computed, the topology of each face must be updated accordingly. New edges may be introduced in four ways (as depicted in Figure 14.6):

1. By splitting existing edges
2. By building a strut (similar to the ones described in Chapter 5)
3. By making a lamina hole (which is made of two edges and a face whose area is zero)
4. By splitting a face.

New edges are introduced, in principle, by means of the high-level polygon and solid operators, which introduce new edges where lines of intersection indicate that faces are to be partitioned. They include SPLIT_EDGE, MAKE_STRUT, CREATE_EDGE, MAKE_HOLE, and SPLIT_FACE. It should be

Figure 14.6. Four ways of adding a new edge: (a) by splitting an edge; (b) by building a strut; (c) by making a lamina hole; (d) by splitting a face.

noted, however, that some geometric tests for establishing the correct parameters for these operators are required, because the topological location of the elements added by the polygon operators to a shape depends on geometric conditions.

Subsequent steps of the algorithm are considerably simplified if all the new edges are identified by a temporary, auxiliary linked list, which we call the "cut list." Every element in this list references one pair of edges, one from each operant solid, which corresponds to the same geometrical segment in the ring of intersection.

The results of performing this splitting operation on all faces of each boundary are (1) an inscribed ring of intersection edges, which partitions the boundary of each solid into faces that are either inside or outside the space occupied by the other solid, and (2) a list of paired cut edges, one from each operant shape.

Merging the Faces

Once the bounding surface of each operant shape has been partitioned, it is necessary to identify and merge into a single face all its parts that will not partake in the final product. In principle, this is done by identifying the relative position of each face with respect to the bounding surface of the other shape (i.e., whether it is outside or inside). Then, depending on the desired set operation, those faces that are outside (for intersection) or inside (for union) the other shape, are merged.

In general, identifying the relative position of the faces of each shape is done by identifying the relative position of a single vertex of one shape with respect to the other one, then propagating this information over the entire boundary.†
Once the relative position of a vertex has been identified, its relative position is assigned to the faces adjacent to it, then propagated to other faces across common edges, while reversing it (from "inside" to "outside" and vice versa) when crossing cut edges. Such propagation is made possible by the well-formedness of the shapes, which guarantees that there exists a path between any two points on the boundary and that the line of intersection is a closed ring. Furthermore, by using the right-hand rule in an extended manner, it is possible to propagate the

---

† If all the vertices of one shape are coincident with the boundary of the other shape, then edges are bisected until a point is found that is unambiguously either inside or outside the other shape.

relative position also over the other shape's boundary, thus eliminating the need to identify the relative position of one of its own vertices with respect to the first shape, as a starting point. The faces of the two shapes that are adjacent to a cut edge have the same relative position (both "inside" or both "outside") if their direction of traversal is topologically *opposite* (when viewed from outside both shapes), as depicted in Figure 14.7.

The identification of the relative positions of the faces of both shapes is, therefore, a matter of traversal, once the relative position of one vertex have been determined.† The determination of this first relative position is a rather complicated geometric operation, which is known as the *point in polyhedron inclusion test* (see the bibliography at the end of this chapter for details).

Once the relative positions of all the faces of each shape have been determined, those faces that will not be part of the final product are merged into a single face by means of procedure MERGE_FACE.

The result of these combined steps is that each operant shape now consists of a well-formed bounding surface, which is made of elements that were left over from the original shapes, some new elements generated by the partitioning process, and two faces (one on each shape) that will be disposed of once the two operandi are joined together in the next step. (These faces, which are the combined result of the merged faces, may not be planar!)

Joining the Operandi into the Final Product

In this final step of the algorithm, the two operandi (or what is left of them) are joined ("glued") together into a single, well-formed shape, which is the product of the algorithm. This is a purely topological operation that consists of extensive

---

† Some complication occurs in the case of multiple disjoint shells, when the relative position of one vertex for each disjoint pair of shells must be determined.

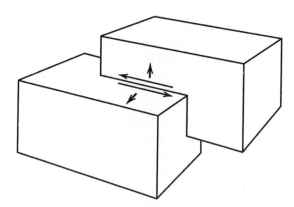

Figure 14.7. Propagating the relative position of one boundary to the other.

re-arrangement of the data structure and in which the merged faces that remain from the previous step are actually expunged, and their bounding edges are combined with the corresponding edges on the other shape.

The advantages of the Hybrid Edge data structure are most evident in performing this otherwise rather awkward "gluing" operation. Because the faces of the solids are really polygons joined by edges, "gluing" the boundaries consists of three steps:

1. Join the lists of faces and the lists of edges of the two solids into one list each in the product solid.
2. Replace the edges joining the merged faces with their adjacent faces by edges that join the segments of the corresponding faces of the other solid.
3. Delete the merged faces.

The first step is trivial. The second step requires only (1) traversal of the cut list of paired edges created by the first part of the algorithm, (2) the removal of the cut edges themselves from the joint list of edges in the product solid, and (3) replacement of the cut edges by new edges that connect corresponding segments of the faces adjacent to the ring of intersection. These operations are performed by means of procedures REMOVE_EDGE, DISPOSE_EDGE, and CREATE_EDGE, whose arguments are taken from the cut list.

The result of this final step of the shape operation algorithm is a well-formed, composite boundary of the two operant solids, joined through the desired set operation. The well-formedness of the product shape is guaranteed, because the operators that are used throughout the algorithm to manipulate the shapes (that is, the high-level polygon and solid operators) are closed under the well-formedness rules. The product shape is thus suitable for use as an operant in successive spatial set operations, thereby facilitating iterative applicability of the algorithm.

It is obvious that this generalized description of the algorithm must be augmented by many special case handling routines. Such routines considerably complicate the algorithm. It is interesting to note that the shape operations algorithm builds a new topological structure from geometrical relationship conditions in a manner that is opposite to the shape construction method described in Chapter 14.

It is also evident why the spatial set operators include the first two inter-solid operators discussed earlier in this chapter: the splitting of a solid by a plane and the splitting of a solid by inscribing a polygon on its boundary. The first can be handled by replacing the first part of the shape operations algorithm with a procedure that splits the boundary of a single solid by a single plane and by not performing the third part of the algorithm. The second can be handled by replacing the first part of the shape operations algorithm with a manual inscription of the cut ring on the boundary of the solid and by not performing the third part of the algorithm. With these additions, the spatial set operation operators can handle most any inter-solid operations applicable to boundary represented shapes.

☐ BIBLIOGRAPHY

Kalay, Y. E., "Determining the Spatial Containment of a Point in General Polyhedra," *Computer Graphics and Image Processing* **19**(4):303–334, August 1982.

Kalay, Y. E., and C. M. Eastman, "Shape Operations: An Algorithm for Combining Boundary-Represented Solids," Technical Report, Computer-Aided Design and Graphics Laboratory, State University of New York at Buffalo, November 1983.

Knuth, D., *The Art of Computer Programming: Fundamental Algorithms,* 2nd ed., Addison-Wesley, Reading, MA, 1973.

Yamaguchi, K., and T. Tokieda, "A Unified Algorithm for Boolean Shape Operations," *IEEE Computer Graphics and Applications*, **4**(6):24–37, June 1984.

15

EXERCISE 2: SOLID MODELING

The boundary of three-dimensional solids can be represented as a collection of connected polygons, provided that certain well-formedness conditions are maintained. In this exercise, you will use the knowledge you acquired through the modeling of polygons to create solid shapes. The projection transforms that will allow you to view the solids are provided in Part 5 of the book.

Your task is to design and implement the data structure of solid shapes composed of connected polygons and the operators that create them. The shapes that are in your model's domain will be restricted to prismatic (extruded) shapes, where the cross section of the form remains the same as its base. The shapes thus consist of two similar, arbitrary (horizontal) polygons that define the base and the top of each shape, connected by (vertical) rectangular polygons. The user should be able to trace the base polygon and specify the desired height to which that polygon should be extruded. The data structure that you use may be as simple as a list of polygons that form the boundary of a solid, or you may add information that will link the individual polygons through connecting edges. If your solid comprises polygons, each edge is represented by two segments (one for each polygon). How would you eliminate drawing the edges twice?

☐ GENERATING A PERSPECTIVE VIEW

To visualize the solids you create, use the perspective transform that is presented in Procedure PERSPECTIVE. The perspective transform, is of type MATRIX:

```
type coords = (x,y,z,w);
     point  = array [coords] of real;
     matrix = array [coords] of point;
```

It is created by procedure **PERSPECTIVE**, given two points: the location of the observer (**OBSV**), and the location of the center of the view (**CNTR**). It assumes a constant view angle of 85 degrees.

```
procedure perspective (var mat : matrix; obsv,cntr : point);
{Create perspective transform matrix mat using observation point
 obsv and center point cntr as inputs. The view angle is a
 constant 85 degrees.}

const   radians     = 0.0174533;
        epsilon     = 10e-6;
        view_angle  = 85.0;       {degrees}
        scale_factor = 5.0;

var     dx,dy,dz,phi,x_rot,y_rot:real;

  function theta (ax,ay : real) : real;
  {Calculate the rotation angle about y. Assume that both ax
   and ay cannot be 0.0 simultaneously.}

  var  t : real;

  begin
    if abs(ay) <= epsilon
      then if ax > 0.0 then t := -90.0 else t := 90.0
      else if abs(ax) <= epsilon
        then if ay > 0.0 then t := 180.0 else theta := 0.0
        else begin
          t := arctan(ax/ay)/radians;
          if ay > 0.0 then t := t + 180.0
        end;
      theta := t
  end; {theta function}

begin {perspective procedure}
  dx := obsv[x] - cntr[x];
  dy := obsv[y] - cntr[y];
  dz := obsv[z] - cntr[z];

  init_matrix (mat);
```

```
if (abs(dx) > epsilon) and (abs(dy) > epsilon)
  then begin
    rotate (mat, x, 90.0);
    y_rot := theta (dx, dy);
    rotate (mat, y, y_rot);
    x_rot := arctan(dz/(sqrt(sqr(dx)+sqr(dy))))/radians;
    rotate (mat, x, -x_rot)
  end
  else begin
    if dz > 0.0
      then x_rot := 0.0
      else x_rot := -180.0;
    rotate (mat, x, x_rot)
  end;

{scale by view angle and put in left-hand coord. system}
phi := (sin(view_angle)/cos(view_angle))*scale_factor;
scale (m, phi,phi,-1)
end; {of perspective procedure}
```

It is up to you to design and implement the user interface to this transform, which includes selecting a point of view, center of view, and optionally clipping plans and view angles (with the appropriate alteration of the constants in procedure PERSPECTIVE to parameters).† It is also up to you to design and implement the means to apply the perspective transform to solids, along the lines explained in Chapter 18. More extensive discussion of computational perspective transformations can be found in the general computer graphics literature, in such books as listed at the end of this chapter.

☐ BIBLIOGRAPHY

Foley, J. D., and A. van Dam, *Fundamentals of Interactive Computer Graphics,* Addison-Wesley, Reading, MA, 1982.

Hearn, D., and M. P. Baker, *Computer Graphics*, Prentice-Hall Inc., Englewood Cliffs, NJ, 1986.

Newman, W. W., and R. F. Sproul, *Principles of Interactive Computer Graphics,* 2nd ed., McGraw-Hill, New York, 1979.

---

†To obtain the perspective depth foreshortening, the x and y coordinate values of each point must be divided by its z coordinate value, after the point was transformed by the perspective matrix.

PART THREE

PLACEMENT

16

PRINCIPLES OF TRANSFORMING SHAPES

The first two parts of this book discussed how the formative elements of shapes (vertices, polygons, edges, and solids) can be represented in the computer by means of abstract data types, which include both data structures and the operators that manipulate them. Parts One and Two concentrated on the *topological* modeling of the data, which defines the relationships between the formative elements. Part Three of the book extends the principles of modeling over the *geometrical* information associated with shapes: the location of shapes in two- and three-dimensional space.

☐ THE RELOCATION OF SHAPES IN SPACE

The purpose of the geometrical modeling operations is to relocate a given shape with respect to its current position within some frame of reference and, at the same time, preserve the geometrical and topological relationships between its components (or change them in a controlled manner). We again distinguish between the data structure and the operators that manipulate it. The data structure is represented by *geometrical transforms* that encapsulate the geometrical change information in a concise form. This information is created and applied to the geometrical components of a shape by *geometrical transformation* operators.

The relocation of points and lines within a given frame of reference is a simple matter of assigning them new coordinate values. These points and lines, however, are members of polygons or solids. It is this membership that considerably complicates their geometrical relocation for two reasons:

1. In most cases we are interested in relocating *all* the points and lines of a polygon or a solid by the *same* amount, such that the result will appear to be the relocation of the entire shape (as depicted in Figures 16.2 and 16.3).

2. The relocation may violate the well-formedness of the shape by reversing its orientation (as depicted in Figure 16.9).

In this part of the book we discuss how to represent the desired relocation and how to apply it to entire shapes in a manner that is efficient and well-formed. We first look at the means to establish a locational *frame of reference* in the form of a coordinate system. Coordinate systems were introduced in Chapters 6 and 13 as the means to uniquely locate points and lines in space. In this part of the book we broaden their scope and see how coordinate systems can be used to establish the location of entire shapes as well as certain dependency relationships between shapes.

Next, we introduce two- and three-dimensional transforms and the operators that apply them to the geometrical attributes of shapes. We then introduce matrix notation of transforms as a means to represent geometrical change, which considerably simplifies the transformation operators. This discussion entails the introduction of homogeneous coordinates, an alternative way to represent lines and points in space, and of matrices and their related operators as the means to concatenate (combine) multiple transforms into one. We conclude this part by discussing locational dependency hierarchies in assembly structures. The user interface to the transformation operators, which is responsible for getting the data (in geometrical or alphanumeric input form) for the subsequent application of transformations, is discussed in Part Five.

☐ LOCATION AND RELOCATION OF POINTS AND LINE SEGMENTS

To symbolically "locate" points and the lines that connect them in the computer's memory, we must use a mathematical notation consisting of numerical and symbolic values, which allows us to "place" points within some abstract frame of reference. As we have seen in Chapters 6 and 13, several different schemes can be used as frames of reference for the purpose of interpreting these values as the geometrical location of a point in the plane or in space. These schemes include the familiar Cartesian and polar coordinate systems. We have been using, and will continue to use here, the Cartesian method, which is the simplest and most widely used.

In two-dimensional space, the Cartesian coordinate system is generated by drawing two perpendicular lines, which we call the *coordinate axes*. Their intersection is known as the *origin* of the coordinate system; it divides each axis into positive and negative halves. Any point p in the plane can be uniquely defined by drawing a line segment from it to each one of the coordinate axes, perpendicular to the respective axis. The coordinates of the point p in the coordinate system are the lengths of these line segments (which may be expressed in some predefined units). The values of the line segment lengths are signed (i.e., positive or negative), depending on which side of the origin they lie, as depicted in Figure 16.1.

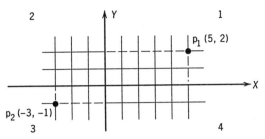

Figure 16.1. The Cartesian coordinate system in two-dimensional space.

The Cartesian coordinate axes also divide the two-dimensional space into four *quadrants,* as depicted in Figure 16.1. (And they divide the three-dimensional space into eight *octants.*) The significance of this division for the purposes of geometrical transformations is discussed later, in the context of scaling.

A line segment can be described geometrically by the location of its two end points (if it is straight). These points can be used (as demonstrated in Chapters 6 and 13) to compute the line equation of which the segment is a part. Because we are interested here in relocating entire shapes without affecting the relationships between their parts, we may limit our discussion to geometrical transformations that apply to points with the understanding that the parameters of lines can be calculated from the end points that bound each segment.

☐ BASIC GEOMETRIC TRANSFORMATIONS

A geometric transformation is the act of relocating all the points of a shape in the same manner, relative to the frame of reference in which the shape is embedded. It thus consists of applying some fixed geometrical data, which describes the nature and quantity of change, to all the points of a shape. For example, the translation of a two-dimensional polygon in the plane would consist of two quantities Dx and Dy, which describe the axial displacement of each point. This information, which we call the *transform,* is applied to all the points of the polygon by a *transformation* operator. For example, in the case of two-dimensional translation, this operator will simply add the quantities Dx and Dy to the coordinates values x, y of each point, respectively, and thereby produce a new set of coordinates x', y' for each point of the polygon:

$$x' = x + Dx$$

$$y' = y + Dy.$$

The effect of applying such transformation (where $Dx = 3$, $Dy = 1$) to all the points of a triangle whose vertices are located at $<1, 1>$, $<3, 1>$, and $<3, 5>$, is depicted in Figure 16.2.

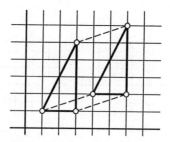

Figure 16.2. Translating a shape in two-dimensional space.

Points (and hence shapes) can be transformed in complex ways. Still, all transformations consist of various combinations of three basic (primitive) transforms:

1. Translation
2. Rotation (about the origin)
3. Scaling (about the origin)

The following sections discuss each of these basic transformations in two and three dimensions and demonstrate their effect on the triangle depicted in Figure 16.2.

Translation

The form of the two-dimensional translation transformation, as noted earlier, is:

$$x' = x + Dx$$

$$y' = y + Dy.$$

where Dx and Dy are the quantities of translation in directions x and y, respectively. In three dimensions, the transformation also includes relocation by Dz in the Z axis, in addition to relocations in X and Y, but it is otherwise similar to the two-dimensional case in all respects:

$$x' = x + Dx$$

$$y' = y + Dy$$

$$z' = z + Dz.$$

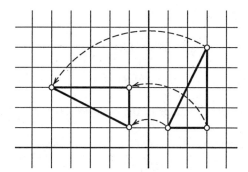

Figure 16.3. Rotating a shape in two-dimensional space.

Rotation

The rotation transformation moves a given point to a new location along a circular arc centered at the origin, as depicted in Figure 16.3. The degree of rotation A is given as an angle that describes (in polar coordinates) the difference between the old angular location B of the point relative to the origin and the coordinate axis and its new angular location $A + B$ (Figure 16.4).

Although degrees, which are a measure on the basis of the polar coordinate system, are a natural way to specify rotation, we must convert them into a set of linear translations in the Cartesian coordinate system which was chosen earlier as the preferred frame of reference in which the location of points is represented. To do so, we use a simple geometrical construction, depicted in Figure 16.4.

First, we note that the distance of the point from the origin does not change due to the rotation. We will denote it r. Second, we observe that:

$$x' = r \cdot \cos(A + B) = r \cdot \cos(B) \cdot \cos(A) - r \cdot \sin(B) \cdot \sin(A)$$

$$\text{(16.1)}$$

$$y' = r \cdot \sin(A + B) = r \cdot \cos(B) \cdot \sin(A) + r \cdot \sin(B) \cdot \cos(A).$$

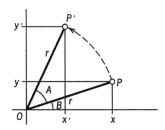

Figure 16.4. Converting angular rotation into linear translation in the two-dimensional Cartesian space.

We also observe in Figure 16.4 that:

$$r \cdot \cos(B) = x$$

$$r \cdot \sin(B) = y.$$

By substituting this pair of values in the equations of (16.1), we obtain:

$$x' = x \cdot \cos(A) - y \cdot \sin(A)$$

$$y' = x \cdot \sin(A) + y \cdot \cos(A).$$

(16.2)

(Note: Positive rotation is counterclockwise about the origin.) Thus, for example, the vertices of the triangle $<1, 1>$, $<3, 1>$, $<3, 5>$ will be relocated to $<-1, 1>$, $<-1, 3>$, $<-5, 3>$, after it has been rotated counterclockwise by 90 degrees about the origin, as depicted in Figure 16.3.

The same principle of rotation is directly extendable to three dimensions, where the rotation of a point about an arbitrary axis which passes through the origin can be decomposed into three angular motions, one about each of the three major coordinate axes: X, Y, and Z (Figure 16.5).

As in the two-dimensional case, the rotations must be converted into three linear translations in three dimensions. Such linear translations amount to translating the two-dimensional *image* of the point as it is projected in one of the major planes (XY, XZ, or YZ), which corresponds to the axis of rotation (Z, Y, and X, respectively).

Rotation by A degrees about the Z axis is thus equivalent to two-dimensional rotation of the projected point in the XY plane, which we discussed earlier. It does not effect the Z coordinate of the point, therefore the two equations in (16.2) are also applicable to rotation about the Z axis in three dimensions.

Rotation about the X axis and about the Y axis differ from rotation about the Z axis only in the coordinate values of the point which they affect: rotation by B degrees about X axis affects the y and z coordinates (but not the x coordinate), therefore it is expressed as:

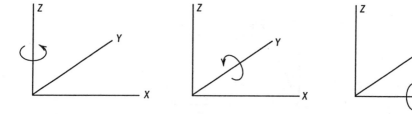

Figure 16.5. Rotational transformations in three dimensions. (Counterclockwise rotation is considered positive when viewed along each of the major axes looking toward the origin.)

$$y' = y \cdot \cos(B) + z \cdot \sin(B)$$

$$z' = -y \cdot \sin(B) + z \cdot \cos(B)$$

(16.3)

which is equivalent to equations (16.2) except that y has been substituted for x, and z for y, and the signs have been adjusted to reflect the positive rotation according to the convention established earlier. Similarly, rotation by C degrees about the Y axis is expressed by substituting y with z in equations (16.2) and adjusting the signs for positive rotation:

$$x' = x \cdot \cos(C) - z \cdot \sin(C)$$

$$z' = x \cdot \sin(C) + z \cdot \cos(C).$$

(16.4)

A point can thus be rotated in three dimensions by using a suitable combination of the three primitive rotations. It is even possible to construct a composite transformation that will rotate a point in three-dimensional space by the three angles A, B, and C all at once. Rotations, however, are not commutative: the order of applying individual rotations to the point is significant. For example, rotation by 90 degrees about X, followed by a rotation of 90 degrees about Y, places the point in a different location in space than the same two rotations applied in reverse order, as depicted in Figure 16.6. To use such a composite trans-

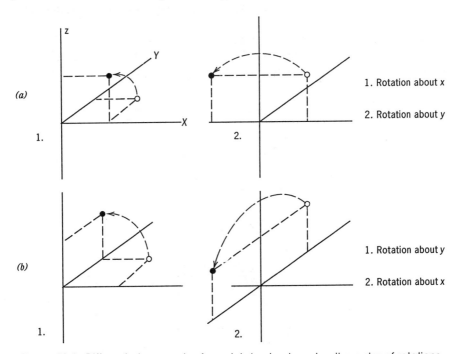

Figure 16.6. Different placements of a point due to changing the order of rotations.

formation, we must order the rotations according the predefined sequence dictated by the transformation. We will, however, find it more convenient to use a freely constructed sequence of individual transformations than have to pre-order the rotations according to the transformation. Therefore, in this book we do not pursue such a composite rotation transformation.

Scaling

The scaling operation moves a point to a new location by multiplying its former coordinates x, y, and z by some constant factors Sx, Sy, Sz:

$$x' = x \cdot Sx$$

$$y' = y \cdot Sy$$

$$z' = z \cdot Sz.$$

Because the coordinates of the point are measured from the origin of the coordinate system, the scaling operation also involves an implicit *translation* of the shape it is applied to, as depicted in Figure 16.7. Thus, for example, to enlarge the triangle we used earlier to twice its original size, we may select $Sx = 2$, $Sy = 2$, which will relocate the end points of the triangle to $<2, 2>$, $<6, 10>$, and $<6, 2>$. Notice that because the scaling is relative to the origin of the coordinate system, the triangle was also translated to the right.

Scaling can be used for a variety of purposes: it can enlarge a shape, or shrink it if Sx, Sy, and Sz are less than one. If they are not equal, the shape will be distorted; it becomes elongated or foreshortened, depending upon its inclination rela-

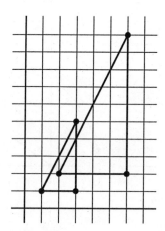

Figure 16.7. Scaling a shape in two-dimensional space.

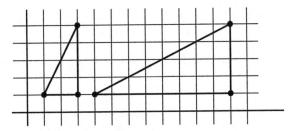

Figure 16.8. Distorting a shape by applying nonuniform scaling to the different coordinate axes.

tive to the coordinate axes, as depicted in Figure 16.8 for $Sx = 4$, $Sy = 1$ *(and the implicit $Sz = 1$).*

A special case of scaling, *mirroring,* occurs when an uneven combination of Sx, Sy, or Sz is negative. The shape will be "mirrored," as depicted in Figure 16.9 for $Sx = -1$, $Sy = 1$, and $Sz = 1$. Mirroring also causes a topological change to the shapes it is applied to, by turning them "inside out." The geometrical mirroring transformation must, therefore, be accompanied by a topological reversal of the shape, or it must not be allowed to happen at all. Mirroring, however, is essential to complete the range of symmetry operations applicable to shapes. Although first quadrant shapes are isomorphic (i.e., — they are congruent) with third quadrant shapes, no transformation consisting of translations and rotations alone can transform first quadrant shapes into congruent second or fourth quadrant shapes without the use of mirroring.

☐ COMPOSITE TRANSFORMATIONS

Taken individually, the basic transformations of translation, rotation, and scaling are rather limited in their modeling powers. To derive more complex shape relocations, several basic transformations must be applied in sequence. For example, the basic rotation transformation revolves a shape about the origin. If the

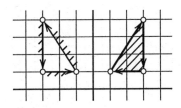

Figure 16.9. Negative scaling causes mirroring of a shape in two-dimensional space.

shape is to be rotated about some arbitrary point in space, a sequence of three transformations must be used:

1. The shape must be translated such that the center of the rotation coincides with the origin.
2. The shape must be rotated as desired.
3. The rotated shape must be "untranslated" by an amount that is equal but opposite to that by which it was translated in step 1.

For example, if the triangle we used earlier is to be rotated by 90 degrees about the point $<1, 3>$, we must use the following sequence of transformations for each of its points (Figure 16.10):

$$x' = x - 1 \qquad\qquad y' = y - 3$$

$$x'' = x' \cdot \cos(90) - y' \cdot \sin(90) \qquad y'' = x' \cdot \sin(90) + y' \cdot \cos(90)$$

$$x''' = x'' + 1 \qquad\qquad y''' = y'' + 3.$$

This multitransformation process is very inefficient because it requires traversing all the points of a shape many times. Transformations, however, are linearly additive; the sequential application of individual transformations have the same effect as the single application of their composite transformation. It is possible, therefore, to combine all the transformations into one composite transformation, which can be applied to the points of the shape only once:

$$x''' = [(x - 1) \cdot \cos(90) - (y - 3) \cdot \sin(90)] + 1$$

$$y''' = [(x - 1) \cdot \sin(90) + (y - 3) \cdot \cos(90)] + 3.$$

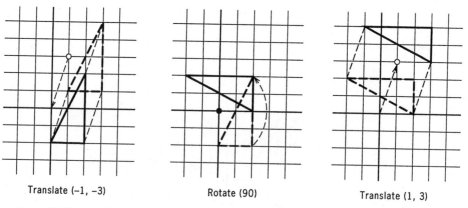

Translate (−1, −3)   Rotate (90)   Translate (1, 3)

Figure 16.10. Rotating a shape by 90 degrees about point $<1, 3>$ in the two-dimensional space.

Similar techniques can be used to control the implicit translation that accompanies scaling, and to perform mirroring about an arbitrary axis.

Even this condensed form of transformation is still rather inefficient because it requires a relatively large number of arithmetical operations to be performed on each point. When dealing with complex shapes, this inefficiency will result in poor run time performance. Furthermore, because each sequence must be pre-designed, it limits the number of transformations available to the designer to some predefined set. As it turns out, transforms can be represented compactly by means of matrix notation, which provides a solution to both problems: it allows us to reduce the number of arithmetical operations that must be applied to each point of the shape by performing many of the required arithmetical operations on the transforms themselves (e.g., by inversion and concatenation), and it simplifies the operations that create composite transforms to the extent where transformations can be created by the designer at run time. Matrix-represented transforms are discussed in Chapter 17.

☐ BIBLIOGRAPHY

Newman, W. M., and R. F. Sproull, *Principles of Interactive Graphics*, 2nd ed., McGraw-Hill, New York, 1979.

Rogers, D. F., and J. A. Adams, *Mathematical Elements for Computer Graphics*, McGraw-Hill, New York, 1976.

17

BASIC GEOMETRICAL TRANSFORMS

The concatenation of transformations is significantly simplified if matrix notation is used to represent the transforms. Although matrix notation is only a change of form, not the substance of the transforms, it is much preferable over nonmatrix representation, because it admits a host of mathematical tools developed for matrix algebra, such as matrix multiplication, inversion, and transposition, and because it provides a uniform basis for the representation of all transformations, regardless of how complex they are.

We begin our discussion of matrix notation for transforms by briefly reviewing the pertinent aspects of matrix algebra, then proceed to show how the basic transforms of translation, rotation, and scaling can be represented in this form. This discussion entails reintroduction of the homogeneous coordinate system, which is needed to justify the uniform representation of two-dimensional transforms by 3 × 3 matrices and of three-dimensional transforms by 4 × 4 matrices.

□ A BRIEF REVIEW OF MATRIX ALGEBRA

A point in two-dimensional Euclidean (E2) space is represented by the coordinates pair $<x,y>$. These coordinates are often referred to as *vectors*: arrows that emanate from the origin and end at the point (Figure 17.1). Vectors are denoted here by the notation *[x y]*.

One of the basic operations that can be applied to vectors is *multiplication*. Algebraically, two vectors **a** and **b** can be multiplied by operating on their components one by one. For example, two vectors $\mathbf{a} = [3 \quad 2]$ and $\mathbf{b} = [-2 \quad 1]$ can be multiplied to yield a scalar $C = -4$. Expressed in vector notation, this operation is known as the *inner product* (or the *dot product*) of the vectors:

$$\mathbf{a} \cdot \mathbf{b} = [3 \quad 2] \cdot \begin{bmatrix} -2 \\ 1 \end{bmatrix} = (3 \cdot (-2) + 2 \cdot 1) = -4 \ .$$

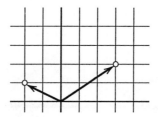

Figure 17.1. Vector representation of points in two-dimensional space.

The inner product operation on vectors is fundamental to matrix algebra in general and to the transformation of shapes in particular. It can easily be implemented computationally, as demonstrated by function INNER_PRODUCT, which computes and returns the scalar inner product of two points, which as we have seen earlier in the book, are represented as vectors of coordinates.

```
type coords = (x,y,z,w);
     point  = array [coords] of real;

function inner_product (pnt1,pnt2 : point) : real;
{Computes and returns the inner product of the vectors
 representing points pnt1 and pnt2.}

var  i        : coords;
     product : real;

begin
  product := 0;
  for i := x to w do
    product := product + pnt1[i]*pnt2[i];
  inner_product := product
end; {inner_product function}
```

A *matrix* is a collection of vectors. The numbers that make up the matrix are known as its *elements*. A matrix of *M* rows and *N* columns is known to be of order $M \times N$. If the number of rows and columns is equal, the matrix is called *square*, such as the following 4×4 matrix:

$$\begin{bmatrix} 2 & 1 & 0 & -1 \\ 3 & 0 & 1 & 2 \\ 3 & 1 & 0 & 0 \\ 0 & 1 & 1 & 2 \end{bmatrix}.$$

   Like the vectors they are made of, matrices can be multiplied by operating on the vectors one by one. For example, two matrices A and B can be multiplied by computing the inner product of every *row* vector in A with every *column* vector in B. The scalar resulting from multiplying the ith row vector of A by the jth column vector of B becomes the ijth element of the product matrix C, as illustrated in Figure 17.2

$$\begin{bmatrix} 2 & 1 & 0 & -1 \\ 3 & 0 & 1 & 2 \\ 3 & 1 & 0 & 0 \\ 0 & 1 & 1 & 2 \end{bmatrix} \cdot \begin{bmatrix} 1 & 0 & 0 & 2 \\ 2 & 0 & 1 & 3 \\ 3 & 1 & 3 & 0 \\ 1 & 3 & 0 & 0 \end{bmatrix} = \begin{bmatrix} 3 & -3 & 1 & 7 \\ 8 & 6 & 3 & 6 \\ 5 & 0 & 1 & 9 \\ 8 & 7 & 4 & 3 \end{bmatrix}.$$

   A matrix in which every element is zero, except those on the diagonal from the upper left corner to the lower right corner whose values are one, is known as the *identity matrix*:

$$\begin{bmatrix} 1 & 0 & 0 & 0 \\ 0 & 1 & 0 & 0 \\ 0 & 0 & 1 & 0 \\ 0 & 0 & 0 & 1 \end{bmatrix}.$$

It has the same role in matrix algebra as the number 1 has in algebra, with respect to multiplication (i.e., multiplying another matrix by the identity matrix is like multiplying a number by 1):

$$\begin{bmatrix} 2 & 1 & 0 & -1 \\ 3 & 0 & 1 & 2 \\ 3 & 1 & 0 & 0 \\ 0 & 1 & 1 & 2 \end{bmatrix} \cdot \begin{bmatrix} 1 & 0 & 0 & 0 \\ 0 & 1 & 0 & 0 \\ 0 & 0 & 1 & 0 \\ 0 & 0 & 0 & 1 \end{bmatrix} = \begin{bmatrix} 2 & 1 & 0 & -1 \\ 3 & 0 & 1 & 2 \\ 3 & 1 & 0 & 0 \\ 0 & 1 & 1 & 2 \end{bmatrix}.$$

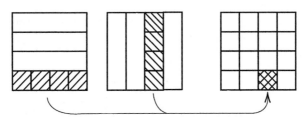

Figure 17.2. An illustration of matrix multiplication.

This rather cumbersome process of multiplication can become very tedious indeed when the multiplying matrices are large. Nevertheless, it can be easily implemented computationally, as demonstrated by Procedure CONCATE-NATE, which multiples two square 4 × 4 matrices *M*1 and *M*2, represented as vectors of points. This procedure must first *transpose M*2, so that the vectors it comprises represent columns rather than rows, as depicted in Figure 17.2. Transposition is an operation that makes the rows of a matrix become its columns and is implemented here by procedure TRANSPOSE.

```
type matrix = array [coords] of point;

procedure transpose (var m : matrix);
{Transpose matrix m by making its rows become its columns.}

var   i,j  : coords;
      mnew : matrix;

begin
  for i := x to w do
    for j := x to w do
      mnew[j,i] := m[i,j];
  m := mnew
end; {transpose procedure}

procedure concatenate (m1,m2 : matrix; var m : matrix);
{Multiply matrix m1 by m2 (M1xM2), and return the resulting
 matrix in m. It first transposes m2.}

var   row,column : coords;

begin
  transpose (m2);
  for row := x to w do
    for column := x to w do
      m[row,column] := inner_product (m1[row],m2[column])
end; {concatenate procedure}
```

A matrix *M* can be multiplied by a vector **v** in a similar manner (after *M* has been transposed), producing a new vector of the same length as the **v**, whose elements are the inner products of **v** with the columns of M. The number of rows in matrix M must, therefore, be equal to the number of elements in vector **v**:

$$[2 \quad 1 \quad 0 \quad -1] \cdot \begin{bmatrix} 1 & 0 & 0 & 2 \\ 2 & 0 & 1 & 3 \\ 3 & 1 & 3 & 0 \\ 1 & 3 & 0 & 0 \end{bmatrix} = [3 \quad -3 \quad 1 \quad 7].$$

Procedure TRANSFORM demonstrates how this process can be implemented computationally.

```
procedure transform (pnt : point;
                     m : matrix;
                     var new_pnt : point);
{Multiply point pnt with matrix m and return resulting point in
 new_pnt. First transpose matrix M.}

var  i : coords;

begin
  transpose (m);
  for i := x to w do
    new_pnt[i] := inner_product (pnt, m[i])
end; {transform procedure}
```

This brief review of matrix algebra, which of course leaves out many important properties of vectors and matrices, describes most of what we need for the purposes of geometric transforms. The only additional matrix operation that we need is matrix inversion, which will be discussed in Chapter 20 in the context of locational hierarchies.

□ REPRESENTING TRANSFORMS IN MATRIX NOTATION

In geometrical transformation, as represented by vectors and matrices, a vector representing the coordinates of a point is multiplied by a transposed matrix representing the transform. We have seen earlier how points can be represented as vectors. The following discussion shows how transforms can be represented as matrices.

Two of the basic transforms, rotation and scaling, can be readily represented in matrix notation. Two-dimensional scaling, for example, is representable by the following 2 × 2 matrix:

$$\begin{bmatrix} Sx & 0 \\ 0 & Sy \end{bmatrix}$$

where Sx and Sy represent the scaling factors for x and y, respectively. This transform, as we have seen earlier, can be applied to a point represented by the vector **[x   y]** to compute the new coordinate values of the point that are also represented in vector notation:

$$[x \quad y] \cdot \begin{bmatrix} Sx & 0 \\ 0 & Sy \end{bmatrix} = [x \cdot Sx \quad y \cdot Sy] \quad.$$

The two-dimensional rotation transform can be similarly represented in matrix notation as:

$$\begin{bmatrix} \cos(A) & \sin(A) \\ -\sin(A) & \cos(A) \end{bmatrix} \quad.$$

However, the two-dimensional translation transform cannot be represented by a 2 × 2 matrix. In contrast to scaling and rotation, which are *multiplication* operators, translation it is an *addition* operator, where the quantities Dx and Dy are added to the x and y coordinates of the translated point, respectively. In order to represent translation in matrix form similar to scaling and rotation, we must find a way to express translation as a multiplication operator. We can do so if the matrix we use to represent two-dimensional translation is a 3 × 3 matrix, rather than the 2 × 2 matrix which we used earlier, and if the two-dimensional point it is applied to is represented by a vector with three elements:

$$[x\ y\ ?] \cdot \begin{bmatrix} 1 & 0 & 0 \\ 0 & 1 & 0 \\ Dx & Dy & 1 \end{bmatrix} = [x + ? \cdot Dx \quad y + ? \cdot Dy \quad ? \cdot 1] \quad.$$

where $? = 1$. But where will this third element (represented here by ?) come from? We could add a third coordinate z, but that would put the point in three-dimensional Euclidean space. Yet, we saw in Chapter 16 that points in the two-dimensional space could be translated without having to resort to the third dimension. So where will the third coordinate come from if the point is to remain two-dimensional? If the two-dimensional Euclidean space cannot accommodate the third coordinate, then we must supplant it with another coordinate system which does. This new coordinate system is known as the *homogeneous* coordinate system, and it is derived from the properties of line equations, discussed in Chapter 6.

The Homogeneous Coordinate System

It was stated in Chapter 6 that the significance of the line equation parameters a, b, and c is in their *ratios* rather than in their *values*. It is this property that allows the derivation of the *normalized* line equation, by scaling a, b, and c such that $c = 1$:

$$(a/c)x + (b/c)y + (c/c) = 0 .$$ (17.1)

Looked at from a more general point of view, such scaling need not produce $c = 1$; it is equally applicable by any constant G:

$$Ga(x) + Gb(y) + G(c) = 0 .$$ (17.2)

Moreover, this scaling may be applied to the variables x and y, rather than the parameters a, b, and c:

$$a(Gx) + b(Gy) + c(G) = 0 .$$ (17.3)

If we now call $x1 = Gx$ and $x2 = Gy$, then Equation (17.3) becomes:

$$ax1 + bx2 + c(G) = 0 .$$ (17.4)

We may also change the name of G to $x3$ ($G = x3$) with no loss of generality, such that Equation (17.4) becomes:

$$ax1 + bx2 + cx3 = 0 .$$ (17.5)

Equation (17.5) is known as the *homogeneous* equation of a line. The parameters a, b, and c still represent a line in two dimensional space, but any point on that line is now given in terms of *three* coordinate values, $x1$, $x2$, and $x3$, rather than two. This is not a mistake, we are no longer dealing with Euclidean space, but rather with homogeneous space. This space has one dimension more than its corresponding Euclidean space: each point $<x, y>$ in two-dimensional Euclidean space is represented by three coordinates $<x, y, w>$ in the homogeneous space. The third coordinate w is called the *scale factor* or the *homogeneous coordinate*. For example, the point $<1, 2>$ will become $<1, 2, 1>$ if we choose $w = 1$, or $<2, 4, 2>$ if we choose $w = 2$, or $<-3, -6, -3>$ if we choose $w = -3$. A point in two-dimensional Euclidean space has, therefore, an infinite number of representations in its corresponding homogeneous space, each corresponding to a different value of w.

A homogeneous point $<x, y, w>$ can be converted back into two-dimensional Euclidean coordinates by dividing the first two coordinate values by the scale factor w $(x/w, y/w)$. This division process is known as *projection*, because we find the n dimensional representation of an $n + 1$ dimensional entity. It is, however, not always possible to perform such a projection. Consider, for example, the homogeneous point $<0, 1, 0>$. Because the scaling factor w is zero, we cannot divide by it the other two coordinates. Instead, we can get a feeling for such points by considering w as an infinitely small value e, which is close to zero but is not zero itself. The Euclidean coordinates of the point now become $<0, 1/e>$. As e approaches zero, the point becomes *infinitely* far away from the origin along the Y axis.

This point at infinity is both a clue to the nature of the homogeneous space and the root of its power. It suggests that problems in the n dimensional Euclidean space that cannot be solved due to special conditions, such as a point at infinity, are easily solvable in the $n + 1$ homogeneous space.

One of the problems homogeneous coordinates enable us to solve, which could not be solved in the Euclidean space, is the representation of points by a vector of three elements:

$$[x\ y\ w] ,$$

where w represents the scaling factor whose value may be chosen arbitrarily. For the sake of simplicity and convenience, we shall choose $w = 1$. The representation of two-dimensional points now becomes

$$[x\ y\ 1] . \tag{17.6}$$

A point represented by this vector can be easily converted back into Euclidean two-dimensional vector representation by simply omitting the scaling factor.

Uniform Representation of Transforms

With the adjustment of the representation of points, the two-dimensional translation transform can now be represented by a 3×3 matrix:

$$\begin{bmatrix} 1 & 0 & 0 \\ 0 & 1 & 0 \\ Dx & Dy & 1 \end{bmatrix}$$

and it can be applied to points represented by the homogeneous coordinate vector (17.6):

$$[x \quad y \quad 1] \cdot \begin{bmatrix} 1 & 0 & 0 \\ 0 & 1 & 0 \\ Dx & Dy & 1 \end{bmatrix} = [x + Dx \quad y + Dy \quad 1].$$

It was mentioned earlier that the purpose of representing transforms in matrix notation was to find a uniform representation that will facilitate their combination. Because translation in two dimensions requires the use of a 3 × 3 matrix, we must also represent the rotation and the scaling transforms by similar 3 × 3 matrices, rather than by 2 × 2 matrices. This is done by adding another row and another column to the 2 × 2 matrices we saw earlier. The 3 × 3 matrix representation of two-dimensional rotation thus becomes:

$$\begin{bmatrix} \cos(A) & \sin(A) & 0 \\ -\sin(A) & \cos(A) & 0 \\ 0 & 0 & 1 \end{bmatrix}, \tag{17.8}$$

and the 3 × 3 matrix representation of two-dimensional scaling becomes:

$$\begin{bmatrix} Sx & 0 & 0 \\ 0 & Sy & 0 \\ 0 & 0 & 1 \end{bmatrix}. \tag{17.9}$$

The extension of these two-dimensional transform matrices into three-dimensional transformations is straightforward. Three dimensional translation is represented by the 4 × 4 matrix:

$$\begin{bmatrix} 1 & 0 & 0 & 0 \\ 0 & 1 & 0 & 0 \\ 0 & 0 & 1 & 0 \\ Dx & Dy & Dz & 1 \end{bmatrix}.$$

Three-dimensional scaling is represented by the 4 × 4 matrix:

$$\begin{bmatrix} Sx & 0 & 0 & 0 \\ 0 & Sy & 0 & 0 \\ 0 & 0 & Sz & 0 \\ 0 & 0 & 0 & 1 \end{bmatrix},$$

and three dimensional rotations are represented by three 4×4 matrices, where:

$$s = \sin(A)$$
$$c = \cos(A)$$

$$\begin{bmatrix} 1 & 0 & 0 & 0 \\ 0 & c & -s & 0 \\ 0 & s & c & 0 \\ 0 & 0 & 0 & 1 \end{bmatrix}$$ for rotation about X axis,

$$\begin{bmatrix} c & 0 & s & 0 \\ 0 & 1 & 0 & 0 \\ -s & 0 & c & 0 \\ 0 & 0 & 0 & 1 \end{bmatrix}$$ for rotation about Y axis,

and

$$\begin{bmatrix} c & -s & 0 & 0 \\ s & c & 0 & 0 \\ 0 & 0 & 1 & 0 \\ 0 & 0 & 0 & 1 \end{bmatrix}$$ for rotation about Z axis.

These matrices can be set up by procedures that, given the parameters of the desired transformation, will return the appropriate transform matrix. We present these procedures in Chapter 18, after discussing how individual transforms can be concatenated (combined) into composite transforms.

☐ BIBLIOGRAPHY

Foley, J. D., and A. van Dam, *Fundamentals of Interactive Computer Graphics*, Addison-Wesley, Reading, MA, 1982.

18

CONCATENATION
OF TRANSFORMS

The utility of representing transforms as matrices is the ability to combine (concatenate) several transforms, each representing a primitive relocation, into one composite transform. This generalizes the construction of the composite transformation and makes its application to many points computationally efficient. In this chapter we discuss the principles of transform concatenations and their application to shapes.

☐ THE PRINCIPLES OF CONCATENATING TRANSFORMS

A complex transform can be described as the product of concatenation (multiplication) of the matrices of the simple transforms which compose it. For example, to derive the transformation that will rotate a shape through a counter clockwise angle of A degrees about an arbitrary point $<x, y>$ in two-dimensional space, we concatenate the following three simple transforms (depicted in Figure 18.1) into a single transform:

1. Translation, which when applied to point $<x, y>$ causes it to coincide with the origin:

$$\begin{bmatrix} 1 & 0 & 0 \\ 0 & 1 & 0 \\ -x & -y & 1 \end{bmatrix}.$$

2. Rotation by A:

$$\begin{bmatrix} c & s & 0 \\ -s & c & 0 \\ 0 & 0 & 1 \end{bmatrix}$$

where $s = \sin(A)$, and $c = \cos(A)$.

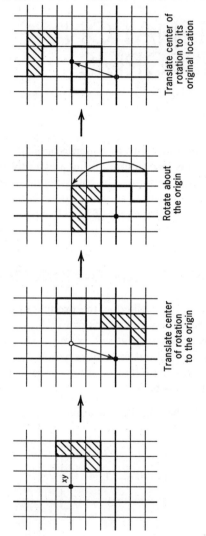

Figure 18.1. Rotation of a shape about an arbitrary point $<x, y>$.

3. Another translation that puts the center of rotation back at location $<x, y>$:

$$\begin{bmatrix} 1 & 0 & 0 \\ 0 & 1 & 0 \\ x & y & 1 \end{bmatrix}$$

The three transforms can be combined into one transform, by concatenation:

$$\begin{bmatrix} 1 & 0 & 0 \\ 0 & 1 & 0 \\ -x & -y & 1 \end{bmatrix} \cdot \begin{bmatrix} c & s & 0 \\ -s & c & 0 \\ 0 & 0 & 1 \end{bmatrix} \cdot \begin{bmatrix} 1 & 0 & 0 \\ 0 & 1 & 0 \\ x & y & 1 \end{bmatrix} \cdot$$

When properly multiplied in the order they have been specified, these transforms yield one compound matrix that represents a rotation by A degrees about a point located at $<x, y>$:

$$\begin{bmatrix} c & s & 0 \\ -s & c & 0 \\ Dx & Dy & 1 \end{bmatrix},$$

where

$$Dx = x - x \cdot c + y \cdot s$$
$$Dy = y - x \cdot s - y \cdot c.$$

The operations needed to compute this matrix are cumbersome, but must be performed only once, whereas the resulting 3×3 matrix may be applied to tens or hundreds of points of the transformed shape, thus saving many arithmetical operations.

☐ PROCEDURAL GENERATION OF TRANSFORMS

The complexity associated with matrix concatenation can be reduced if the matrices are created *procedurally* and if the new transforms are multiplied with some global transform T (which is initialized to the identity matrix). The creation of a composite transform thus becomes a sequence of procedure calls. Although the responsibility for properly sequencing individual transforms remains with the programmer (or the user), the procedures can assume responsibility for proper matrix multiplication. The procedures needed to create the basic transforms are **INIT_MATRIX**, which initializes the global transform T to the identity matrix, **TRANSLATE**, **ROTATE**, and **SCALE**. Each procedure takes a number of parameters, creates the corresponding 4×4 matrix, and multiplies it with the global transform T.

```
procedure init_matrix (var m : matrix);
{Create and return the identity matrix.}

var  i,j : coords;

begin
  for i := x to w do
    for j := x to w do
      if i = j
        then m[i,j] := 1
        else m[i,j] := 0
end; {init_matrix procedure}

procedure translate (var t : matrix; dx,dy,dz : real);
{Create a 4x4 translation matrix and multiply it with the global
 matrix T.}

var  m : matrix;

begin
  init_matrix (m);
  m[w,x] := dx; m[w,y] := dy; m[w,z] := dz;
  concatenate (t,m,t)
end; {translate procedure}

procedure rotate (var t : matrix; axis : coords; angle : real);
{Create a 4x4 rotation matrix about the given axis, and multiply
 it with the global matrix T.}

const  radians = 0.0174533;
var    a,s,c   : real;
       m       : matrix;

begin
  a := angle*radians; {convert from degrees into radians}
  s := sin(a); c := cos(a);
  init_matrix (m);

  case axis of
    x : begin
      m[y,y] := c; m[y,z] := -s;
      m[z,y] := s; m[z,z] := c
    end;
```

```
 y : begin
       m[x,x] := c; m[x,z] := s;
       m[z,x] := -s; m[z,z] := c
     end;
 z : begin
       m[x,x] := c; m[x,y] := -s;
       m[y,x] := s; m[y,y] := c
     end
 end;

 concatenate (t,m,t)
end; {rotate procedure}

procedure scale (var t : matrix; sx,sy,sz : real);
{Create a 4x4 scaling matrix and multiply it with the global
 matrix T.}

var  m : matrix;

begin
  init_matrix (m);
  m[x,x] := sx; m[y,y] := sy; m[z,z] := sz;
  concatenate (t,m,t)
end; {scale procedure}
```

These procedures can also be used for two dimensional transformations, if the values for the z coordinate are set correspondingly (i.e., 0 for translation and rotation, and 1 for scaling, and the rotation axis is set to Z). For example, the two-dimensional rotation by A degrees of a shape about an arbitrary point $<x, y>$, which we discussed earlier, can be implemented by the following sequence of procedure calls:

```
init_matrix (t)
translate(t, -x, -y, 0)
rotate(t, z, A)
translate(t, x, y, 0)
```

A similar sequence of transformations can be used to reflect (mirror) a shape about an arbitrary line in two dimensions. The algorithm for such reflection (depicted in Figure 18.2) comprises the following steps:

1. Translate the shape such that the line of reflection passes through the origin.
2. Rotate the line of reflection about the origin such that it aligns with the Y axis.
3. Reflect the shape about the Y axis (by scaling with $Sx = -1$ and $Sy = 1$).

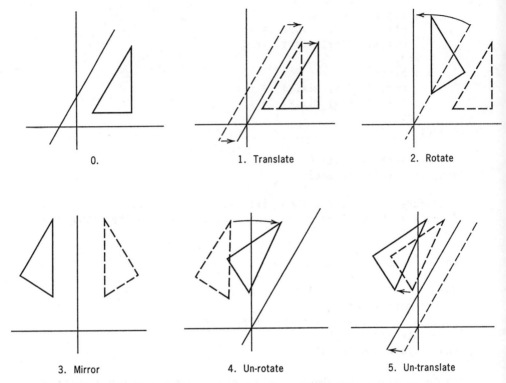

Figure 18.2. Reflecting a shape about an arbitrary line in two dimensions.

4. Rotate the shape by same quantity as in step 2 but in the opposite direction.
5. Translate the shape by the same amount as in step 1 but in the opposite direction.

The amount of translation along the X axis, such that the line of reflection passes through the origin, is the distance of the point where the line intersects the X axis from the origin. Given the line equation $ax + by + c = 0$, this distance is $Dx = -c/a$, and the angle of rotation such that it aligns with the Y axis is $A = -b/a$. The sequence of transforms is thus:

```
init_matrix (t)
translate(t, -Dx, 0, 0)
rotate(t, z, A)
scale(t, 1,-1, 1)
rotate(t, z, -A)
translate(t, Dx, 0, 0)
```

The same principles can be applied to scaling a three-dimensional shape about an arbitrary point $<x, y, z>$, without translating the shape, as demonstrated by the following sequence of transformations:

```
init_matrix (t)
translate(t, -x, -y, -z)
scale(t, sx, sy, sz)
translate(t, x, y, z)
```

□ APPLYING THE TRANSFORM TO A SHAPE

Having set up the global transform matrix T, we now want to apply it to each point of the shape to be transformed. We do so by multiplying the vectors representing the current locations of the vertices of the shape by the transform matrix T. We can use for this purpose procedure TRANSFORM, which was presented earlier in this chapter, although we may find it too expensive, in terms of computing time, when applied to the many points of which typical shapes are made. Still, for the sake of simplicity, we shall continue to use it in this book. We will demonstrate how shapes can be transformed by applying procedure TRANSFORM to a polygon.

To transform a polygon p by the global transform T, we must apply T to each point of p and recompute the line equations of all the segments of p, as demonstrated by procedure TRANSFORM_POLYGON. It uses the polygon data structure, discussed in Part One, and procedure PLACE_SEGMENT to compute the line equation of its segments, which was introduced in Chapter 6.

```
procedure transform_polygon (p : pptr; t : matrix);
{Transforms polygon p by the global transform T. First,
 transform all the vertices, then recompute the line equations
 of all the segments.}

var  g : gptr;
     v : vptr;

begin
  {transform all the vertices of p}
  g := p^.glist;
  repeat
    v := g^.gvert;
    transform (v^.form, t, v^.form);
    g := g^.gnext
  until g = p^.glist;
```

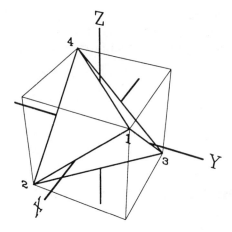

Figure 18.3. Generating a tetrahedron fit inside a cube and transforming it into a more "conventional" position. Reprinted with permission from *IEEE Computer Graphics and Applications.* This drawing first appeared in *IEEE Computer Graphics and Applications* in November 1987.

```
{recompute line equations of all segments of p}
repeat
   place_segment (g);
   g := g^.gnext
until g = p^.glist
end; {transform_polygon procedure}
```

Transformations of this kind allow us to exercise the modeling capabilities of the system with greater ease and flexibility than would be possible otherwise. In particular, they allow us to move shapes that were generated earlier to new locations in space, and re-scale and re-orient them as needed. They also allow us to generate complex shapes in the most convenient inclination (with regard to the coordinate axes), then place them in their actual position in space. A tetrahedron, for example, can be generated conveniently if it is fit inside a cube centered at the origin, parallel to the major coordinate planes (Figure 18.3). Its vertex coordinates will be $(1, 1, 1), (1, -1, -1), (-1, 1, -1),$ and $(-1, -1, 1)$. After it has been generated, the tetrahedron can be transformed into a more "conventional" orientation (e.g., centered at the origin with one of its faces flush with the XY plane) by rotation of 45 degrees about the Y axis, rotation of arctan $\sqrt{2}/2\,(=35.2644)$ degrees about the X axis, and translation of $\sqrt{1/3}\,(=0.57735)$ units along the Z axis.

☐ BIBLIOGRAPHY

Newman, W. M., and R. F. Sproull, *Principles of Interactive Graphics,* 2nd ed., Mc-Graw-Hill, New York, 1979.

19

LOCATIONAL DEPENDENCY HIERARCHIES

The concept of *assemblies* is similar to that of shapes, only at a higher level of abstraction. It introduces structure and relationships between individual shapes. One major use of such relationships is making the location of shapes depend on the location of other shapes in the assembly, such that relocations (transformations) can be automatically propagated. This chapter discusses the concept of assemblies as it applies to locational dependencies and develops the means to implement them.

□ THE CONCEPT OF ASSEMBLIES

The complexity of artifacts and environments rarely allows them to be represented by a single polygon or solid. Rather, hundreds or even thousands of shapes are often needed for this purpose. For example, several tetrahedra of the kind modeled in Chapter 18 can be combined with pyramids of appropriate sizes to construct a structure known as a *space frame,* which is a common structure for lightweight roofing of large spans (Figure 19.1).

Assemblies of shapes are characterized by two important properties:

1. They are composed of individual shapes, whose locations in space depend on the locations of other shapes in the assembly.
2. The assembly as a whole can be treated as one entity for the purposes of combining it with other assemblies and for the purposes of its relocation in space.

The first property is depicted in Figure 19.1, where a number of tetrahedra and pyramids (each generated in the manner discussed in Chapter 18) have been translated and placed in positions relative to each other, such that together they make a space frame. The second property is depicted in Figure 19.2, where sev-

237

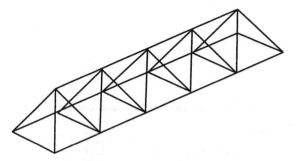

Figure 19.1. A space frame composed of rotated and translated tetrahedra and pyramids.

eral space frames have been positioned in such a way that they roof a given structure.

As designers of CAD systems capable of handling assemblies, we are faced with questions similar to the ones appearing earlier in the book, relating to modeling individual shapes:

1. How to represent an assembly of shapes?
2. How to manipulate assemblies of shapes?

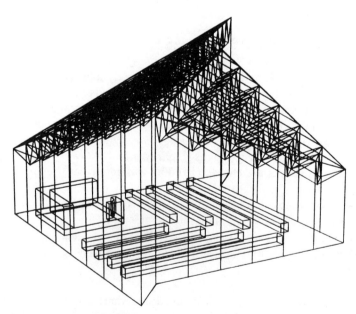

Figure 19.2. Using space frames to roof a structure. Figure courtesy of Bruce R. Majkowski, Computer-Aided Design and Graphics Laboratory, State University of New York at Buffalo.

Again we see the composite nature of an abstract data type, which is made of a data structure and its related operators, although at a higher level. We are concerned here with an *assembly of shapes,* rather than with the elements of a single shape. As before, we find these two components to be inseparable: A particular data structure can make certain operations easier to implement than others and vice versa. Hence, before we present a particular data structure for representing assemblies of shapes, which occurs in Chapter 20, we must consider the operations that will be performed on the assembly. These operators bear close resemblance to the operators we find in high-level programming languages for the manipulation of structured data types, such as arrays and records in Pascal. They include operators to *construct* an assembly given its parts, *select* individual shapes within a given assembly for special treatment, and *manipulate* the assembly as a whole.

The single most important property of an assembly is the *relative placement* of its parts. Without this property, the collection of parts is just that: a collection of parts. An assembly, on the other hand, is a collection of *related* parts: One part depends on the location of others parts, and the collection as a whole depends on the proper association of its parts. In the automotive industry, for example, we regard *cars* as singular entities, although each car is made of many parts. The car, as an entity, is much more than the sum of its parts: It is a highly organized collection of interdependent components, and it functions as no single part can. This higher functionality is due to the proper relative placement of the components and their complementing individual functions. Each component can itself be an assembly of parts, which comprises a subassembly of the whole and could, under certain circumstances, be manipulated independently from the whole. For example, the engine of the car is made of pistons, spark plugs, carburetor, and many other components, all working in concert. The engine of the car, as an entity, could be replaced without substantially affecting the function or composition of the higher level assembly (the car). In other words, the notions of assemblage and relative placements are *hierarchical:* An assembly of related parts may itself be a component within a larger (higher level) assembly.

The functional and locational hierarchical relationships between the components of an assembly are considered its most important characteristics, so much so that they virtually dictate the form of the assembly representation data structure. In this chapter and in Chapter 20, we shall address only the *locational* hierarchical dependencies of parts in an assembly. We shall study *functional* dependencies in Part Four, where we are concerned with objects.

☐ RELATIVE LOCATIONS

To illustrate the concepts of relative locations and locational dependency hierarchies, consider the floor plan depicted in Figure 19.3. Its shows two furnished offices and a reception area, represented by a collection of polygons.

An obvious way to represent this floor plan in the database would be through

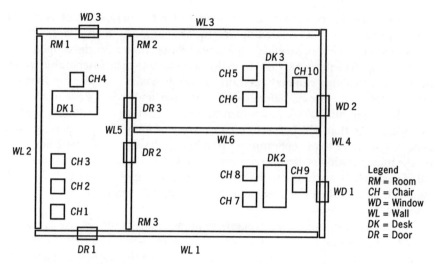

Figure 19.3. A floor plan represented as an assembly of polygons.

a simple linked list of polygons. Such representation is adequate if the floor plan will not be modified, such as for the purposes of display or storage. However, it is not adequate for the purposes of *design*, where the composition, size, and relative placement of the components undergo many changes.

Suppose, for example, that we wish to increase the reception area by reducing the length of the two offices. This change amounts to translating wall *WL5* rightward, as depicted in Figure 19.4. Obviously, doors *DR2* and *DR3*, which are located in this wall, must also be relocated by the same amount, and wall *WL6* must be shrunk by the same amount as the relocation of wall *WL5*. If we use the simple linked-list method for representing the floor plan, the designer will have to perform these adjustments manually.

Such changes could be managed by the system if the relationships between the shapes were established before wall *WL5* is relocated. Such automatic consistency maintenance can be likened to spreadsheet software, where the sums of rows and columns are automatically adjusted when numbers are changed anywhere in the table. Automatic design consistency maintenance, or at least the detection and flagging of inconsistencies, could save the designer much time and reduce the likelihood of design errors while the best placement for the wall is being considered.

Some of the relationships needed to support such automatic consistency maintenance describe the locational dependencies between the components of the assembly. The locations of doors *DR2* and *DR3* *depend* on the location of wall *WL5*. Similarly, the desk and three chairs in each office are functionally related, and therefore, they are related geometrically. This relationship will be useful if the designer wishes to increase the area of one office and reduce the area of the other by displacing wall *WL6*, a change that might require the relocation of the furniture in one or both offices (Figure 19.5).

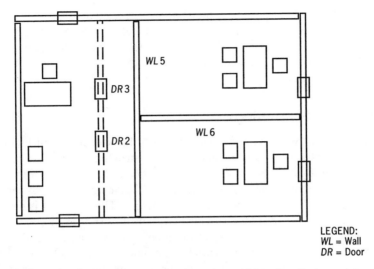

LEGEND:
WL = Wall
DR = Door

Figure 19.4. Design changes may introduce inconsistencies that must be fixed manually.

☐ REPRESENTING LOCATIONAL DEPENDENCY HIERARCHIES

Computational structures that can be used to represent locational dependency hierarchies are characterized by two properties:

1. They are capable of representing hierarchical relationships between the components of the structure.
2. They are capable of representing locational dependencies between the components of the structure.

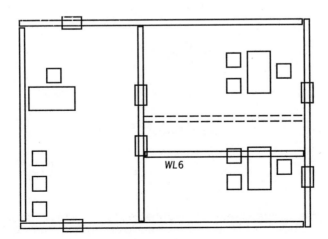

Figure 19.5. Relocation of wall *WL6* requires relocation of the furniture in the offices.

The two properties are not the same. The first is a method of structuring the elements of an assembly to reflect their hierarchical relationship, and the second is the method of representing their relative locations. We shall examine first the hierarchical structuring of assemblies and then the locational dependencies between their elements.

Hierarchical Structuring

The most widely used computational structure that can represent hierarchical relationships between data elements is the *tree* structure, which is discussed in detail in Appendix B. Tree structures represent *branching relationships* and are a special case of more general graph structures. Unlike graphs, trees contain no cycles (i.e., their branches split but do not merge). This property is convenient for representing a variety of hierarchical relationships. For example, a building can be represented as a hierarchy of architectural, mechanical, and electrical systems; each of which is composed of additional subsystems. Figure 19.6 depicts two possible hierarchical relationships between the components of the offices depicted in Figures 19.3 through 19.5: Figure 19.6a depicts a relationship based on the structure of the building, and Figure 19.6b depicts a relationship based on the functions of the offices.

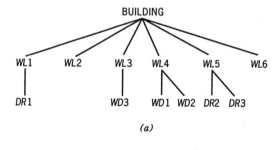

(a)

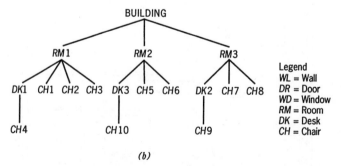

(b)

Figure 19.6. Different tree representations of the hierarchical relationships between the components of a building: (a) structural relationship and (b) functional relationship.

Tree structures are particularly useful for representing the spatial nestedness of components in an assembly, where the components are classified as being *subjoint, conjoint,* or *disjoint* to other elements. *Subjoint* means the elements are part of another element. *Disjoint* means the elements are not part of each other. *Conjoint* means the elements are partially part of and partially not part of each other. In using a tree to represent spatial nestedness, we assume that conjoint relations between entities are not allowed. If they were allowed, they would introduce cycles in the graph that are not representable by tree structures. Rather, we shall require that the elements be subjoint to at most one nesting element. The nesting element will be referred to as the *parent,* and the nested elements as its *children.* Every element can thus be the child of at most one parent and can be the parent of many children. All the children of one parent are called *siblings.* The one and only element that has no parent is called the *root* of the tree. Each element, however, is considered the root of a subtree, which consists of its children and their children. The tree structure, then, is an effective means of organizing the locational dependency relationships of elements.

Hierarchical structuring of assemblies is, in fact, a statement of dependency, or componential buildup. An object can be said to be made of multiple parts, each of which may contain other parts. This structuring allows us, therefore, to refer to and manipulate entire assemblies or subassemblies by applying some operation to their parent element. For example, when the reader is referred to a certain chapter in the book, the reference is really to all its sections and paragraphs. Similarly, when moving a wall, the designer is also interested in moving all its doors, windows, studs, and other components. By treating each subassembly in the hierarchy as a unit, such operations need to be applied only once at the appropriate level of the tree and can be propagated automatically to the component shapes.

Locational Dependencies

Locational dependencies represent the method for propagating transformational changes throughout the hierarchical structure. Two methods can be used for this purpose:

1. A stored (static) method
2. A functional (dynamic) method

In the first case, the transformation that was used to relocate the root of a subtree must also be applied to all its children. This means that each time a shape is transformed, the subtree rooted by it must be traversed, and every shape must be transformed. Both tree traversal and transformation of the shapes are expensive operations and should be avoided if possible. Some unnecessary traversals and shape transformations can be avoided if updating the location of the children is delayed until the "final" location of their parent has been decided, rather than updating their locations for each intermediate design alternative.

Traversal and update cannot be avoided, however, if the intermediate alternatives are to be displayed. Once the locations of all the shapes in the assembly have been updated, no further traversals are needed, because each shape is stored in the project's global frame of reference (hence the term *static method*).

The second method relies on separating the geometrical definition of the shape from its location in space. Rather than associating each point, line, or plane with its geometrical location in the project space, elements are defined in some *local* frame of reference. To find its location in the project space, the shape must be transformed from its local frame of reference to the project's frame of reference. For example, the elements of each door in a building can be defined in the door's own frame of reference (Figure 19.7a). To place the door in its proper location in the building we must apply to it the proper transformation (Figure 19.7b). Once this transform has been applied, the door's project location is found (Figure 19.7c).

The separation of the shape's internal geometric definition from its location in space has two advantages:

1. In defining the shape, we may concentrate on issues pertinent to the shape itself rather than to the assembly as a whole.
2. It facilitates relative placement.

The first property is easy to appreciate when we must design shapes that are placed in the project space far from its origin or are rotated in some "inconvenient" manner (as depicted in Figure 19.8).

The second property underlies the concept of *relative placement*. The transform associated with the shape could place it in space *relative to another shape* rather than relative to the project's global frame of reference. When this concept is combined with the concept of hierarchical relationships, it defines the shape's relative placement in the assembly. In other words, the location of each shape

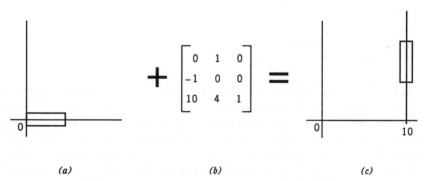

(a)   *(b)*   *(c)*

Figure 19.7. Transforming a shape from its local frame of reference (a) by a transform (b) to the project space (c).

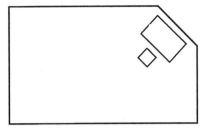

Figure 19.8. Shapes are more easily designed in a local frame of reference and then transformed to their project space than designed in the project space itself.

can be made dependent on the location of its parent shape (except for the root shape, which is defined in the project's global frame of reference). Hence, when the parent shape is displaced, so are its children. Such relocation is automatic, because the frame of reference of the children has not been modified. (They still relate to their parent shape as they did before.) To demonstrate this dependent relationship, consider the diagrams depicted in Figure 19.9. They depict four polygons, A, B, C, and D, each, which represent an office, a desk, a chair, and a bookcase, respectively. We are interested in the effect that relocating the office (polygon A) has on the furniture (polygons B, C, and D). In Figure 19.9a, the polygons are not hierarchically dependent. Therefore, relocating A has no effect on B, C, and D. In Figures 19.9b and 19.9c, the polygons are hierarchically related, therefore relocation of A causes the same relocation to apply to B, C, and D (Figure 19.9b). The relocation of B causes the relocation of C, but not of D (Figure 19.9c).

The functional placement method requires no traversal and no updating of the location of the children. However, displaying the shapes requires both traversal and application of the transformation every time. This is achieved by placing each shape in its own frame of reference (coordinate system) and storing with it the transform that relates the shape's own frame of reference to that of its parent shape in the hierarchy. When a shape is transformed, only the transform that relates it to its parent's frame of reference must be updated. The children of the transformed shape are not affected by the change, because their location relative to their parent's frame of reference has not been changed. To display each shape, we must calculate the shape's location in the project's frame of reference, which is the cumulative product of the transforms of its ancestors, and apply this transform to the shape. The cumulative transform is computed by traversing the tree and concatenating the transforms stored with each shape. This method requires the definition of each shape in its local frame of reference, storage of the relative transform with each shape, and application of the concatenated transformation to the shape every time the shape is displayed (hence the term *dynamic method*).

We will choose the dynamic method of representing and operating on loca-

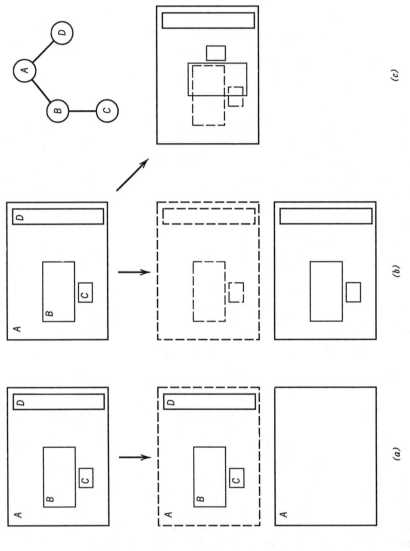

Figure 19.9. The difference between relocating (a) hierarchically independent and (b) hierarchically dependent polygons.

(a) (b) (c)

tional dependencies and describe this method in more detail in the Chapter 20 through the concept of *location trees*.

☐ BIBLIOGRAPY

Blinn, J. F., "Nested Transformations and Blobby Man," *IEEE Computer Graphics and Applications,* **7**(10):59–65, October 1987.

20

LOCATION TREES

This chapter describes how the concept of hierarchical shape assemblies can be computationally implemented using tree structures, and how locational dependencies can be represented by separating the internal geometry of shapes from their location in space. We call this implementation a *location tree*.

☐ REPRESENTING LOCATION TREES

A location tree is a binary tree, as discussed in Appendix B, in which each node represents a *shape* located in its own frame of reference, the *transform* that relates this shape to its parent shape's frame of reference, and the tree relationships of the node:

```
type  nptr = ^node;
      node = record
               shape    : pptr;
               location : matrix;
               sibling,
               parent,
               child    : nptr
             end;
```

The location tree is based on the concept that frames of reference (coordinate systems), like shapes, are themselves subject to placement. We can thus construct *local* coordinate systems, which define the frame of reference for their own shapes, and *place* them within more global frames of reference. These coordinate systems are related to the more global coordinate systems that embed them through transforms similar to the ones discussed in Chapter 18. These transforms, however, are not applied to the coordinate system itself. Rather, they are applied to the shapes that use the coordinate system as their frame of reference.

To find the global, "project" location of a shape that uses a local frame of reference, we *concatenate* the transforms of the shape's ancestor coordinate systems with the transform of the shape itself.

For example, consider Figure 20.1: the office (polygon *A*) is located in its own frame of reference (Figure 20.1a). To locate it in the project's global frame of reference, it must be transformed by the transformation that locates its own frame of reference within that of the project's. That transformation, in this case, is the identity matrix. The desk (polygon *B*) is also located in its own frame of

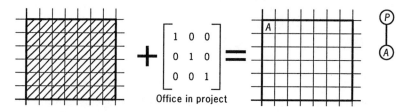

(a) Locating the office (A) in the project's global frame of reference:

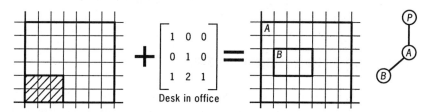

(b) Locating the desk (B) in the project's global frame of reference:

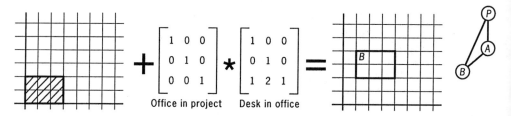

(c) Locating the desk in the project's global frame of reference:

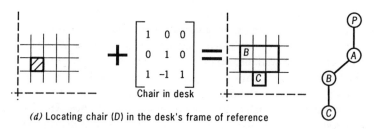

(d) Locating chair (D) in the desk's frame of reference

Figure 20.1. Relative and global placement of office, desk, chair, and bookcase.

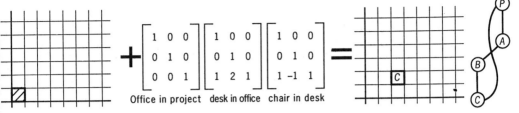

$$
+ \begin{bmatrix} 1 & 0 & 0 \\ 0 & 1 & 0 \\ 0 & 0 & 1 \end{bmatrix} \begin{bmatrix} 1 & 0 & 0 \\ 0 & 1 & 0 \\ 1 & 2 & 1 \end{bmatrix} \begin{bmatrix} 1 & 0 & 0 \\ 0 & 1 & 0 \\ 1 & -1 & 1 \end{bmatrix} =
$$

Office in project   desk in office   chair in desk

(e) Locating the chair in project's global frame of reference:

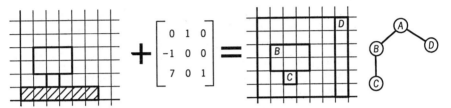

$$
+ \begin{bmatrix} 0 & 1 & 0 \\ -1 & 0 & 0 \\ 7 & 0 & 1 \end{bmatrix} =
$$

(f) Locating the bookcase (D) in office's frame of reference:

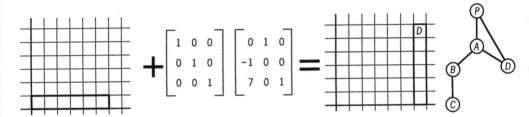

$$
+ \begin{bmatrix} 1 & 0 & 0 \\ 0 & 1 & 0 \\ 0 & 0 & 1 \end{bmatrix} \begin{bmatrix} 0 & 1 & 0 \\ -1 & 0 & 0 \\ 7 & 0 & 1 \end{bmatrix} =
$$

(g) Locating the bookcase in the project's global frame of reference:

Figure 20.1 Continued.

reference, as depicted in Figure 20.1b. To place it in its relative position in the office (polygon A), it must be translated by $Dx = 1$, $Dy = 2$ (Figure 20.1b). If we are interested in its location within the project's global frame of reference (e.g., for the purposes of display), it must also be transformed by the transform that places the office in the project's frame of reference (Figure 20.1c). Like the desk, the chair (polygon C) is also defined in its own coordinate system. To locate it in the coordinate system of the desk, it must be translated by $Dx = 1$, $Dy = -1$ (Figure 20.1d). The location of the chair in the project's global frame of reference is found by concatenating its local transform ($Dx = 1$, $Dy = -1$) with the transform that locates the desk in the office ($Dx = 1$, $Dy = 2$), and with the transform that locates the office in the project's space (Figure 20.1e). Likewise, the bookcase (polygon D) is located in its own frame of reference. To place it in the office's frame of reference it must be translated and rotated, as shown in Figure 20.1f. To find the location of the bookcase in the project space, this transform must also be concatenated with the transform that places the office in the project space (Figure 20.1g).

If we now decided to transform the entire office (e.g., rotate it by 90 degrees), the only transform that must be changed is the one that locates the office in the project space. The project locations of the desk, chair, and bookcase will be updated automatically, as soon as their own transforms are concatenated with the new office transform.

□ CONSTRUCTING A LOCATION TREE

The construction of a location tree is a process controlled by the designer, who must decide when one shape is subjoint to another, such as the desk and the bookcase are to the office, and the chair is subjoint to the desk in Figure 20.1. Once decided by the designer (e.g., for functional reasons), two computational issues must be resolved:

1. The appropriate data structure must be constructed.
2. The appropriate transform must be associated with the subjoint shape.

Using tree operators of the kind presented in Appendix B, the first issue is easily resolved. It is the second issue that is of interest to us in this context: the assignment of an appropriate transform to the newly subjoint shape.

The principle underlying the computation of a relative placement transform is that the location of a shape B within the project's global frame of reference is not changed when it is assigned a location relative to some other shape A. What does change is the *composition* of transformations that place shape B where it is. If shape B were defined in the project's global frame of reference, there is only one transform (the one associated with shape B itself) responsible for its global placement. After becoming subjoint to shape A, part of the responsibility for placing it is transferred to the transforms that place shape A. The location of shape B consists, therefore, of the concatenated product of all the transforms in the path leading from shape B to the root of the tree (which represents the project's global frame of reference). For example, if the chair in Figure 20.1 were located in the project's global frame of reference, it would be associated with a translation transform $Dx = 2, Dy = 1$. Because it is subjoint to the desk, which is subjoint to the office, part of the chair's global placement has already been accomplished by the transforms of the office and the desk. Those transforms (which are $Dx = 0, Dy = 0$, and $Dx = 1, Dy = 2$, respectively) place the chair in a position which is no longer at the origin of the project's frame of reference. If the chair is to remain in its former location, the transform associated with it must be modified to $Dx = 1, Dy = -1$, as shown in Figure 20.1e.

The new (relative) transform of the shape can be computed from the old (global) one by "factoring out" the transforms of its ancestors. Such computation is akin to subtracting the amount shape B has been transformed by its parent shape A and the other nodes in the path from it to the root of the tree, leaving only the difference in placement that must be accomplished by the transform of shape B itself.

Computing the Project Location of a Shape

The concatenated product of the transforms that must be subtracted from the shape's original project location is, in fact, the project location of its parent shape. This location can be computed by concatenating the transforms associated with the shapes in the path leading from the shape to the root of the location tree. Procedure PROJECT_LOCATION performs this concatenation.

```
procedure project_location (n : nptr; var m : matrix);
{Computes and returns the project location transform m of the
 shape stored by node n in the location tree, by concatenating
 the transforms stored by n and all its ancestors.}

var  t : nptr;

begin
  m := n^.location;
  while n^.parent <> nil do
    begin
      n := n^.parent;
      concatenate (n^.location, m, m)
    end
end; {project_location procedure}
```

Computing the Inverse of a Transform

Once the project location of the shape's parent has been calculated, it must be "subtracted" from the shape's own project location. In matrix algebra, "subtraction" is replaced by multiplying the shape's own transform with the *inverse* of the concatenated transforms of its ancestors.

Inversion of a matrix is equivalent to computing the reciprocal of a number. When a matrix M is multiplied by its inverse M^{-1}, the result is the identity matrix. (Similarly, when a number is multiplied by its reciprocal, the result is 1.) For example:

$$
\begin{bmatrix} 0 & -1 & 0 \\ 1 & 0 & 0 \\ 2 & 4 & 1 \end{bmatrix} \cdot \begin{bmatrix} 0 & 1 & 0 \\ -1 & 0 & 0 \\ 4 & -2 & 1 \end{bmatrix} = \begin{bmatrix} 1 & 0 & 0 \\ 0 & 1 & 0 \\ 0 & 0 & 1 \end{bmatrix} .
$$

Many methods exist for computing the inverse of a matrix (provided it has one). Procedure INVERT_MATRIX implements the determinant-cofactor method for inverting a nonsingular 4 × 4 matrix.

```
procedure invert_matrix (t : matrix; var inverse : matrix);
{Compute the inverse of the 4×4 matrix t using the determinant/
 cofactor method. t must not be singular.}

var  i,j : coords;
     d   : real;

  function cofactor (i,j : coords) : real;
  {Compute cofactor of 3×3 matrix.}

  var  k,n  : coords;
       sign : integer;
       m    : matrix;

    function det3 : real;
    {Computes determinant of 3×3 matrix m.}

    var  d1,d2 : real;

    begin
      d1 := m[x,x]*m[y,y]*m[z,z] +
            m[x,y]*m[y,z]*m[z,x] +
            m[x,z]*m[y,x]*m[z,y];
      d2 := m[x,x]*m[y,z]*m[z,y] +
            m[x,y]*m[y,x]*m[z,z] +
            m[x,z]*m[y,y]*m[z,x];
      det3 := d1 - d2
    end; {det3 function}

  begin {cofactor}
    {set up 3×3 matrix}
    for k := x to pred(i) do
      begin
        for n := x to pred(j) do m[k,n] := t[k,n];
        for n := succ(j) to w do m[k,pred(n)] := t[k,n]
      end;
    for k := succ(i) to w do
      begin
        for n := x to pred(j) do
          m[pred(k),n] := t[k,n];
        for n := succ(j) to w do
          m[pred(k),pred(n)] := t[k,n]
      end;
```

```
{compute cofactor of m2}
if odd (ord(i)+ord(j))
   then sign := 1 else sign := -1;
cofactor := sign*det3
end; {cofactor function}

function det4 : real;

var  d : real;
     j : coords;

begin
  d := 0;
  for j := x to w do d := d + t[x,j]*cofactor(x,j);
  det4 := d
end; {det4 function}

begin {invert procedure}
  d := det4;
  for i := x to w do
    for j := x to w do
      inverse[i,j] := cofactor(j,i)/d
end; {invert_matrix procedure}
```

Reparenting Shapes in the Location Tree

We could now conclude the location tree construction process by combining the two steps of concatenating the shape's transform with the inverse project location of its parent and the restructuring of the tree to reflect the new hierarchical relationships. Yet, the construction of a location tree from shapes that were previously located in the project's global frame of reference represents merely a special case within the universe of manipulating a location tree (Figure 20.2a). The more general case of location tree restructuring is *reparenting:* the process whereby a shape and all its children are moved to a new parent (Figure 20.2b).

Reparenting can construct the location tree from a nonhierarchical assembly of shapes (i.e., all the shapes are located in the project's global frame of reference), or modify the tree once it exists, as depicted by Figure 20.2. Such modifications are initiated by the designer and are caused by different functional associations of the shapes in the assembly. For example, the designer may wish to change the hierarchical relationships depicted in Figure 20.2a by disassociating the chair from the desk, such that the chair will not be relocated when the desk is. This disassociation requires that both the *structure* of the location tree and the *transform* associated with the chair be changed. As discussed earlier, such modification of the location tree does not affect the chair's location within the project's global frame of reference. Therefore, the new transform of a relocated

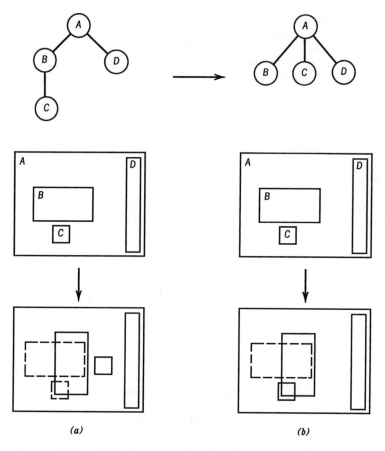

By reparenting chair (c) it is no longer affected by a transform applied to desk (b)

Figure 20.2. Restructuring a location tree by reparenting chair *C* so it becomes a child of office *A* rather than desk *B*.

shape *A* can be calculated using the following algebraic representation of the transforms involved:

[project location of *A*] = [project location of new parent of *A*] ×
[new transform of *A*]

hence:

[new transform of *A*] = *inverse of* [project location of new parent of *A*] ×
[project location of *A*].

This change is only marginally more complicated than the initial parenting process we described earlier; therefore, we can effect it by a similar process. To move a shape *A* from its current frame of reference to the frame of reference of another shape *B*, we follow these steps (which are implemented in procedure REPARENT_SHAPE):

1. Compute the project location transform of shape *A*, using Procedure PROJECT_LOCATION.
2. Compute the *inverse* of the project location transform of the new parent shape *B*, using procedures PROJECT_LOCATION and INVERT_MATRIX.
3. Concatenate the transform as computed in step 2 with the transform computed in step 1, and assign the resulting transform to shape *A*.
4. Change the structure of the location tree to reflect the new hierarchical relationship.

```
procedure reparent_shape (node, new_parent : nptr);
{Computes new location transform for re-parenting node with
 new_parent, and restructures location tree.}

var  n,p : matrix;

begin
   {compute new location transform of node}
   project_location (node, n);
   project_location (new_parent, p);
   invert_matrix (p, p);
   concatenate (p, n, node^.location);

   {reparent node}
   move_node (node, new_parent)
end; {reparent_shape procedure}
```

New shapes that are added to the assembly must be treated as located in the project's global frame of reference before they are assigned to a particular subtree, then reparented as discussed above.

☐ TRAVERSING THE LOCATION TREE

The binary tree structure we chose for representing the location tree also lends itself well for displaying the shapes in their project locations, through the use of recursive traversal. Such traversal is required whenever the global location of all shapes must be determined (as is the case in their display) and, hence, when the transforms stored in the path leading from each shape to the root of the tree must be concatenated and applied to the shape.

Procedure PROJECT_LOCATION, which was discussed earlier, performs such concatenation. Its usefulness, however, is limited to computing the project location of individual shapes, such as in displaying the shape stored by one particular node. When an entire assembly (or subassembly) is to be displayed, the use of this procedure will become prohibitively expensive. Not only must we perform a full tree traversal, which is an expensive but unavoidable operation, but the "visiting" function which is applied to each node will itself traverse all the ancestors of that node. The transform stored in the root of the tree, for example, will in this case be concatenated $n!$ times ($n! = n$ factorial $= 1 \cdot 2 \cdot 3 \cdot 4 \ldots \cdot n$). Clearly, the transforms that have already been concatenated must not be concatenated again. For example, the individual transforms of all the children of a particular node will be concatenated with the same project location transform of their parent, which need not be recalculated.

Such "top-down," nonredundant concatenation can be achieved if the intermediate transforms that were concatenated up to, but not including, the transform of the node currently being visited are stored in some way. As such, the only additional concatenation needed is that of the particular transform of the visited node.

A particularly convenient structure for storing the transforms that have already been concatenated is provided by a data structure known as a *stack* and its associated operators PUSH and POP. The stack is a LIFO (last-in-first-out) structure, like a stack of trays in a cafeteria: The most recently placed tray on the stack will be the first to be removed. The operators PUSH and POP place an element on (i.e., add an element to) the stack and remove the top element from the stack, respectively, as depicted by Figure 20.3.

A stack of matrices can keep track of the sequence and intermediate results of the transform concatenation process by storing the product of the concatenated transforms from the root of the location tree down to the node that is currently being visited by the tree traversal process. The stack of matrices can be represented by the a linked list of transforms of the following form:

```
type  kptr = ^stack_record;
      stack_record = record
                       transform : matrix;
                       link      : kptr
                     end;
```

Procedure PUSH_TRANSFORM will add a matrix to the stack each time a child is visited, and procedure POP_TRANSFORM will remove the top (first) transform from the stack each time the recursion process backtracks to a higher level in the tree.

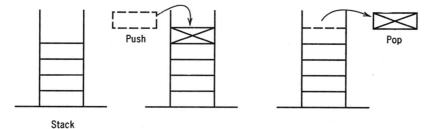

Figure 20.3. The stack data structure and operators.

```
procedure push_transform (m : matrix; var stack : kptr);
{Concatenates the transform represented by matrix m with the
 transform stored by the first element in the stack, and add it
 to the stack as a new element.}

var  item : kptr;
     mtop : matrix;

begin
  {get transform stored at the top of the stack}
  mtop := stack^.transform;

  {create new item and link it to the stack}
  new (item);
  item^.link := stack;
  stack := item;

  {concatenate transform and store it in stack}
  concatenate (m, mtop, stack^.transform)
end; {push_transform procedure}

procedure pop_transform (var stack : kptr);
{Remove top element of the stack.}

var  item : kptr;

begin
  item := stack;
  stack := stack^.link;
  dispose (item)
end; {pop_transform procedure}
```

The stack must be initialized by pushing onto it the identity matrix, so that the project's global frame of reference is established. It can then be used to represent the sequence and products of concatenation as the location tree is recursively traversed. This process is implemented here for polygons by procedure DISPLAY_TREE.

```
procedure display_tree (node : nptr);
{Display the polygons stored in the location tree recursively.
 Push new transforms onto a stack as the recursion visits
 children of nodes, and pop them as the recursion backtracks.
 Note: the global variable STACK which is used by this
 procedure must be initialized to the identity matrix outside
 this procedure.}

begin
  {transform and display current node}
  transform_polygon (node^.shape, stack^.transform);
  display_polygon (node^.shape);

  {traverse the current node's children}
  if node^.child <> nil
    then begin
      push_transform (node^.location, stack);
      display_tree (node^.child);
      pop_transform (stack)
    end;

  {traverse the current node's siblings}
  if node^.sibling <> nil
    then display_tree (node^.sibling)
  end; {display_tree procedure}
```

☐ IMPLEMENTATION OF LOCATION TREES

By locating each shape in its own frame of reference, its global location is not explicitly stored. Instead, it must be computed (by applying to it the concatenated transform) whenever the shape's global location is needed, such as when it is to be displayed. Yet, the purpose of the location tree is to eliminate the need for traversing the tree and applying to its nodes the same transform applied to the root node, when the root is relocated. It would seem, therefore, that location trees present no significant advantage over the traversal of the tree each time a node is relocated. This problem can be reduced in two ways.

First, some redundant computations can be avoided if not all the shapes are displayed each time a shape is relocated. Rather, the user can choose to display only the relevant parts of the tree by displaying only the *subtree* of a particular node or displaying the ancestors of a node but not its children. For example, if

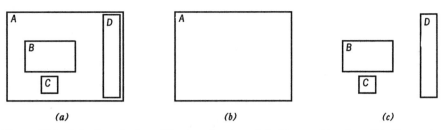

Figure 20.4. Selective display of the location tree. (*a*) office and furniture (*b*) office only (*c*) furniture only.

an entire room is being moved, the designer may choose to display the building but not the furniture contained in the rooms. If, on the other hand, the furniture has been rearranged, the designer may selectively display the content of the room but not the entire building (Figure 20.4).

Second, we can store a *second transform* with each node, representing its *project location,* which is the result of concatenating all the transforms in the path of this node to the root of the tree. This transform, however, must be updated whenever the location of any node in the path is changed. This can be facilitated by a flag that indicates whether a node was relocated. The flag must be tested before the shapes are displayed.

□ BIBLIOGRAPHY

Behnke, H., F. Bachmann, K. Fladt, and H. Kunle, eds., *Fundamentals of Mathematics,* Vol. 1, MIT Press, Cambridge, MA, 1974.

Eastman, C. M., "The Design of Assemblies," Institute of Physical Planning, Technical Report 11, Carnegie-Mellon University, Pittsburgh, PA, 1980.

21

EXERCISE 3: GEOMETRICAL TRANSFORMS

Your task in this exercise is to design and implement the geometric operators that transform and place polygons. They include two-dimensional transformation operators (translation, rotation, and scaling) and locational dependency operators.

First, you are to design and implement the three *transformation* operators such that they apply to a given polygon:

1. TRANSLATE a polygon by distances Dx, Dy, along the X, Y coordinate axes, respectively.
2. ROTATE a polygon by an angle θ about an arbitrary point $<x, y>$.
3. SCALE a polygon by factors Sx, Sy, about an arbitrary point $<x, y>$.

The user must be able to access the three transformation operators though a graphical interface invoked through appropriate menu boxes, as described in Part 5. The graphical interface will accept user-defined points and convert them into the respective input types required by the operators. The number of types of input and their significance is as follows:

1. For TRANSLATION: two points. The difference between their x and y coordinates will be interpreted as Dx and Dy, respectively.
2. For ROTATION: three points. The first point will be interpreted as the center of rotation $<x, y>$, and the other two, together with the first one, will determine the angle of rotation. (A Function ANGLE that calculates and returns the angle formed by three points was described in Chapter 6.)
3. For SCALING: three points. The ratio of the distances between them will be interpreted as the scaling factor (scaling along X and Y axes should be separate operations). In order to avoid translation due to scaling, you should calculate the center of gravity of the polygon (which is just the mean of all x's and all y's of its points) and use it as the center about which scaling is performed (or you may let the user define the center of scaling).

Your second task in this exercise is to *place* the polygons relative to other polygons in a locational dependency hierarchy, implemented as a location tree. Such locational dependency will ensure that when one shape is displaced, all the shapes whose locations depend on it are also properly displaced. For example, if we translate a wall, all its studs must move along with it.

The property of relative location can be represented most conveniently by a hierarchical tree structure, in which higher levels in the tree represent larger aggregations of shapes. Using the stud wall example, all studs can be represented as children of a wall, all the walls as children of a floor, and so on. The construction of tree structures is discussed in Appendix B.

In some cases it may be desirable to change the parental association of shapes, depending on the particular operation which is applied to them. For example, for certain purposes it may be desirable to represent a pipe as an element (child) of a wall. But if the wall is to be translated, we may want the pipe to remain where it is, because of its connections to other pipes in adjacent walls. To facilitate such reparenting, the user should be able to pick shapes and assign them to new parents.

PART FOUR

ASSOCIATION

22

MODELING OBJECTS

In the previous chapters we have concentrated on the formative attributes of real-world objects and environments. But objects and environments are made of more than just shapes. Their properties also include the materials from which they are made, their manufacturers, model numbers, dates of completion, their colors and textures, their functions, and any other properties that are pertinent to the applications using the model. In addition to their intrinsic properties, objects are connected to other objects in a variety of ways. We have seen how objects form assembly structures in Part Three. Objects can also be related in other ways: a group of objects may have been manufactured by the same manufacturer, or made of the same materials, or have related functions.

To be truly useful for design applications, both nonshape properties and the relationships between objects must be modeled (i.e., represented in a manipulable way). Without the explicit modeling of attributes and relationships, the model is incomplete; it is restricted to geometric modeling only, which is important but not sufficient to support applications such as energy consumption computation, structural analysis, and so on. The principles and techniques of modeling attributes and associations are the concerns of this fourth part of the book.

☐ THE PROPERTIES OF OBJECTS

The modeling of objects, as such, is the most recent development in CAD. It has arisen with the advent of database management systems and with the growing need to computationally represent and operate on more than just the formative attributes of entities in order to support applications such as energy analysis and structural analysis. Few references to object modeling exist in the literature, and practically no object modeling techniques have yet been established. Objects, however, are gaining importance as the need for the computational integration of design synthesis and analysis grows and as programming practices are being developed in other fields, in the form of object-oriented languages.

An object, for the purposes of computer-aided design, can be defined as:

A collection of attributes that describe some physical or abstract entity that can be computationally represented and operated on.

These attributes include the shape of the object as well as any other pertinent nonshape information that is used by applications that rely on the model, such as material, cost, color, and function.

In addition to the composition of physical artifacts and environments, objects also reflect the structural and functional relationships of the organization to which they belong. Objects thus provide access to related *collections* of entities at varying levels of the representational hierarchy. For example, a single stud is an object that has shape and material attributes. It is also part of a wall assembly, which is part of the structure of a house, and so on.

The attribute and assembly properties distinguish objects from the singular, formative entities discussed in Parts One through Three. Unlike the topological and geometric properties, which are difficult to model because of their complexities and interdependencies, attribute and assembly properties are difficult to model for the following two reasons:

1. The list of attributes is open ended, and individual attributes take many different forms. Therefore, a single record structure may not be capable of representing all types of attributes. Alternatively, generality in representation may come at the expense of the descriptive power of the model or require too much processing.

2. Assembly is context-sensitive: it depends on run-time preferences. For example, the wall assembly mentioned earlier can be associated with the room it bounds, if the spaces of the house are of current interest, or it can be associated with the general structural scheme of the house, if construction and structure are of interest. In many cases, multiple simultaneous associations are needed.

Attributes and assembly are related properties. In many cases, the attributes of objects are dependent on the manner by which they are assembled. For example, the *function* attribute of a door is typically a "connector of two spaces." If, however, the door is blocked by a piece of furniture that prevents it from functioning as a connector, its function may become "a partition between two spaces," which is similar to the function of a wall. The linkage between objects thus may influence their attribute values, which may otherwise provide incorrect information to the applications that use them (consider, for example, how a fire egress evaluation application may be mislead by considering the blocked door to be a viable means of egress). In fact, assembly structures provide channels for propagation of attribute value changes in the modeling system.

We first look at how nonshape attributes can be added to the representation of objects, and we quickly discover that the computational cost of fully repre-

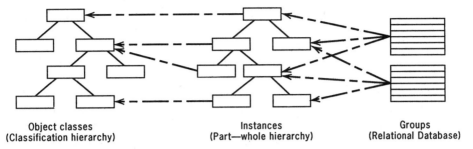

| Object classes
(Classification hierarchy) | Instances
(Part—whole hierarchy) | Groups
(Relational Database) |

Figure 22.1. The logical relationships between objects, instances, and groups.

senting objects is rather high. To make the *representation* of individual objects tractable within the confines of finite computational resources, we shall group them in classification hierarchies, which allow the definition of objects as specialized subclasses of more general objects and, hence, allow the definition of shared properties by *inheritance*. To make the *manipulation* of objects similarly tractable, we classify individual objects as *instances* of some master object. To model the relationships between objects, we assemble them in related *groups*. The logical relationships between objects defined in hierarchical classes and sub-classes, their instances, and the grouping of instances are depicted in Figure 22.1.

Finally, we shall see that grouping, as a means of accessing aggregations of related objects, is a useful tool also at subobject levels, where a collection of faces, edges, and vertices representing a particular portion of the object must be accessed (e.g., a hole in a beam). These collections of parts are known as *features*. The concept of aggregation at the subobject level is also extendable to the geometrical data underlying the shape's representation, where a collection of points or lines must be manipulated as one. We shall discuss the grouping of geometrical information in the context of *parameters*.

☐ THE REPRESENTATION OF OBJECTS

The physical artifacts and environments we model in the context of computer-aided design are characterized by several properties, which include:

1. A *name*, which uniquely identifies the object
2. A *shape*, which consists of topological and geometric entities
3. A list of geometric *parameters*
4. A list of topological *features*
5. A list of nonshape *attributes*

In addition to these properties, which are *intrinsic* to the object, the data structure must also support some of the relationships that will be used by operators that manipulate objects. In particular, it must support the *hierarchical* relationships that define the inheritance path for defining objects by classes and subclasses and *instantiation* of objects by "cloning."

Inheritance of properties permits considerable saving in storage by enabling definition of objects as specialized subclasses of a more general class. For example, a car can be defined as a specialized subclass of motorized means of transportation, which may also include aircraft and ships. By belonging to the class of motorized means of transportation, car-objects are known to have the capacity of carrying people over relatively long distances, and they are known to require some type of fuel. They are also known to pollute and to constitute a certain hazard to people. All these properties need not be repeated when representing cars as a subclass of motorized means of transportation, because they can be *inherited* from the more general class. Only the specialization that restricts the definition cars to an earth-bound means of transportation needs to be added, as well as any other specializations not included in the superclass definition. For example, such additional specialization includes information about the relatively smooth, often special track that cars need. A train, for example, would be another specialized earth-bound motorized means of transportation that differs from cars in ways that include restriction to a fixed rail. A Ferrari, on the other hand, would constitute a specialized subclass of car-objects. Inheritance hierarchies are implemented by making objects part of a binary tree structure, which is similar to the locational hierarchies discussed in Chapter 20.

Instancing is a concept that has no parallel in manual design practices, where once an object is "made," it is no longer dependent on its "maker." For example, although all Ford Model T's were made from the same template, some well preserved cars still survive today even though the assembly line that made them was scraped a long time ago. The computer, on the other hand, allows us to link an instance to its master object throughout the existence of that master. In fact, the instance ceases to exist when the master does.

The grouping relationships provided by instancing are both means of representation and of manipulation of similar objects. As a means of representation, instancing enables storing many copies of a master object without duplicating the information. For example, all windows in a building can be considered instances of one master window (e.g., the one described in the manufacturer's catalog). As a means of manipulation, instancing permits wholesale modification of all the objects in the group, without exception. Because all the instances of one master object are dependent on the master, when it is modified, so are its instances. If, for example, the designer decided to replace all the windows by a different type, only one change is needed. Instancing thus reduces the verbosity of the data base and enhances its consistency (when the master object is modified, no instance is left unmodified).

To allow for local variations, each instance may have its own "private" list of attributes, which must not conflict with the attributes the instance inherits from its master object. For example, *color* could be defined as a private attribute of an instance, in which case it could be modified independently for each instance. It is not always easy to decide which attributes should belong to the master object, and thus be shared by all instances, and which ones should belong to the instances, and thus be "local." Although private attributes allow customization of instances, too many of them will define the instance as an entity substantially different from another instance of the same object, thereby rendering the intent behind instancing impotent. On the other hand, removing all private attributes from the instances will necessitate creating a new master object for each minor modification, such as change of color. Only the user can determine the right balance between global and local attributes and use them judiciously for achieving both unity and variety.

The instances share the shape and the nonshape attributes of the master shape, but differ in their locations in space (and their own attributes). Locations are defined through a transformation matrix, which multiplies the coordinates and parameters stored by the shape's geometry. They can be made hierarchically dependent, as discussed in Chapter 20, where the location of certain instances depends on the location of other instances.

These properties define the data structure underlying object and instance representations, which may take the following form:

```
optr        = ^object;
tptr        = ^instance;
aptr        = ^attribute;
text_string = array [1..20] of char;

object = record
            name           : text_string;
            shape          : sptr;
            alist          : aptr; {attribute list}
            tlist          : tptr; {instance list}
            sibling        : optr; {nil-end list}
            parent,child   : optr  {inheritance tree}
         end;

instance = record
              master         : optr;
              location       : matrix;
              alist          : aptr; {own attributes}
              tnext          : tptr; {circular list}
              parent,child   : tptr  {location tree}
           end;
```

It is obvious that representation alone will not support the functionality associated with hierarchical structuring and instancing. Rather, it must be augmented by the proper operators. These operators are discussed in Chapter 23. In the remainder of this chapter we shall discuss how nonshape attributes can be represented.

☐ NONSHAPE ATTRIBUTES

An object may have attributes other than shape. Such attributes describe an open-ended list of object characteristics, which are used by various applications systems. They include, for example, the material objects such as walls and windows are made of, which are used by energy evaluation programs and by structural analysis programs. Attributes may include cost, which can be used by budgeting and cost-estimation programs, and they may include manufacturers names and delivery dates used by project management applications.

Nonshape attributes are characterized by diversity and by quantity. Consider, for example, the following collection of nonshape attributes that describes a telephone:

Color: white
Type: rotary
Manufacturer: AT&T
Cost: $27.95
Functional: no (broken)

It is evident that no single record type can store the numerous different attributes of even simple objects, let alone all objects. Instead, it is necessary to find some means that will be sufficiently flexible to store different collections of attributes, yet will not reduce them to meaninglessness.

A means that is commonly used to represent collections of related attributes is found in database management systems. These systems are designed to store and operate on collections of attributes that are defined by the user. The database systems provide user interface tools, data representation tools, and operators such as query languages and report generators. It is conceivable, therefore, to adopt a database management system as the means to represent and manipulate the nonshape attributes of objects. Furthermore, if the shape of an object is considered an attribute (albeit a more complicated one than most others), then the database management system could become the modeling environment itself. This approach has, in fact, been adopted by at least one computer-aided design system, and explored by others.

Yet, while a database management system provides some convenient means for storage and retrieval of nonshape attributes, it often lacks the means that allow dynamic linkage of objects and the means to identify and store relationships in a way that will be amenable for rapid, dynamic processing. In fact, most database management systems assume that the data are relatively static and concentrate their main effort in providing good means to query it. In computer-aided design systems, on the other hand, the data are often transient, and queries, for the purposes of applications, are relatively infrequent. Moreover, changes may be induced not only by the user, but also by the data, through propagation of changes in the network. It is necessary, therefore, to develop the means for representing and operating on nonshape attributes that are much more dynamic in nature than the means offered by conventional database management systems.

In developing such means, it is possible to begin by defining the least common denominator between different attribute types and to identify their common features. One such common feature is the attributes' composition. Most nonshape attributes are three-tuples of *name-value-units*. For example, the attributes we used earlier to describe a telephone can be classified as:

Name	Type	Value	Units
Color	(Text string)	White	
Mode	(Text string)	Rotary	
Manufacturer	(Text string)	AT&T	
Cost	(Numerical—Real)	27.95	Dollars
Functional	(Logical)	False	

The classification in the preceding table assumes that a small number of types of attributes (text string, real, and logical, in the above example) can represent all types of attributes. It also assumes that these types are associated with operators to create, delete, and most important, *understand* the attributes they represent. In a way, these types can be likened to the standard types provided by a programming language such as Pascal, which allows the compiler to type-check and to understand the meaning of the expressions they make.

One way to implement an open-ended, dynamic attribute handling capability using a limited number of generic attribute types is given by the following data structure:

```
aptr        = ^attribute;
text_string = array [1..20] of char;
att_type    = (int, rel, txt, log);

attribute   = record
                anext : aptr;
                name : text_string;
                units : text_string;
                case kind : att_type of
                    int : (i_value : integer);
                    rel : (r_value : real);
                    txt : (t_value : text_string);
                    log : (l_value : boolean)
              end;
```

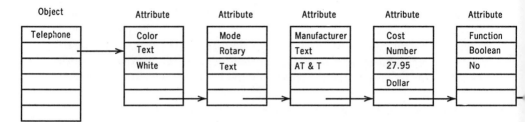

Figure 22.2. A linked list of attributes.

This method of representation uses the Pascal variant record type to represent four different types of values in one record. It can easily represent most any type of attribute, composed of name, type, and value triplets. Variant records are a union of several record types, although there can "be" only one record type at any given time. Their advantage is that we need not create a separate record for each type and can, therefore, reference any one of the possible types by means of a single pointer. In the above example, the KIND field in the record defines its type and provides access to the specific field in the variant part of the record. Only one such field is accessible at any given time.

The above record can contain the telephone example information in the following form (depicted in Figure 22.2):

```
var telephone = optr;
    a           = aptr;

begin
 telephone^.alist := nil;

 new (a);
 a^.name := 'color';
 a^.kind := txt;
 a^.t_value := 'white';
 a^.next := telephone^.alist;
 telephone^.alist := a;

 new (a);
 a^.name := 'cost';
 a^.kind := rel;
 a^r._value := 27.95;
 a^.units := 'dollars';
 a^.next := telephone^.alist;
 telephone^.alist := a;

 {and so on}
end;
```

☐ BIBLIOGRAPHY

Cox, B., *Object Oriented Programming,* Addison-Wesley, Reading, MA, 1987.

Date, C. J., *An Introduction to Database Systems,* Addison Wesley, Reading, MA, 1977.

Ingalls, O. H. H., "The Smalltalk-76 Programming Language: Design and Implementation," *Proceedings of the 5th Annual ACM Symposium on Principles of Programming Languages,* pp. 9–16, Tucson, AZ, January 1978.

Kalay, Y. E., "A Relational Database for Non-Manipulative Representation of Solid Objects," *Computer-Aided Design* 15(5):271–276, September 1983.

Kalay, Y. E., "Redefining the Role of Computers in Architecture: From Drafting/Modeling Tools to Knowledge-Based Design Assistants," *Computer-Aided Design,* 17(7):319–328, September 1985.

Keirous, W. T., D. R. Rehak, and I. R. Oppenheim, "Object-Oriented Programming for Computer-Aided Engineering," Working Paper EDRC-12-09-87, Engineering Design Research Center, Carnegie-Mellon University, Pittsburgh, PA, 1987.

Lafue, G. M. E., "Integrating Language and Database for CAD Applications," *Computer-Aided Design* 11(3):127–130, May 1979.

Ullman, J. D., *Principles of Database Systems*, Computer Science Press, Potomac, MD, 1980.

Yaski, Y., "A Consistent Database for an Integrated CAAD System: Fundamentals for an Automated Design Assistant," Ph.D. Dissertation, Carnegie-Mellon University, May 1981.

23

MANIPULATING OBJECTS

Among the more important and unique characteristics of objects that were discussed in Chapter 22 are inheritance of attributes and instancing. *Inheritance* is the property that allows definition of objects as specialized subclasses of more general object classes. A new object class is thus defined by inheriting the properties of its parent object class and by adding its own unique properties. The inherited properties need not be repeated. New properties may not override the inherited ones, because that would constitute redefinition of the parent object class. *Instancing* permits cloning of objects while maintaining their affinity: When one instance is modified, so are all the others. In this chapter we discuss the principles of inheritance and instancing operations and their possible implementations.

□ INHERITANCE

The list of nonshape attributes that characterizes objects is potentially very large. It has been our approach throughout this book to try and manage prolific information by its hierarchical ordering. This approach worked well for the management of shape information, in the form of layering and hierarchical abstraction, and it seems prudent to reuse it here for managing nonshape information as well. Yet, the difference between shape information and nonshape information is the lack of apparent structure. This deficiency requires that the structure be imposed explicitly by the user rather than by some intrinsic properties of the model, as is the case with shape information.

Probably the most straightforward, explicit hierarchical structuring that can be imposed on a collection of seemingly unstructured attributes is *generalization*. Objects, as collections of related attributes, can be considered specialized *classes* of more general collections of attributes. Figure 23.1, for example, depicts hierarchical specialization of information, which leads from a general hex-

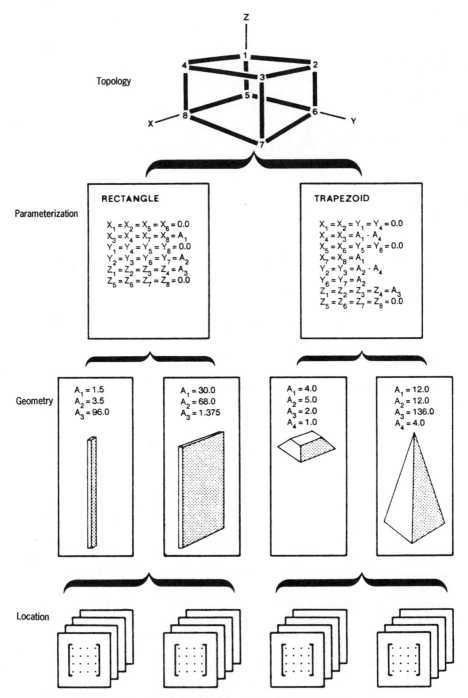

Figure 23.1. Specialization hierarchy of formative information.

ahedral topology to studs, doors, and various pyramidal objects located in particular locations in space. The lower levels in the hierarchy *add* information to that which is included in their parent levels. Thus, for example, all second-level (geometry) objects "inherit" the hexahedral topology of the first level. The studs and the doors of the third level inherit both hexahedral topology *and* parallelepiped geometry. They only differ in the *values* assigned to the height, length, and width parameters of that geometry. The fourth-level entities are exact copies of the third-level objects, located in different places in space. They inherit all other attributes from their parents in the hierarchy.

The hierarchical inheritance of attributes permits considerable saving in storage space, because only the specialization attributes must be added to the structure. For example, the stud object depicted in Figure 23.1 must include only its particular parametric value attributes. Its topology and parameterization are inherited from the more general class of hexahedral objects. The choice and definition of attributes in various levels of the inheritance hierarchy are completely at the user's discretion.

The OBJECT record data structure introduced in Chapter 22 can support inheritance of properties only partially, for inheritance is implemented mostly by operators that traverse the tree structure. Such operators include not only addition and deletion of attributes, but more important, operators that access the entire lineage of attributes inheritable by an object and operators that test for conflict between newly added attributes and ones inherited from higher level object classes.

The inheritance operators are based on principles similar to those of the stack operators discussed in Chapter 20 for the manipulation of locational dependencies. The attributes associated with object classes in the inheritance hierarchy can be considered *stacked*. The most specialized attributes are at the top of the stack, and the most general ones are at its bottom. All the attributes possessed by an object are represented by the entire stack. Using the example depicted in Figure 23.1, the hexahedral topology would be at the bottom of the stack, whereas the location of the object in space would be at the top of the stack, as depicted in Figure 23.2.

The operators that initialize, dispose of, create, delete, add, and remove objects are similar to the tree manipulation operators discussed in Appendix B; therefore, they will not be repeated here. Only three additional operators are needed to implement the hierarchical inheritance of attributes. The first is FIND_ATTRIBUTE, the second is SHOW_OWN_ATTRIBUTES, and the third is SHOW_ALL_ATTRIBUTES.

The first operator is used whenever a new attribute is to be added to an existing object or instance or when objects are reparented in the hierarchy. In both cases it is necessary to make sure that attributes particular to the object or the instance do not conflict with the attributes they inherit. Function FIND_ATTRIBUTE searches the inheritance hierarchy from the given object up to the root of the tree and compares the name of the attribute in question with the

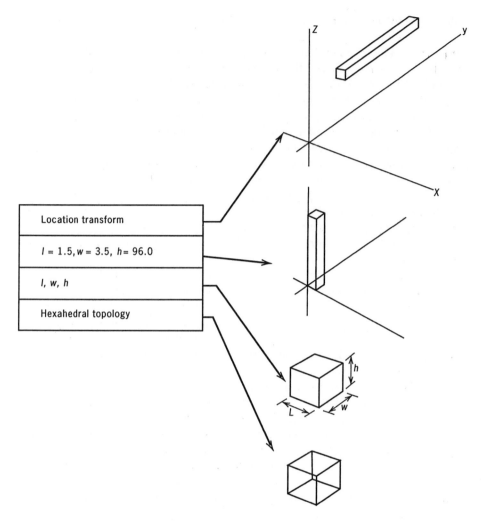

Figure 23.2. A stack representation of inherited attributes.

names of all the attributes the object inherits (the name of an attribute is considered its unique identifier).

```
function find_attribute (a : aptr; o : optr) : boolean;
{Search tree recursively from object o up to the root. Return
 true if an attribute with the same name as a's exists in o's
 attribute list or in the attributes it inherits, otherwise
 return false.}

var  atemp : aptr;
     found : boolean;
```

```
    function same_name (att, a : aptr) : boolean;
    {Compare the names of att and a. Return true if they are
     the same, else return false.}

    var  i : 1..20;

    begin
      same_name := true;
      if (a <> nil) and (att <> nil)
        then for i := 1 to 20 do
          if att^.name[i] <> a^.name[i]
            then same_name := false
    end; {same_name function}

begin {find-attribute}
  find_attribute := false;
  if o <> nil
    then begin
      {test all attributes of object o}
      atemp := o^.a_list;
      while (atemp <> nil) and not same_name (a,atemp) do
        atemp := atemp^.anext;
      if atemp <> nil
        then find_attribute := true
        else begin
          found := find_attribute (a, o^.parent);
          find_attribute := found
        end
    end
end; {find_attribute function}
```

Procedure SHOW_OWN_ATTRIBUTES, as its name implies, is used to review the particular attributes of a given object or instance. It consists simply of traversing the attribute list of the object or the instance and showing them on the screen.

```
procedure show_own_attributes (a_list : aptr);
{Traverse list of attributes a_list and show them.}

var  a : aptr;
     i : 1..20;

begin
  a := a_list;
  while a <> nil do
    begin
      for i := 1 to 20 do write(a^.name[i]);
```

```
      case a^.kind of
        int : write('numerical', a^.i_value:10);
        rel : write('numerical', a^.r_value:10:2);
        txt : begin
                 write('text string');
                 for i := 1 to 20 do write(a^.t_ value[i])
              end;
        log : write('logical', a^.l_value)
      end;
    a := a^.anext
  end;
  writeln
end; {show_own_attributes procedure}
```

When procedure SHOW_OWN_ATTRIBUTES is combined with a traversal mechanism, such as that used by function FIND_ATTRIBUTE, it can be used to show all the attributes of an object, including the inherited ones, as implemented in procedure SHOW_ALL_ATTRIBUTES.

```
procedure show_all_attributes (o : optr);
{Traverse tree recursively from object o to the root and show
 all attributes inherited by o.}

begin
  show_own_attributes (o^.alist);
  if o^.parent <> nil
    then show_all_attributes (o)
end; {show_all_attributes procedure}
```

To show all the attributes of an instance, we would call SHOW_OWN_ATTRIBUTES with the instance's ALIST field value as parameter, then call SHOW_ALL_ATTRIBUTES with the instance's master object pointer as parameter.

These three operators, together with operators that create, delete, and modify the inheritance tree of object classes, and with operators that create, add, remove, and delete individual attributes, are all that is needed for implementing nonshape attribute modeling.

The following function COPY_OBJECT demonstrates some of these operations as they apply to creating a new object by copying an existing one. This copy becomes a sibling of the copied object in the inheritance tree. As described later in this chapter, such copies are useful when the user wishes to modify some instances of the object but not all, at which time a new object, which is a copy of the old one, must be created, so the old one can be modified.

```
function copy_object (o : optr; new_name : text_string) : optr;
{Make a copy of object o, under new_name. Return pointer to new
 object.}

var  onew : optr;
     a    : aptr;

begin
  new (onew);
  onew^.name := new_name;
  a := o^.alist; {copy own attributes}
  while a <> nil do
    begin
      new (anew);
      anew^ := a^; {copy all fields of a}
      anew^.anext := onew^.alist;
      onew^.alist := anew;
      a := a^.anext
    end;

  onew^.shape := o^.shape;      {same shape as o     }
  onew^.tlist := nil;          {no instances yet    }
  onew^.sibling := o^.sibling; {onew is sibling of o}
  o^.sibling := onew;
  onew^.parent := o^.parent;   {same parent as o    }
  onew^.child := nil;          {no children, yet    }
  copy_object := onew
end; {copy_object function}
```

It should be noted that the shape property of objects was excluded from the inheritance hierarchy because, in contrast to nonshape attributes, it comprises an indivisible entity. If it were inheritable, all objects that belong to one inheritance hierarchy would have had one and only one shape. Nonshape attributes, on the other hand, can be distributed in the hierarchy, so object classes have more freedom in their selective inheritance. Therefore, the sharing of shape is handled directly by pointers, rather than by indirect inheritance. Several objects that share a shape could simply reference the same shape data structure.

□ INSTANCING

Instancing, as discussed in Chapter 22, is the process of "cloning" objects. It serves three purposes:

1. It provides an efficient means for making copies of objects without replicating all the data they contain, but rather by adding only the information unique to each copy (i.e., its location and orientation in space and its own attributes).

2. It provides a means for enhancing the semantic integrity of the model by ensuring that all the copies of an object are identical, and when changes are made to the object, all its copies are also updated.

3. It provides a means whereby objects can be grouped in assemblies other than inheritance hierarchies.

The first purpose is representational; the second is operational; and the third is associative. In the following, we discuss each purpose and see how each can be implemented computationally.

Instancing as a Means of Representation

The first property is a means of representation, which is implemented by the data structure itself in the form of a pointer from the instance record to the object record. The instance's own attributes do not duplicate the ones stored by the object it "instantiates," hence data redundancies are avoided. The avoidance of redundancies is also the key to enhancing the model's semantic integrity: data are modified and updated in only one place for each object and instance; therefore, inconsistencies between different sets of data representing the same object cannot occur.

The only operational functionality needed to implement the first property of instancing is the identification of the master object when an instance is created. In addition, in many cases all the instances of one object need to be accessed (e.g., for display purposes); therefore, a circular list of all the instances of one object is also maintained. This list is referenced by the TLIST field in the OBJECT record.

```
procedure init_instance (var t : tptr);
{Create a new instance record and initialize its fields.}

begin
  new (t);
  with t^ do
    begin
      master := nil;
      alist := nil;
      init_matrix (location);
      tnext := t; {circular list}
      parent := nil; child := nil
    end
end; {init_instance procedure}
```

```
procedure create_instance (o : optr; var t : tptr);
{Create an instance t of object o.}

begin
  init_instance (t);
  t^.master := o;
  if o^.tlist = nil
    then o^.tlist := t
    else begin
      t^.tnext := o^.tlist^.tnext;
      o^.tlist^.tnext := t
    end
end; {create_instance procedure}

procedure delete_instance (var t : tptr);
{Delete instance t. Note: assume t has already been removed from
 the location tree. If t is the last instance of its master
 object, delete the master object too.}

var  tpred : tptr;
     a     : aptr;

begin
  {test if t is the only instance of its master object}
  if t = t^.tnext
    then delete_object (t^.master)
    else begin {remove t from list of master's instances}
      tpred := t^.master^.tlist;
      while tpred^.tnext <> t do tpred := tpred^.tnext;
      tpred^.tnext := t^.tnext;
      t^.master^.tlist := tpred
    end;

  {delete own attributes}
  while t^.alist <> nil do
    begin
      a := t^.alist; t^.alist := a^.anext;
      dispose (a)
    end;
  dispose (t); t := nil
end; {delete_instance procedure}
```

Note that the creation of an instance does not automatically locate it in space, because the location of the new instance depends on the hierarchical relationships it forms with instances of other objects, as we shall discuss next. Also, the creation of an instance does not include ADD and REMOVE operations, as we have seen with other modeling entities (e.g., polygons). The reason for this omission is that instances cannot exist on their own; they exist only when they are related to a master object. Therefore, the "addition" of an instance to the list of instances of a master object is made automatically when it is created, and when an instance is "removed" from its master, it must also be deleted.

Instancing as a Means of Manipulation

As a means of manipulation, instancing permits wholesale modification of all the objects in the database, without exception. If, for example, the designer decides to replace all the windows by a different type, only one change is needed. Instancing thus reduces the verbosity of the data structure and enhances its consistency. (When the master object is modified, no instance is left unmodified.)

The implementation method we have chosen in Chapter 22 for objects and instances allows access to the master object-class through any one of its instances. In effect, it means that the boundary between instances and the master is intentionally invisible. The designer can change *all* instances by changing any one of them without going to the particular "master" in order to do so.

In many cases, however, the designer may wish to exclude certain instances from the change. Such exclusion, in effect, creates a *new master object* and associates the excluded instances with it rather than with the one that is being modified. This operation is demonstrated by the following procedure EXCLUDE_INSTANCE, which uses function COPY_OBJECT (discussed earlier in this chapter). It also calls ADD_INSTANCE, which is merely an adaptation of procedure ADD_NODE that is discussed in Appendix B for the manipulation of trees and, therefore, is not repeated here.

```
procedure exclude_instance (t : tptr);
{Create a new master object which is a copy of the master of
 instance t. Make an instance of this new master and add it
 to the locational hierarchy as sibling of t.}

var   o    : optr;
      tnew : tptr;

begin
  o := copy_object (t^.master, new_name);
  create_instance (o, tnew);
  tnew^.location := t^.location;
  add_instance (tnew, t^.parent) {to the assembly}
end; {exclude_instance procedure}
```

Instancing as a Means of Association

The instances share all the attributes of the master shape, but differ in their locations in space. It is this separation of the instance's location from the rest of the object's attributes that allows instances to be grouped in locational hierarchy assemblies of the kind discussed in Chapter 20. The location of each instance is defined through a transform matrix, which multiplies the coordinates of the

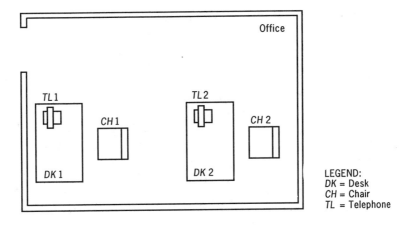

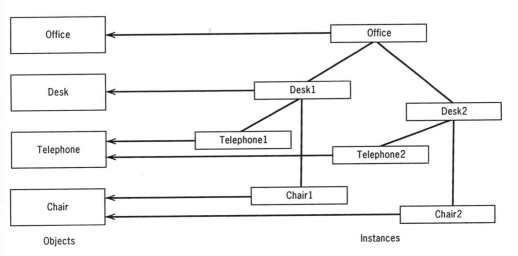

Figure 23.3. Inheritance hierarchy and instance assembly of office furniture.

master object's shape geometry. These transforms can be made hierarchically dependent, as discussed in Chapter 20, where the actual location of the instance in space is the concatenated product of the locations of its parent instances in the locational hierarchy. This location can be calculated by means of the stack operators PUSH_TRANSFORM and POP_TRANSFORM, and the instances can be displayed by means of procedure DISPLAY_TREE as discussed in Chapter 20.

The association of instances in assemblies can be performed by operators that are similar to the tree manipulation operators discussed in Appendix B. They include operators to ADD an instance to the assembly structure, operators to

REMOVE it from that structure, and operators to RE_PARENT an instance in the assembly. These operators affect only the relationships between the instances themselves in the assembly and should not be confused with the operators that were discussed earlier in this chapter, which CREATE instances and DELETE them. Those operators affect the relationship between an instance and its master object, not its place within the locational hierarchy.

The locational hierarchy of the instances is completely separate from the inheritance hierarchy of the object-classes (discussed earlier) that serves to pass attributes from parent objects to their children. The locational hierarchy of instances does not affect the attributes. Therefore, different instances of the same object can form a locational hierarchy all by themselves, or instances of different objects can form a locational hierarchy, representing an assembly of parts. Figure 23.3 depicts (schematically) an example of such an assembly, formed by office workstation furniture: a telephone that sits on a desk and a chair that is associated with the desk. Each one of these entities is an instance of a different master object and forms part of the workstation assembly.

The advantages of this dual hierarchical structure is in the ability to manipulate each independently from the other. For example, it is possible to modify the brand of the desk without affecting the assembly structure, in the previous example, and it is possible to separate the chair from the assembly without modifying its master object. The disadvantage is that the assembly structure as a whole is not an object; therefore, it cannot be instantiated—only its separate members can. This representational deficiency can, however, be easily overcome by providing appropriate assembly-copying operators, which will be functionally equivalent to the instancing of objects. The logical clarity gained by the separation is more than an adequate compensation for the inconvenience of writing some additional operators.

☐ BIBLIOGRAPHY

Eastman, C. M., "The Design of Assemblies," Institute of Physical Planning, Technical Report 11, Carnegie-Mellon University, Pittsburgh, PA, 1980.

24

GROUPING OBJECTS

Objects and instances are units of information that represent real or abstract entities. They are interdependent: objects inherit properties from more general object classes, and instances share all the attributes of a master object except for its location. Locational dependencies allow instances to form assemblies of related parts. In addition to these intrinsic relationships, objects and instances are also related through *extrinsic* relationships, which provide means of identification and access to *groups* of instances that share some common property. In this chapter we discuss such group relationships and draw parallels to them from relational database theory and practice.

☐ TYPES OF RELATIONSHIPS BETWEEN OBJECTS

Five types of relationships between objects and their instances can be readily identified:

1. Class-subclass relationship: one object is a specialized subclass of a more general object class. For example, casement windows are a specialized subclass of windows, and windows are a specialized subclass of openings.

2. Master-instance relationship: an object is an instance of a master object. Instances of the same master object share all its attributes except location (and optionally some private attributes). For example, all casement windows in a building are instances of the master window that appears in the manufacturer's catalog, although they are located in different places in the building.

3. Part-whole relationship: an object is part of an assembly of objects. For example, the window is part of a wall, which is part of the building.

4. Group relationship: objects (or rather their instances) can be grouped according to some common property other than the first three. For example,

all wooden objects make a group, as do all the objects delivered after a certain date, as do all the objects whose price exceeds $2,500.

5. Dimensional relationship: the size of one object can depend on the size and location of another object.

The first three types of relationships are *intrinsic* to the object or instance; they are part of its very definition (i.e., its data structure). Their implications and possible implementations have, therefore, been discussed in Chapters 22 and 23, as part of the object and instance definition and related operations.

The fourth type of relationship is *extrinsic* to the objects and their instances. A group relationship is implemented through additional data structures that reference objects and instances, but do not partake in their definition. This type of relationship provides, therefore, a structured means to *group* and *access* objects that share some common property. This type of relationship is the subject matter of this chapter.

The fifth type of relationship—dimensional dependence—implies that the size of one object is dependent on another one. It is, therefore, a relationship that is both extrinsic and intrinsic to the object. This type of relationship, which we call *parameterization,* is discussed in Chapter 26.

Variations on these five basic relationship schemes are abundant. Furthermore, objects can be associated in more than one way. For example, all Ford Model T's were instances of the master Model T. They were also a class in the hierarchy of motor vehicles, which is a subclass of more general means of transportation. They are also members of a group of objects identified by the property of having been the first assembly line car ever produced and a group of objects whose color is black.

□ THE CONCEPT OF GROUPING

Grouping is a term used here to define a means of identifying, and hence accessing, a collection of instances that share some common property. This identification and access can be used for a variety of purposes, such as for applying to the members of the group some common operation (e.g., display) or for answering queries that concern them. Grouping, for the purpose of identifying and accessing objects, relies on *representation* of the relationships between the grouped objects and on *operators* to create, modify, and delete these relationships.

Group relationships form an important part of general set theory. They differ from the part-whole, master-instance, and classification hierarchy relationships discussed earlier in that they are more flexible and membership in them is "voluntary." Because they add no new information to the model, only facilitate access to existing information, a member in one group can also be a member in other groups at the same time without risking data conflicts or inconsistencies.

The generality of groups complements the restrictive nature of the more specialized relationships. Yet, this generality requires that the binding property, which is the criteria for membership in the group, be explicitly defined. Generality also diminishes the functionality of the group relationship, compared with the other type of associations, to the point where the group becomes merely a means of identification and access to the members.

The representation of related instances as a group could be done in a variety of ways that allow for collecting a variable number of members. Sets and linked lists are examples of such collection mechanisms. Whichever method is chosen, it must be capable of referencing instances without affecting them. That is, the GROUP structure must be *extrinsic* to the instances (e.g., a group pointer in the instance record is not acceptable). This will permit each instance to participate (be a member of) several different groups.

The groups we are interested in are dynamic structures. Their memberships may grow or shrink as the objects represented by the model evolve, and the groups themselves may be split and combined in well-defined ways to form new groups. The group operators must, therefore, facilitate the well-defined modeling of groups and their members.

The problem of grouping objects in a structured manner is similar to many other data management problems that require storage of and access to related information. Specifically, *database management systems* (DBMSs) have been developed that do precisely that: They provide structured means to store, query, and update information.

☐ THE RELATIONAL DATABASE CONCEPT

Many database management systems have been developed in the past two decades. They include the *network,* the *hierarchy,* and the *relational* models. These models and the principles they are based on are described in numerous textbooks. Of the three, the *relational* model represents the relationships among the units of information it stores in the logically simplest manner: in the form of two-dimensional tables (Figure 24.1).

The relational database model was derived in 1971 by E.F. Code at IBM from the well-established mathematical set theoretic concept of *relations.* † It consists of tabulated collections of objects and their properties (attributes). Tables represent two types of relationships:

1. Relationships that are internal to an object, represented by the attributes that make up an object. This relationship is represented by the rows in the table, each of which is a collection of attributes (called *domains* in relational DBMS nomenclature).
2. Relationships that are external to the objects, represented by the table as a whole, which is called a *relation* in relational DBMS nomenclature.

†E.F. Code, "A Database Sublanguage Founded on the Relational Calculus," *Proc. of SIGFIDET Workshop,* San Diego, CA, November, 1971.

FACE LIST

face no	ring on F
1	1
2	2
3	3
4	4
5	5
6	6

RING LIST

ring no	next R/f	face	edge on R
1	1	1	1
2	2	2	1
3	3	3	2
4	4	4	3
5	5	5	4
6	6	6	5

EDGE LIST

edge no	ring 1	Esucc1	Epred1	vert 1	ring 2	Esucc2	Epred2	vert 2
1	1	2	4	1	2	9	10	2
2	1	3	1	2	3	10	11	3
3	1	4	2	3	4	11	12	4
4	1	1	3	4	5	12	9	1
5	6	8	6	6	2	10	9	5
6	6	5	7	7	3	11	10	6
7	6	6	8	8	4	12	11	7
8	6	7	5	5	5	9	12	8
9	5	4	8	5	2	5	1	1
10	2	1	5	6	3	6	2	2
11	3	2	6	7	4	7	3	3
12	4	3	7	8	5	8	4	4

VERTEX LIST

vertex no	Xcord	Ycord	Zcord
1	−0.5	−0.5	0.5
2	−0.5	0.5	0.5
3	0.5	0.5	0.5
4	0.5	−0.5	0.5
5	+0.5	−0.5	−0.5
6	−0.5	0.5	−0.5
7	0.5	0.5	−0.5
8	0.5	−0.5	−0.5

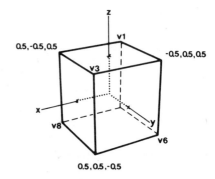

Figure 24.1. A relational database representation of shape information.

The example depicted in Figure 24.1 demonstrates the properties of the relational model. It shows how the geometric information associated with shapes can be represented in simple tabular form. Each table (relation) contains only one class of shape components; the components share the same set of attributes.

The only limitation imposed by the relational model on the represented information is that every item and attribute in each relation must be unique. There is no limit, however, on how many relations can be used; therefore, it is possible to expand the information to include as many properties and items as needed.

While this representation does not lend itself to *manipulating* shape information, it does support *querying* shapes. Such queries are made by rearranging the relations by extracting rows and columns and by combining them into new relations that include the information needed to answer the query. For example, to find all the vertices (in order) that define the polygon bounding FACE 3 of the cube depicted in Figure 24.1, the following sequence of steps can be used:

1. Find the rings of edges that bound FACE 3 (in this case there is only one, namely R3).
2. Find all the edges that constitute the rings identified in step 1 (in this case, there are four edges: 2, 6, 10, and 11). This step can be formulated as the creation of a new relation, which is a subset of the original EDGE-LIST relation.
3. Sort the relation created in step 2 by end point-matching edges into a list of succeeding vertices, then create a new relation from the remaining vertices joined by the locational information (x, y, z coordinates) that is associated with each of them, as stored in the original VERTEX-LIST relation.

This rather lengthy process is facilitated by a set of universal operators unique to the relational model, which are called the *selection, projection,* and *join* operators. They provide the necessary "cut" and "paste" tools for identifying and extracting subsets of the original relations and their combination in new ones.

The concept of *relation* is formally defined as a *subset of the Cartesian product of a list of domains,* where the domains, as noted earlier, are the attributes of the objects. The power of the relational database model is in its ability to represent and operate on inter-object relationships, by collecting objects and their attributes in *relations.* Each relation represents a single class of objects. In relational database terminology, columns, which represent one type of attribute each, are called *domains*, and the rows are called *tuples.*

The *selection* operator is a means to identify tuples (rows) that include a particular domain (attribute). The *projection* operator is a means to split an existing relation into two or more relations, each of which contains a subset of the rows and columns of the original one. The *join* operator is a means to combine two or more separate relations into one, while eliminating data redundancy (i.e., attributes that are common to the joined relations).

In the following, we shall use the principles of the relational database model in developing the GROUP relationship representation and operators. We will, however, adapt these principles to our specific needs.

☐ THE REPRESENTATION OF GROUPS

A group, as defined earlier, is a collection of instances that share some common property. The representation of a group, therefore, consists of two elements:

1. A means to represent the property shared by members in the group
2. A means to identify members of the group

The first means may simply be a reference to the common attribute shared by all members in the group. The second means can be provided in a variety of ways, such as linked lists, arrays, or sets. It must not rely on some field in the instance itself, because each instance can be part of many groups, and as noted earlier, group relationship is extrinsic to the instance. A data structure for representing groups can thus be implemented as follows:

```
type  rptr  = ^group;
      group = record
                 attr  : aptr; {common attribute    }
                 inst  : tptr; {instance            }
                 mnext : rptr; {next member in group }
                 rnext : rptr  {pointer to next group}
              end;
```

New groups can be initialized, created, and added to the existing group list, removed from it, and deleted by a set of operators that follow the design principles that were discussed throughout the book. They will not be repeated here. Only operators that are specific to the group concept and rely on the relational database model will be discussed in the next section.

☐ OPERATING ON GROUPS

Selection

The *selection* operator identifies in a given group (relation) all the instances with attribute lists that include a particular attribute value. For example, if all the windows were members of one group, we could *select* the casement windows.

```
procedure select_instance (a : aptr; r : rptr; var m : rptr);
{Traverse group r starting at its member m and return pointer to
 its next member that includes attribute a. If m=nil start
 with the first member in the group.}

var  found : boolean;

begin
  found := false;
  if m = nil then m := r;
  while not found and (m <> nil) do
    if m^.attr^ = a^ then found := true else m := m^.mnext;
  select_instance := m
end; {select_instance procedure}
```

Projection

The projection operator constructs a new group from instances identified by the
selection operator. It does not affect the former group. For example, the casement windows identified earlier could become a new group of their own, while
still being members of the more general group of windows. The common property of all the instances in this group is referenced by the ATTR field in the
GROUP record. Procedure ADD_MEMBER takes care of creating new members and adding them to the list of instances referenced by the group.

```
procedure add_member (t : tptr; a : aptr; r : rptr);
{Add instance t as new member to list of members in group r. The
 common attribute is a.}

var  new_member : rptr;

begin
  new (new_member);
  with new_member^ do
    begin
      attr := a; {common attribute}
      inst := t; {instance        }
      mnext := new_group;
      new_group := new_member
    end
end; {add_member procedure}
```

```
function project_group (r : rptr; a : aptr) : rptr;
{Create new group from the instances of group r which have
 attribute a. Return pointer to new group.}

var  new_group, m : rptr;

begin
  new_group := nil;

  m := nil;
  repeat
    select_instance (a,r,m);
    if m <> nil then add_member (m^.inst, a, new_group)
  until m = nil;

  project_group := new_group
end; {project_group function}
```

Join

The join operator combines two groups into one by creating a new group which is the union of the two. It eliminates redundancy by testing members of one group to see if any are already members of the other group, in which case they are not added to the list of members of the joined group.

```
function join_groups (r1,r2 : rptr) : rptr;
{Combine the instance lists of groups r1 and r2, which share a
 common attribute, without duplications. The common attribute
 referenced by the new group is the same that is referenced
 by each of the input groups.}

var  new_group, m : rptr;
     a            : aptr;

     function member (t : tptr; r : rptr) : boolean;
     {Return true if instance t is member in group r.}

     var  m     : rptr;
          found : boolean;

     begin
       m := r; found := false;
       while not found and (m <> nil) do
         if m^.inst = t
           then found := true
           else m := m^.mnext;
       member := found
     end; {member function}
```

```
begin {join_groups function}
  new (new_group);
  a := r1^.attr; {common attribute}

  {add all members of r1 to new_group}
  m := r1;
  while m <> nil do
    begin
      add_member (m^.inst, a, new_group);
      m := m^.mnext
    end;

  {add non-redundant members of r2 to new_group}
  m := r2;
  while m <> nil do
    begin
      if not member (m^.inst, r1)
        then add_member (m^.inst, a, new_group);
      m := m^.mnext
    end;

  join_groups := new_group
end; {join_groups procedure}
```

The *select, project,* and *join* operators are means to manipulate grouping relationships between objects. The relationships themselves are used as permanent
means of access to instances that share some common property. The permanency of the access is useful only if the instances are to be accessed more than
once and if it would cost too much to re-identify them each time. Such is the case
for permanently identifying all the furniture produced by one manufacturer or
all the engine assembly parts. If the group of instances is temporary, it may be
computationally cheaper to traverse the database and identify the instances as
needed. Such is the case for displaying a particular group of objects or their
relocation.

Permanency, however, is transient, as is the composition of the group. In particular, attention must be paid to updating the groups when the instances they
reference are modified. Some instances may be deleted altogether, or their properties may be altered so they should no longer be part of the group. Such testing
obviously complicates the grouping of objects, but it does not alter it
conceptually.

☐ "INTELLIGENT" DESIGN DATABASES

The representation and manipulation of inter-object relationships, as discussed
in this chapter, is the first step toward the development of an "intelligent" de-

sign database, which will not only represent the designed artifact, but also actively assist the designer by managing its own semantic integrity. This can be done by automatically propagating design changes, which are applied by the designer or by high-level design operators to one part of the database, to its other parts.

This concept of an "intelligent" database can be implemented using a network of objects, of the kind discussed here, where objects are also associated with integrity and self-maintenance knowledge base, operators, and data, in addition to their representational descriptions. The network will be used by the objects to communicate with each other through broadcast messages. The knowledge base associated with each object will be responsible for interpreting and responding to these messages.

In addition to relieving the designer and the high-level design operators from the database management responsibilities which they currently assume, such object-centered, decentralized database management scheme will lend itself to extension and modification and may facilitate the application of parallel processing methods to computer-aided design and database management.

☐ BIBLIOGRAPHY

Date, C. J., *An Introduction to Database Systems,* Addison-Wesley, Reading, MA, 1977.

Kalay, Y. E., "A Relational Database for Non-Manipulative Representation of Solid Objects," *Computer-Aided Design* 15(5):271–276, September 1983.

Lafue, G. M. E., "Integrating Language and Database for CAD Applications," *Computer-Aided Design* 11(3):127–130, May 1979.

Ullman, J. D., *Principles of Database Systems,* Computer Science Press, Potomac, MD, 1980.

25

FEATURES

Features are prominent shape properties, made of the primitive components of shapes, such as faces, edges, and vertices, that bound a hole or that define a protrusion. Their identification and grouping in a manner similar to the grouping of instances provide recognition of, and direct access to, the shape elements that partake in their definition. The concept of features and their representation are the subject matter of this chapter.

☐ THE CONCEPT OF FEATURES

The purpose of the various object grouping schemes that were discussed in Chapter 24 is to provide the user or the application programmer with means to identify and classify sets of objects that share some common property (e.g., the objects that make up a bridge assembly). This classification provides immediate access to groups of related objects (i.e., it requires no search). In many cases, however, particular *subsets* of the faces, edges, and vertices, which form the shape attributes of objects, describe important *partial properties* of the object. Consider, for example, the wide-flanged beam (W-beam) depicted in Figure 25.1: it is represented as a highly structured collection of faces, edges, and vertices. Yet, some of these components are identifiable as important subparts of the whole. For example, the "vertical" part of the beam is important for determining its load-bearing capacity, and the flanges determine its resistance to torque and twist. The holes on both sides are important for determining the size and number of bolts that will be needed to attach the beam, and their distances from the ends of the beam determine certain shear resistance properties. These subcomponents are significant enough to warrant special attention, because they describe the load-bearing and attachment properties of the beam. They are known as *features*.

The origin of the term *features* arises from its general use in computer-aided design as a means of specification of *portions* of a model that are of particular

299

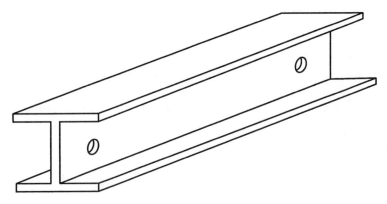

Figure 25.1. A wide-flanged beam.

interest. It denotes a *subset* of the shape primitives (faces, edges, and vertices) that make up an object representation. For example, a hole in the W-beam can be considered a feature. It comprises many faces, edges, and vertices, which are part of the beam's general shape representation. Their uniqueness is only in that they represent a part of the beam that has some particular semantical importance for certain applications. Features thus have several important properties:

1. They comprise a particular *grouping* of a subset of the shape primitives that are also used for representing the shape as a whole.
2. Similarly to objects, features may have other *attributes,* in addition to shape (e.g., name, properties, parameters).
3. Features have meaning only in *particular circumstance.* A collection of parts that is considered a feature for some applications may not be considered as such for some other applications.
4. Features are *hierarchical.* A feature, which comprises certain parts of a shape, could itself be made of other features.

The great utility of feature hierarchies lies in their *independence* of the whole object representation. Features need not exhaustively reference every entity in the model to which they are applied. Rather, they identify and provide access to aggregated parts of the object, which are of interest to a particular application. Thus features help customize the object representation to the application's particular needs, without affecting the model as a whole and without interfering with the model's generality. Features thus provide a *denotational* mechanism for describing the structure or function of generalized object representations from the application's particular point of view.

Like instances, features are members of *aggregation hierarchies.* Unlike instances, features represent a selective aggregation hierarchy, which describes objects in terms of their more significant parts. Features thus offer a flexible way for structuring information: they provide immediate access to parts that are of interest to the application programmer, making search unnecessary or even the need to know about parts of the model that are of no interest to him. By combining the denotational capabilities of features with particular operators, the model as a whole is protected from unauthorized manipulative actions by the application programmer (or the application program itself). Using the W-beam as an example, an application that must design the bolts to fasten the beam will only be interested in the size of the holes. If the holes were not explicitly referenced, this application would have no way of finding them without explicit help from the user. If the holes were referenced by a feature hierarchy, then direct access is provided, and no help is needed. Furthermore, if the feature were equipped with an operator to compute the parameters of the holes (in terms of their radius and depth), the querying application would not need to know how the shape information was structured and would not have to provide its own geometric calculation operators but could, instead, rely on the model's geometric operators (which probably would be needed by other applications as well).

☐ THE REPRESENTATION OF FEATURES

The list of feature properties given earlier also defines their computational representation. A feature record must allow grouping of a subset of the shape primitives (faces, edges, and vertices). It must include other attributes, in addition to the shape primitives, and it must include means for hierarchical structuring. In the following discussion we shall limit the shape description powers of features to polygons, which represent themselves or the faces of solids. They can be used to infer the other shape primitives by localized search or pointer dereference. A FEATURE record, for our purposes, can thus be described by the following declarations:

```
const  poly_max = 100;

type   ftptr   = ^feature;
       feature = record
                  name    : text_string;
                  alist   : aptr;
                  pmax    : 0..poly_max;
                  plist   : array [1..poly_max] of pptr;
                  parent,
                  child,
                  sibling : ftptr
                end;
```

The operators that are needed to support features include, in addition to the obvious ones which create, add, and delete a feature from the hierarchy, operators that allow addition and removal of polygons to the list referenced by a feature. The addition and removal of features is similar to the tree structure manipulations discussed in Appendix B. The addition and removal of polygons referenced by a feature are implemented here by means of a stack-like mechanism, which allows a feature to reference up to 100 polygons. The stack itself is implemented as an array, which simplifies the addition and removal of polygons referenced by a feature record, as demonstrated by procedures ADD_ FEATURE_POLYGON and REMOVE_FEATURE_POLYGON.

```
procedure add_feature_polygon (p : pptr; ft : ftptr);
{Add polygon p to list of polygons referenced by feature ft,
 unless p is already part of that list.}

var  i     : 1..max_poly;
     found : boolean;

begin
  i := 1; found := false;
  while not found and (i <= ft^.pmax) do
    if ft^.plist[i] = p
      then found := true
      else i := i + 1;

  if not found and (ft^.pmax < poly_max)
    then begin
      ft^.pmax := ft^.pmax + 1;
      ft^.plist[ft^.pmax] := p
    end
end; {add_feature_polygon procedure}


procedure remove_feature_polygon (p : pptr; ft : ftptr);
{Remove polygon p from list of polygons in feature ft, and close
 the gap in the array. Assume p is in the list.}

var  i,j : 1..poly_max;

begin
  i := 1;
  while ft^.plist[i] <> p do i := i + 1;

  for j := i to (ft^.pmax - 1) do
    ft^.plist[j] := ft^.plist[j + 1];
  ft^.pmax := ft^.pmax - 1
end; {remove_feature_polygon procedure}
```

To demonstrate the use of features as implemented here, we shall again use the W-beam structure. As discussed earlier, the W-beam is characterized by the following features:

1. "Vertical" part
2. Flanges
3. Holes

Using the FEATURE data structure, several records will be needed to describe them. We shall also make these features part of another feature, which describes the entire W-beam. This particular feature is used only for accessing the others; therefore, it will contain no polygon pointers:

```
var  ft0,ft1,ft2,ft3,ft4 : ftptr;
new (ft0);
with ft0^ do
  begin
    name:= 'W-beam';
    pmax:= 0;
    parent:= nil;
    child:= nil;
    sibling := nil;
  end;
new (ft1);
with ft1^ do
  begin
    name:= 'vertical part';
    pmax:= 2;
    plist[1] := {ptr to first polygon of vertical part};
    plist[2] := {ptr to second polygon of vertical part};
    parent:= ft0; ft^.child := ft1;
    child:= nil;
    sibling := nil;
  end;
new (ft2);
with ft2^ do
  begin
    name:= 'top flange';
    pmax:= 4;
    plist[1] := {ptr to first polygon of flange};
    .

    .
    plist[4] := {ptr to fourth polygon of flange};
    parent:= ft0; ft^.child := ft2;
    child:= nil;
    sibling := ft1;
  end;
```

```
new (ft3);
with ft3^ do
  begin
    name:= 'bottom flange';
    pmax:= 4;
    plist[1] := {ptr to first polygon of flange};
      .
      .
    plist[4] := {ptr to fourth polygon of flange};
    parent:= ft0; ft^.child := ft3;
    child:= nil;
    sibling := ft2;
  end;

new (ft4);
with ft4^ do
  begin
    name:= 'hole';
    pmax:= 36;
    plist[1] := {ptr to first polygon of hole};
      .
      .
    plist[36] := {ptr to 36th polygon of hole};
    parent:= ft0; ft^.child := ft4;
    child:= nil;
    sibling := ft3;
  end;
      .
      .
      .
```

The feature hierarchy can be made part of the OBJECT record that was discussed in Chapter 22, which will enable the instances of the object to access and use it.

□ BIBLIOGRAPHY

Peterson, D. P., "A Naive Definition of Features," Technical Report, Sandia National Laboratories, New Mexico, January 1986.

26

PARAMETERIZATION

Features, as discussed in Chapter 25, are means for identification and access of related *topological* entities of shapes. Related *geometrical* entities of a shape can be similarly identified and accessed through the use of *parameters*. Unlike features, parameters are both a means of access and a geometrical constraint that enforces the relationship upon the entities it groups. Parameters can thus be viewed as "handles" that allow shape modification according to certain constraints and that automate the propagation of the changes applied to one geometric entity over its related geometric entities. This chapter discusses the concept of parameterization and its possible implementations.

☐ THE CONCEPT OF PARAMETRIZATION

Parameterization is *the imposition of constrained relationships on the shape of objects*. It enables shape manipulation by adjusting several geometrical attributes in some fixed relation to each other, or in relation to explicit changes applied to other shapes, or the location of other objects. A rectangle, for example, can be characterized as a four-sided figure constrained by the following relationships: it is of length L and width W; its opposite sides are parallel to each other; and its adjacent sides are perpendicular to each other (Figure 26.1).

This parametric characterization contains more information about the shape than a definition in which the x, y locations of the four vertices are defined explicitly because it implies that certain *geometric relationships* between the vertices are fixed. These relationships are incorporated in the values L and W, which are known as the *parameters* of the rectangle, and in the name *rectangle* itself, which incorporates the facts that the shape is made of four sides, of which the opposite ones are parallel and the adjacent ones are perpendicular to each other. Moreover, the shape of the rectangle could be *modified* by changing only L and W (Figure 26.2).

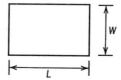

Figure 26.1. The parametric characterization of a rectangle.

Parameterization is thus both a means to enhance the well-formedness of a shape and a powerful tool for its manipulation. It enhances well-formedness by incorporating some *semantic* information in the shape's definition and aids its manipulation by reducing the number of changes the designer must explicitly apply to the shape. Together, the incorporation of well-formedness semantic information in the shape's definition and the support this added information lends to the shape's manipulation relieves the designer from the need to explicitly manage the *implications* of applying changes to the shape of an object. Instead, the *propagation* of changes applied to one part of the object to its other parts becomes the responsibility of the system itself. Thus for example, to elongate the rectangle the designer would have to change only one attribute (L), rather than move two vertices and ensure that the new locations assigned to them comply with the definition of the rectangle (parallel opposite sides and perpendicular adjacent sides).

Another, more complicated type of parameterization comes in the form of constraints that link the form of one shape to the form or location of other shapes. For example, the length of a wall may depend on the location of other walls it abuts, and the size of a beam depends on the length it spans (as well as the loads it must support). Such dependencies are common in assemblies, such as structural frames, windows, and motors. The length L of the beam depicted in Figure 26.3, for example, depends on the location of the supports $S1$ and $S2$, as does its depth D.

☐ KINDS OF PARAMETERIZATION

Parameterization of shapes can be classified according to the following categories:

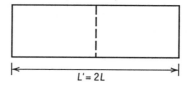

Figure 26.2. Modifying a parametric rectangle.

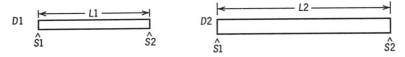

Figure 26.3. The parametric definition of a beam.

1. Cause and effect of the change
2. The extent to which the shapes are affected

Cause and Effect

The change that affects a parameterized shape could be caused by direct means, or it could be caused by changes applied to other shapes. The effect of the change could apply to the entire shape, or it can be restricted to some selected parts of the shape. Different causes and effects interact with each other, as depicted in the following diagram:

		cause	
		direct	indirect
effect	whole shape		
	part of shape		

Scaling, for example, can be regarded a direct, whole-shape parameterization, as depicted in Figure 26.4. When a shape is scaled by some factor that is applied to the value of one of its coordinates, *all* the vertices are affected.

Indiscriminate scaling, however, cannot achieve the effects depicted in Figure 26.5, where the dimensional changes do not affect all the vertices of the shape in the same manner.

Partial parameterization is more difficult to achieve than whole shape parameterization, because it requires explicit identification of the elements of the shape that are to be affected. The combination of indirect and partial parameterization, which is depicted in Figure 26.3, is the most difficult one to implement and to manage.

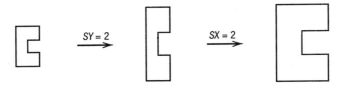

Figure 26.4. Scaling as direct, whole-shape parameterization.

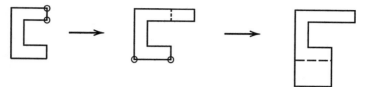

Figure 26.5. Dimensional changes that cannot be achieved by indiscriminate scaling.

Extent of Change

The effects of changes caused by parameterization can fall under the following two categories:

1. Topologically invariant
2. Topologically variant

Topologically invariant parameterization modifies only the geometry of a shape, leaving its topological interrelationships intact. For example, elongating the rectangle depicted in Figure 26.2 only affects the geometrical attributes of the vertices. Topologically variant parameterization affects both the geometry of the shape and its topology. For example, extruding the rectangle into a solid results in a topologically variant parameterization.

Topologically invariant parameterization allows us to control the shape without having to position each element separately. It is, therefore, the most common type of parameterization. For example, the hexahedral topology depicted in Figure 26.6 can be parameterized by length (L), width (W), and height (H), in the following form:

$$x1 = x2 = x5 = x6 = 0$$

$$x3 = x4 = x7 = x8 = L$$

$$y1 = y4 = y5 = y8 = 0$$

$$y2 = y3 = y6 = y7 = W$$

$$z1 = z2 = z3 = z4 = 0$$

$$z5 = z6 = z7 = z8 = H.$$

By assigning different values to L, W, and H, any hexahedral parallelepiped can be generated. Note that this parameterization also implies parallel pairs of opposite faces and orthogonal pairs of adjacent faces. It also positions the shapes such that one of their vertices is at the origin.

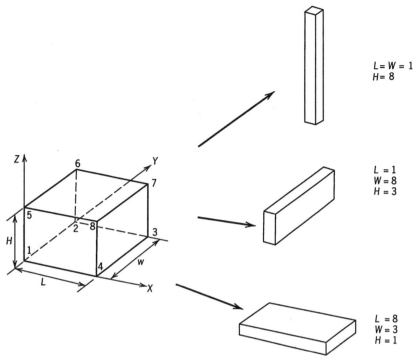

Figure 26.6. Topologically invariant parameterization of a hexahedron.

Another common use of parameterization prevails in the definition of certain curved surfaces. A limited number of so called "control points" serve as parameters that define the shape of the surfaces as a whole. Their effect is purely geometrical, and it is applied to all the points in the surface through a mathematical transformation. The particular transformation depends on the type of surface we use. Figure 26.7 depicts a bicubic surface patch, defined through the Bernstein–Bezier parameterization transform.

Topologically variant parameterization, on the other hand, affects both the topology of the shape and its geometry. As such, topologically variant parameterization can be used as a powerful means for generating a family of shapes called *swept shapes*, which include extruded and revolved solids, as well as swept polygons. A given line can be "swept" in the plane to form a polygon by moving it along a given trajectory or in space to create a so-called "ruled surface." A polygon can be swept in space to create an extruded, three-dimensional prismatic solid (or a form of revolution), as depicted in Figure 26.8.

The parameters, in these cases, are the starting line or polygon and the trajectory of the sweep (the height of the extrusion or the axis of the rotation). Obviously, topologically variant parameterization is much more difficult to implement than topologically invariant parameterization, but it is also much more powerful.

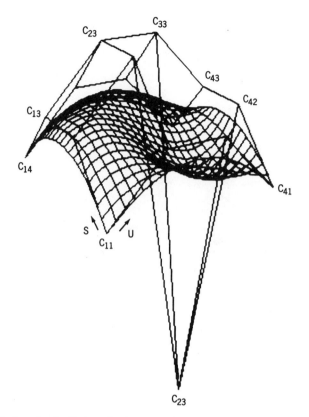

Figure 26.7. Topologically invariant parameterization of a bicubic Bezier patch.

□ IMPLEMENTATION

Shape parameterization of all types can be implemented in two ways or by their combination:

1. By means of *functions* (or procedures) that use the parameters as input, such as in the case of extruding a polygon into a solid
2. By means of *stored parameters* that represent related geometrical values, such as in the case of the parameterized hexahedron

Functional Parameterization

Functional parameterization is easier to implement than stored parameterization. It is typically written to create a predefined shape, given certain values as parameters. Consider, for example, procedure MAKE_HEXAHEDRON, which generates a parameterized hexahedron:

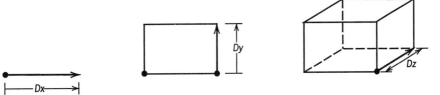

Figure 26.8. Sweep-generated line segments, polygons, and solids are parametrically variant shapes.

```
procedure make_hexahedron (l,w,h : real; var s : sptr);
{Make a hexahedron whose length is l, width is w, and height is
 h. Return pointer to the new shape.}

var f_top : pptr;
    e,enew : eptr;
    g      : gptr;
    v1,v2  : vptr;
    pnt    : array [1..8] of point;
    i      : 1..8;

begin
  {initialize geometry}
  for i := 1 to 8 do
  begin
    case i of
      1,2,5,6 : pnt[i,x] := 0;
      3,4,7,8 : pnt[i,x] := l
    end;
    case i of
      1,4,5,8 : pnt[i,y] := 0;
      2,3,6,7 : pnt[i,y] := w
    end;
    case i of
      1,2,3,4 : pnt[i,z] := 0;
      5,6,7,8 : pnt[i,z] := h
    end
  end;

  create_solid (s);
```

```
{make base face}
e := s^.elist;
e^.eseg[1]^.gvert^.form := pnt[1];
for i := 2 to 4 do
  begin
    split_edge (e,enew, v1,v2);
    v2^.form := pnt[i];
    e := enew
  end;

{extrude}
extrude_base (s^.plist, f_top);
g := f_top^.glist;
for i := 5 to 8 do
  begin
    g^.gvert^.form := pnt[i];
    g := g^.gnext
  end;

  {assign geometry to all segments}
  e := s^.elist;
  while e <> nil do
    begin
      place_segment (e^.eseg[1]);
      place_segment (e^.eseg[2]);
      e := e^.enext
    end
end; {make_hexahedron procedure}
```

This procedure produces a shape with six faces, where opposite faces are parallel to each other and where adjacent faces are orthogonal to each other. Its dimensions are determined by the parameters L, W, and H. However, once created, this shape looses its parameterization: it is not possible to elongate it by specifying a different value for L, W, or H.

Stored Parameterization

To facilitate parametric manipulation of existing shapes, the parameters must be stored. That is, there must be some means to identify and access a certain set of vertices, which is similar to the means for identifying and accessing features. In fact, the only difference between parameters and features is in their purposes: Features are a generalized means of identifying and accessing related shape information, and parameters are specific means for identifying and accessing geometrical attributes. Their specialization allows the implementation of parameters to be simpler than the implementation of features. To store the parameters of the hexahedron, for example, we could employ the following data structure, in which a set of vertices is stored together with the parametric value that relates them to each other.

```
const vert_max = 100;

type prptr      = ^parameter;
     parameter = record
                    name    : char;
                    value   : real;
                    coord   : coords; {x, y, or z}
                    vmax    : 0..vert_max;
                    vlist   : array [1..vert_max] of vptr;
                    prnext  : prptr
                 end;
```

The length, width, and height parameters of the hexahedron could be stored in the following (stylized) manner:

name = L0	name = L1
value = 0	value = l
coord = x	coord = x
vlist[1] = ↑v1	vlist[1] = ↑v3
vlist[2] = ↑v2	vlist[2] = ↑v4
vlist[3] = ↑v5	vlist[3] = ↑v7
vlist[4] = ↑v6	vlist[4] = ↑v8
prnext = L1	prnext = W0
name = W0	name = W1
value = 0	value = w
coord = y	coord = y
vlist[1] = ↑v1	vlist[1] = ↑v2
vlist[2] = ↑v4	vlist[2] = ↑v3
vlist[3] = ↑v5	vlist[3] = ↑v6
vlist[4] = ↑v8	vlist[4] = ↑v7
prnext = W1	prnext = H0
name = H0	name = H1
value = 0	value = h
coord = z	coord = z
vlist[1] = ↑v1	vlist[1] = ↑v5
vlist[2] = ↑v2	vlist[2] = ↑v6
vlist[3] = ↑v3	vlist[3] = ↑v7
vlist[4] = ↑v4	vlist[4] = ↑v8
prnext = H1	prnext = NIL

After it has been set up, this parameterization can be applied to the parameterized shape using procedure **APPLY_PARAMETERS**.

```
procedure apply-parameters (s : sptr; prlist : prptr);
{Apply the parameters stored in prlist to the vertices and
 segments of shape s.}

var pr : prptr;
    i  : 1..vert_max;
    e  : eptr;

begin
  pr := prlist;
  while pr <> nil do
    begin
      for i := 1 to pr^.vmax do
        pr^.vlist[i]^.form[pr^.coord] := pr^.value;
      pr := pr^.prnext
    end;

  {update the geometry of all segments}
  e := s^.elist;
  while e <> nil do
    begin
      place_segment (e^.eseg[1]);
      place_segment (e^.eseg[2]);
      e := e^.enext
    end
end; {apply_parameters procedure}
```

Stored parameterization is more flexible than predefined, functional parameterization, because it preserves the parameterization throughout the "life" of the shape. Its implementation requires, however, an appropriate data structure and a full set of operators to create, modify, and delete parameters, as well as operators that apply them to the vertices they reference.

☐ PARAMETERIZATION OF ASSEMBLIES

Although much more complicated, the parameterization of assemblies shares the same goals as the parameterization of individual shapes, and hence it can be implemented in a similar manner. Parameterized assemblies of shapes are either:

1. Topologically invariant (where topology is used metaphorically to denote the number and relationships of the shapes that comprise the assembly)
2. Topologically variant (which is the more prevalent form and the more difficult to implement of the two)

Topologically invariant parameterized assemblies are typically closed systems, such as window frames and structural frames, as depicted in Figure 26.9. They are characterized by a set of shapes that always come as a set and comprise a particular object that may take different sizes.

Parameterization of such assemblies requires definition of the parameters that control the global appearance of the object while maintaining its internal consistency. For example, modifying the size of the window frame which is depicted in Figure 26.9 does not change the width of its members nor the connectivity of the different components. Topologically invariant assemblies can be constructed functionally through procedures that predefine the assembly. The functional construction method is effective for well-defined objects, such as walls and windows, but does not lend itself to constructing customized assemblies or their parametric modification once constructed.

Topologically variant parameterized assemblies, on the other hand, are open systems that can be constructed *by the user* rather than by the programmer. They are a product of the design process itself, evolving and changing with it. Examples of topologically variant parameterized assemblies include abutting walls, assemblies of electrical wiring or piping systems, and staircases. In such cases it is not possible to predefine all the relationships between the constituent shapes. Rather, both the number of shapes and the relationships between them are consequences of the design process itself. It is the *user*, therefore, who must make such associations *dynamically* and possibly modify them as the design evolves. The user must be provided, therefore, with tools to create, modify, and delete associations.

Topologically variant parameterization of assemblies is similar, in some re-

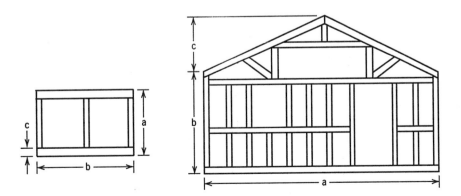

Figure 26.9. Topologically invariant parameterized assemblies.

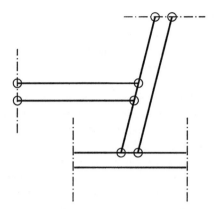

Figure 26.10. Dynamic parameterization of an architectural floor plan by computing the intersection of walls with other walls.

spects, to the association of shapes in locational hierarchies, where shapes are located in relation to other shapes. The main difference is in that locational hierarchies relate whole shapes, whereas parameterized assemblies are able to relate *parts* of shapes.

A limited solution to the problem of dynamically associating parts of an assembly was proposed by Yaski for architectural purposes. In his model, each wall is bounded at both its ends by another wall or by a "virtual wall" (which is a line that intersects the wall). The end of the wall is calculated as an intersection between the lines of one wall with the other, as shown in Figure 26.10.

A more general approach would be to allow the user to define sets of related vertices, which could be implemented by using the method discussed earlier for the stored parameterization of individual shapes, as depicted in Figure 26.11. It shows the parametric relationships between a column and three walls. The relocation of column C to the right will cause elongation of wall $W1$, shrinkage of wall $W2$, and relocation of wall $W3$, by updating the geometric values associated with their respective vertices.

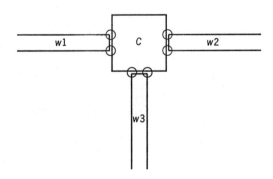

Figure 26.11. Stored parameterization of assemblies.

Features and parameterization extend the notion of association and grouping over parts of shapes, as well as whole shapes, and complete our discussion of this subject. It should be noted that instancing, which was discussed in Chapter 23, may conflict with parameterization. Parameterization can be construed as "customization" of shapes, while instancing is based on the notion of uniformity— the ability to replicate one shape without exceptions. Consider, for example, instancing walls to form an architectural floor plan. While all the walls of a certain kind could be regarded as instances of some master wall, all their lengths will be different. Methods for reconciling parameterization with instancing, without simply ignoring either one, are yet to be developed.

☐ BIBLIOGRAPHY

Yaski, Y., "A Consistent Database for an Integrated CAAD System: Fundamentals for an Automated Design Assistant," Ph.D. Dissertation, Carnegie-Mellon University, May 1981.

27

EXERCISE 4: OBJECT MODELING

In this part of the book we have discussed methods for associating shapes with nonshape attributes, thereby forming *objects*. We have also discussed methods for associating objects with other objects in *inheritance hierarchies* and with *instances*.

Your first task in this exercise is to design and implement an abstract data type called OBJECT. It includes shape and nonshape attributes and supports generalization hierarchies for the purpose of inheriting attributes from more general object classes. Objects should be identifiable by name. The operations that are needed to support objects and attributes are:

1. Creation of new a new object, which is a specialized subclass of a more general object class
2. Deletion of an object (along with its subclasses)
3. Creation of new attributes
4. Addition/removal of attributes of an object class

Your second task is to implement an abstract data type called INSTANCE. An instance references a master object and is part of a locational hierarchy of the type discussed in Part Three. In fact, you should use the code developed for Exercise 3 as you complete the current one. The operations that are needed to support instancing include the following:

1. Creation/deletion of an instance of a given object
2. Placement and relocation of an instance in the locational hierarchy of the assembly
3. Together with the object operators, separation of an instance from its current master object by creating a new master and assigning the instance to it.

PART FIVE

INTERFACE

28

DISPLAY

The interface allows users to visualize and manipulate the model stored in the system's database. Each user interface operation involves the selection of the *operant* to which some operation should be applied (e.g., a specific object, solid, polygon, segment, or vertex), the specification of the *action* itself (e.g., addition or removal of segments or holes), and the provision of the *data* needed to complete the operation (e.g., indication of the location where a new vertex should be placed).

The information conveyed by these components could be provided in any order. Depending on the nature of the operation, some of the components may not be needed at all. Such information could be provided *graphically*, by indicating the desired location on the screen, or *alphanumerically*, by typing a pair of $<x, y>$ coordinate values. Furthermore, alphanumeric input could be *absolute*, as in typing the desired coordinate values, or it could be *relative*, in which case a *direction* and a *magnitude* must be provided.

The design of user interfaces involves a host of functional, ergonomic, and psychological issues, which cannot be elaborated upon in this book. Here we shall concentrate on *functional* characteristics alone, providing only the means to graphically display and pick shapes and their components, and graphically indicate the desired actions and data that should be applied to them.

□ USER INTERFACE OPERATORS

The operators that allow users to manipulate shapes and their components can be classified in two groups:

1. Operators that allow the user to *display* the shapes and visualize the results of actions applied to them. These operators also facilitate the selection of operandi by operators of the second group by visually confirming the system's recognition of elements picked by the user.

323

2. Operators that allow the user to *pick* a shape or one of its components, to which some modeling operation can then be applied.

These operators can be combined in many ways, allowing the user to *make* new shapes, to *modify* them by adding and deleting components or relocating them, and to *kill* (delete) shapes and their components. They also provide the necessary interface to *add* and *remove* elements in assembly structures and to *place* them in space.

All user interface operators are based on some means of communicating between the user and the computer, which includes the ability to indicate screen locations by registering the cursor's location. The nature of such means differs widely between various implementations and depends, to a large degree, on particular hardware characteristics. Here we shall use a simple menu-driven graphical approach, where the user can choose desired actions and operandi from a menu that is displayed on the screen. A generic technique for selecting options from a menu and for picking operandi on the screen is presented in Appendix C. The user interface operators that require point input and the selection of menu options are based on that discussion.

□ DISPLAY OPERATORS

Display operators fulfill two important user interface functions:

1. They allow the user to *visualize* the shapes as they are created and manipulated.
2. They provide visual *confirmation* to the picking operations of vertices, segments, polygons, and solids.

Both functions are carried out by traversing the data structure and directing the computer to trace the traversal graphically on the screen. In this book we shall use for this purpose the tools developed in the first volume in this book series.† These tools include display drivers that facilitate the tracing of lines on the screen of a graphics workstation, by means of procedures MOVE_TO and DRAW_TO:

```
procedure move_to (x,y : integer); {external}
procedure draw_to (x,y : integer); {external}
```

†Y. E. Kalay, *Graphic Introduction to Programming* Wiley, New York, 1987

These procedures are used in this context by procedure SHOW_LINE, which displays a line segment connecting two given points.

```
procedure show_line (pnt1, pnt2 : point);
{Display line connecting pnt1 and pnt2 on the screen.}

begin
  move_to (pnt1[x], pnt1[y]);
  draw_to (pnt2[x], pnt2[y])
end; {show_line procedure}
```

Displaying the shape information that is stored in the model's three-dimensional database on the screen of a graphics workstation, nevertheless, involves more than just traversing the data structure and showing it on the screen. Rather, it involves a process of *mapping* between two different frames of reference: the three-dimensional frame of reference where the shapes are stored, which we shall refer to as the "world," and the two-dimensional frame of reference of the screen, where the shapes are displayed. Furthermore, the entire world cannot be displayed on the screen without considerable reduction of scale. Thus, the display of shape information entails at least a change of scale, but often also a projection that reduces the three-dimensional shape information into two-dimensional graphical information. This mapping from the world to the screen is accomplished by means of *windows* and *views*.

Windows and Views

A *window* is the area on the screen in which the information is displayed. It may encompass the entire screen or only a part of it. Furthermore, it is possible to display information simultaneously in multiple windows, which may partially or completely overlap.

A *view* is the content of a window. It represents the transformed and projected portion of the world which is visible through the given window. If multiple windows are displayed simultaneously, each one is associated with a particular view, as depicted in Figure 28.1.

Windows are represented by rectangles on the screen and by a particular record that contains the information pertinent to their manipulation. Views, on the other hand, are more abstract concepts: although they correspond to rectangular, volumetric boxes in the world, they are more often represented by the transforms that map their content to the window. As such, only one record is needed to store both the window and the view associated with it:

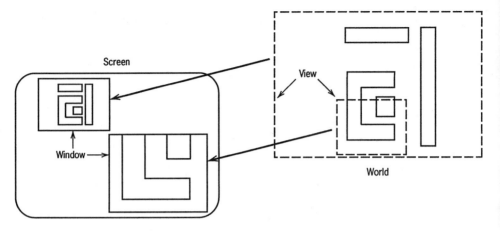

Figure 28.1. The concept of windows and views.

```
type view_type = (top,right,left,front,back,axon,persp);
     wptr      = ^window;
     window    = record
                    w_min,w_max      : point; {location of window
                                                on the screen}
                    view_kind        : view_type;
                    world_to_screen,
                    screen_to_world  : matrix; {transforms}
                    wnext            : wptr
                 end;
```

Like all data structure entities, windows are associated with operators that create, delete, and modify them. The creation of a window entails specifying its location on the screen (w_min, w_max), the kind of view seen through it (top, right, left, front, back, or perspective),† and its relationship to a view (the transforms from world to screen and from screen to world). These transforms, which are inverses to each other, are the essence of the window-view concept. They prescribe how the shape information in the world appears on the screen and where the locations indicated by the user on the screen are in the world. The transformations themselves are carried out by procedures like SCREEN_ TO_WORLD and WORLD_TO_SCREEN, which use the same operators that were discussed in Chapter 18 for the relocation of shapes.

---

†These views can be extended to include projections that are not parallel to the major planes of the coordinate system.

```
procedure screen_to_world (var ps,pw : point; w : wptr);
{Transform screen point ps to its corresponding world location
 pw through window w.}

begin
  transform (ps, w^.screen_to_world, pw)
end; {screen_to_world procedure}

procedure world_to_screen (var pw,ps : point; w : wptr);
{Transform world point pw to its corresponding screen location
 ps through window w.}

begin
  transform (pw, w^.world_to_screen, ps)
end; {world_to_screen procedure}
```

Before we discuss how to set up and control these transforms, we must first deal with an issue that is a by-product of the window-view concept: the problem of clipping.

Clipping

When a line segment is mapped from the world to a particular window on the screen, it may not show in its entirety: parts of the line segment may be mapped to areas of the screen that are outside the window. For that matter, it is possible that none of the line segment will show. The parts of the line that do not show in the window must be trimmed, or *clipped*, as depicted in Figure 28.2.

Given that we map a particular *view* onto a particular *window*, and that the entire content of a view appears in the window, line segments can be clipped either against the boundary of the window or against the boundary of the view. The difference between the two methods is in whether the line segments are first transformed from the world to the screen and are then clipped (against the win-

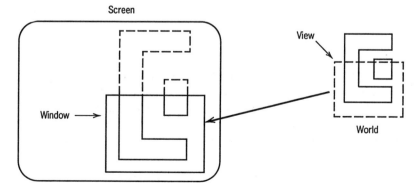

Figure 28.2. Clipping line segments to the boundary of a window.

dow), or whether they are first clipped (against the view) and then transformed from the world to the screen. The two methods are logically equivalent. However, apart from the fact that we chose not to explicitly represent the boundaries of the view in the world, the transformation of line segments before they are clipped against the window is preferred for two reasons:

1. It allows us to treat three-dimensional line segments in the same manner as two dimensional lines: the three dimensional lines will become two-dimensional after the projection transformation and before they are clipped.
2. Because of numerical imprecisions, this method is more accurate than the other. Errors due to clipping are not amplified by the mapping transformation.

The disadvantages of transforming before clipping are that some of the line segments that have been transformed from the world to the screen will be clipped away, thereby wasting the effort invested in their transformation. The performance of fore and back-plane clipping must be treated separately.

Clipping is a well-known problem that has been solved in many different ways by computer graphics researchers. Because the focus of this book is modeling rather than graphics, we shall demonstrate here only one clipping algorithm, by Liang and Barsky[†]. The reader is referred to the readings recommended at the end of this chapter for a more comprehensive discussion of the subject.

The Liang and Barsky clipping algorithm is based on representing line segments parametrically, in the following form:

$$x = x1 + (x2 - x1) \cdot u \qquad u = 0 \cdots 1$$
$$y = y1 + (y2 - y1) \cdot u$$

or

$$x = x1 + Dx \cdot u \qquad u = 0 \cdots 1$$
$$y = y1 + Dy \cdot u, \qquad\qquad (28.1)$$

where $<x1, y1>$ and $<x2, y2>$ are the end points of the line segment, and u is a parameter whose value is 0 at $<x1, y1>$ and 1 at $<x2, y2>$. Each point $<x, y>$ on the line segment thus corresponds to a particular value of u between 0 and 1.

Every point $<x, y>$ of the line segment which is inside the boundary

[†]See D. Hearn and M. P. Baker, *Computer Graphics*, Prentice-Hall, Inc., Englewood Cliffs, NJ, 1986.

of a window defined by the coordinates $<w\_min[x], w\_min[y]>$ and $<w\_max[x], w\_max[y]>$ must satisfy the following inequalities:

$$w\_min[x] \leq x \leq w\_max[x]$$
$$w\_min[y] \leq y \leq w\_max[y]. \qquad (28.2)$$

When the equations of (28.1) are combined with inequalities (28.2) we get:

$$w\_min[x] \leq x1 + Dx \cdot u \leq w\_max[x]$$
$$w\_min[y] \leq y1 + Dy \cdot u \leq w\_max[y]. \qquad (28.3)$$

These inequalities can be expanded into four inequalities of the form:

$$p_i \cdot u \leq q_i,$$

where $i = 1, 2, 3, 4$ correspond to the left, right, bottom, and top boundaries of the window, respectively, and where

$$p_1 = -Dx \qquad q_1 = x1 - w\_min[x]$$
$$p_2 = Dx \qquad q_2 = w\_max[x] - x1$$
$$p_3 = -Dy \qquad q_3 = y1 - w\_min[y]$$
$$p_4 = Dy \qquad q_4 = w\_max[y] - y1$$

Line segments that are parallel to the boundaries of the window have $p_i = 0$ (i.e., their Dx or Dy are 0). Such lines pass through the window only if their corresponding $q_i \geq 0$, otherwise they do not pass through the window at all and can be rejected from further consideration. Line segments whose p_i is nonzero intersect the extended boundaries of the window that corresponds to i at a point defined by the value of the parameter u:

$$u = q_i / p_i$$

Thus, we can calculate the points (defined by two parameters $u1$ and $u2$) where line segments intersect the extended boundaries of the window. If $u1 > u2$, the line segment intersects the extended boundaries outside the window itself and can be rejected.

In procedure CLIP_LINE, the values of $u1$ and $u2$ are initialized to 0 and 1, respectively. The corresponding values of p and q are calculated for each window boundary and are used to determine if the line segment can be rejected or if the values of $u1$ and $u2$ must be adjusted.

```
function clip_line (var pnt1, pnt2 : point; w : wptr) : boolean;
{Liang and Barsky line clipper: given two points pnt1 and pnt2
 in screen coordinates, return line clipped to the boundaries
 of window w. Return true if any part of the line shows in the
 window.}


var  u1,u2, dx,dy : real;

  function clip_test (p,q : real; var u1,u2 : real) : boolean;
  {Test if the line segment can be rejected, or adjust the
   values of the parameters u1 and u2.}


  var  r : real;


  begin
   if p <> 0 then r := q/p;
   if p < 0
     then if r > u2
             then clip_test := false
             else if r > u1 then u1 := r
       else if p > 0
             then if r < u1
                     then clip_test := false
                     else if r < u2 then u2 := r
             else if q < 0 then clip_test := false
  end; {clip_test function}


begin {clip_line}
 u1 := 0; u2 := 1;
 dx := pnt2[x] - pnt1[x]; dy := pnt2[y] - pnt1[y];
 if clip_test (-dx, pnt1[x] - w^.w_min[x], u1, u2) and
    clip_test ( dx, w^.w_max[x] - pnt1[x], u1, u2) and
    clip_test (-dy, pnt1[y] - w^.w_min[y], u1, u2) and
    clip_test ( dy, w^.w_max[y] - pnt1[y], u1, u2)
   then begin
         if u1 > 0
            then begin
              pnt1[x] := pnt1[x] + u1*dx;
              pnt1[y] := pnt1[y] + u1*dy
            end;
```

```
        if u2 < 1
            then begin
                pnt2[x] := pnt1[x] + u2*dx;
                pnt2[y] := pnt1[y] + u2*dy
            end;
            clip_line := true
        end
    else clip_line := false
end; {clip_line function}
```

☐ VIEW TRANSFORMATIONS

A window-view pair is set up by specifying a rectangle on the screen, which defines the boundary of the window, and by specifying the particular projection that will be used by that window in transforming world entities to the screen. These two factors—the boundary and the type of view—are used to construct the *world-to-screen* and the *screen-to-world* transforms themselves. Initially, the view in a newly created window is centered on the origin of the world. This can be changed through *panning*, as depicted in Figure 28.3a. Moreover, the ratio of scales between the window and the view is initially set to one. However, this scale can be modified by *zooming*, as depicted in Figure 28.3b. The view can be one of the predefined types (top, right, left, front, back, axonometric, or perspective) or any other type of projection that is supported by the system. These operations are listed here in procedures CREATE_VIEW, PAN, and ZOOM.

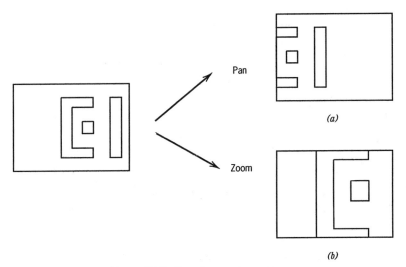

Figure 28.3. Panning and zooming.

```
procedure create_view (w : wptr; view : view_type);
{Determine world-to-screen and screen-to-world transform
 matrices of the view in window w, of the specified type.}

var  o,c : point;

begin
  with w^ do
    begin
      init_matrix (world_to_screen);
      init_matrix (screen_to_world);
      dx := (w_max[x] + w_min[x])/2;
      dy := (w_max[y] + w_min[y])/2;

      case view of
        top   : begin
                    translate (world_to_screen, dx, dy, 0);
                    translate (screen_to_world, -dx,-dy, 0);
                 end;
        right : begin
                   rotate (world_to_screen, x, 90);
                   rotate (world_to_screen, y, 90);

                   translate (world_to_screen, dx, dy, 0);
                   translate (screen_to_world, -dx,-dy, 0);

                   rotate (screen_to_world, y, -90);
                   rotate (screen_to_world, x, -90)
                 end;
        left  : begin .. end;
        front : begin .. end;
        back  : begin .. end;
        axon  : begin .. end;
        persp : begin .. end
      end {case}
  end; {with}

  w^.view_kind := view
end; {create_view procedure}

procedure pan (w : wptr; dx,dy,dz : integer);
{Translate the transforms in window w by dx, dy and dz.}

begin
  translate (w^.world_to_screen, dx, dy, dz);
  translate (w^.screen_to_world,-dx,-dy,-dz)
end; {pan procedure}
```

```
procedure zoom (w : wptr; factor : real);
{Scale the transforms in window w by factor, without
 translation.}

var  midw, midv : point;

begin
  {determine center of view from center of window}
  for ax := x to w do
     midw[ax] := (w^.w_min[ax] + w^.w_max[ax])/2;
  screen_to_world (midw, midv, w);

  {translate center of view to world origin}
  translate  (w^.world_to_screen,-midw[x],-midw[y],-midw[z]);
  translate (w^.screen_to_world,-midv[x], -midv[y],-midv[z]);

  {scale view by factor}
  scale (w^.world_to_screen, factor, factor, factor);
  scale (w^.screen_to_world, 1/factor, 1/factor, 1/factor);

  {translate view back}
  translate (w^.world_to_screen, midw[x], midw[y], midw[z]);
  translate (w^.screen_to_world, midv[x], midv[y], midv[z])
end; {zoom procedure}
```

☐ DISPLAYING VERTICES, SEGMENTS, POLYGONS, AND SOLIDS

Procedure SHOW_LINE, which was mentioned earlier in this chapter, is the basis for displaying vertices, segments, polygons, and solids. It must, however, be combined with the transformation and clipping operators to produce line segments that show in particular windows. This combination is achieved through procedure DISPLAY_LINE.

```
procedure display_line (pnt1,pnt2 : point; w : wptr);
{Transform the line connecting pnt1 and pnt2 from world to
 screen coordinates, then clip it to the boundaries of window
 w and display it.}

var  new1,new2 : point;

begin
  world_to_screen (pnt1, new1, w);
  world_to_screen (pnt2, new2, w);
  if clip_line (new1, new2, w) then show_line (new1, new2)
end; {display_line procedure}
```

A vertex, which is only a point, can be displayed by showing a cross centered on it. The lines that comprise the cross are subject to clipping themselves, as shown in procedure DISPLAY_CROSS.

```
procedure display_cross (pnt : point; w : wptr);
{Draw a cross centered at point pnt.}

const size = 3; {arbitrary half-size of cross}

var  n,n1,n2,n3,n4 : point;

begin
  world_to_screen (pnt, n, w);
  n1[x] := n[x] - size; n1[y] := n[y] - size;
  n2[x] := n[x] + size; n2[y] := n[y] + size;
  n3[x] := n[x] - size; n3[y] := n[y] + size;
  n4[x] := n[x] + size; n4[y] := n[y] - size;
  if clip_line (n1, n2, w) then show_line (n1,n2);
  if clip_line (n3, n4, w) then show_line (n1,n2)
end; {display_cross procedure}
```

The display of segments, polygons, and solids follow similar principles. Their display can also be used to ERASE vertices, segments, polygons, and solids by changing the color used in the process of their display from *normal* (typically white) to the *erasure* color (typically black) or to the *mark* color (typically red) for their highlighting, as discussed in Chapter 30.

```
procedure display_segment (g : gptr; w : wptr);
{Show line connecting the two vertices bounding segment g in
 window w.}

var  v1,v2 : vptr;

begin
  v1 := g^.gvert; v2 := other_vertex (g);
  display_line (v1^.form, v2^.form, w)
end; {display_segment procedure}
```

```
procedure display_polygon (p : pptr; w : wptr);
{Display all segments of polygon p in window w, recursively.}

var  g : gptr;

begin
  if p <> nil
    then begin
      {display polygon p}
      g := p^.glist;
      repeat
        display_segment (g, w);
        g := g^.gnext
      until g = p^.glist;

      {display all holes in p}
      if not p^.hole
        then display_polygon (p^.child, w)
        else display_polygon (p^.pnext, w)
    end
end; {display_polygon procedure}

procedure display_solid (s : sptr; w : wptr);
{Display all edges of solid s in window w, recursively.}

var  e : eptr;

begin
  if s <> nil
    then begin
      {display solid s}
      e := s^.elist;
      repeat
        display_segment (e^.eseg[1]);
        e := e^.enext
      until e = nil;

      {display all cavities in s}
      if not s^.cavity
        then display_solid (s^.child, w)
        else display_solid (s^.pnext, w)
    end
end; {display_solid procedure}
```

All the elements that are visible in a particular window can be displayed by calling procedures DISPLAY _ POLYGON and DISPLAY _ SOLID for each of the database elements, with the same window parameter, as shown in procedure DISPLAY _ VIEW.

```
procedure display_view (w : wptr);
{Display all database solids and polygons in window w.}

var  s : sptr;
     p : pptr;

begin
  s := solid_list; {global list of all solids}
  while s <> nil do
    begin
      display_solid (s, w);
      s := snext
    end;

  p := polygon_list; {global list of all polygons}
  while p <> nil do
    begin
      display_polygon (p, w);
      p := pnext
    end
end; {display_view procedure}
```

☐ BIBLIOGRAPHY

Foley, J. D., and A. van Dam, *Fundamentals of Interactive Computer Graphics,* Addison-Wesley, Reading, MA, 1982.

Hearn, D., and M. P. Baker, *Computer Graphics*, Prentice-Hall Inc., Englewood Cliffs, NJ, 1986.

Lane, J. M., L. C. Carpenter, T. Whitted, and J. F. Blinn, "Scan Line Methods for Displaying Parametrically Defined Surfaces," *Communications of the ACM* 23(1):23–34, January 1980.

Phong, B. T., "Illumination for Computer Generated Pictures," *Communications of the ACM*, 18(6):311–317, June 1975.

Sutherland, I., W. Sproull, and M. Schumacker, "A Characterization of Ten Hidden Surface Algorithms," *Computing Surveys*, 6(1), March 1974.

Warnock, J. E., "A Hidden Surface Algorithm for Computer Generated Halftone Pictures," technical report, Department of Computer Science, University of Utah, Salt Lake City, 1969.

29

DISPLAY LISTS

The considerable effort needed to display a view must be re-invested every time the view is displayed. In particular, this effort is noticeable when a large number of shapes, or one complex shape, is redisplayed in order to change its color. Such change in color confirms that the shape has been identified by the system, and some modeling operation can be applied to it. Much computational effort could be saved if the transformed and clipped images of the shapes that are visible in a particular window were stored (in addition to their storage in the world). The data structure that stores such images is known as the *display list*.

The display list is a relatively simple, two-dimensional data structure that captures the transformed and clipped images of the shapes that are produced by the DISPLAY procedures and that acts as a buffer between the world and the screen. To use a display list, the output of the DISPLAY procedures that were presented in Chapter 28 must be redirected into the display list rather than into the screen. The content of the display list is subsequently drawn on the screen. This buffering slows down the initial display of the shapes, but considerably speeds up their redisplay. As we shall see in Chapter 30, it also facilitates the picking of shapes. Obviously, when the list of shapes that are visible through the window changes because of panning, zooming, or modifying the shapes themselves, the display list must be updated. Furthermore, its compatibility and consistency with the world data structure must be strictly maintained. This chapter discusses the concept of display lists and their possible implementation.

☐ REPRESENTING DISPLAY LISTS

The display list stores transformed and clipped images of polygons and solids as they appear in a particular window; therefore, it is specific to that window. In fact, the display list can be stored as part of the window's definition. This can be done by adding, to the window record introduced in Chapter 28, pointers to its particular display lists:

```
window = record
           w_min,w_max : point;
           view_kind : view_type;
           world_to_screen,
           screen_to_world : matrix;
           dp_list : dpptr; {polygon display list}
           ds_list : dsptr; {solid display list}
           wnext : wptr
         end;
```

where DPPTR and DSPTR are pointers to the polygons and solids display lists, respectively. (Both lists are initialized to nil when a window is created.) The display lists themselves are made of two-dimensional elements that store the transformed and clipped images of segments, as well as pointers to the world entities (segments, polygons, edges, and solids) from which they were generated:

```
dgptr           = ^d_list_segment;
dpptr           = ^d_list_polygon;
dsptr           = ^d_list_solid;

d_list_segment = record
                   pnt                 : array [1..2] of point;
                   dgnext              : dgptr;
                   case seg_of_poly    : boolean of
                     true    : (dpoly  : dpptr;       {screen}
                                seg     : gptr);       {world}
                     false   : (dsolid : dsptr;       {screen}
                                edg     : eptr)        {world}
                 end;

d_list_polygon = record
                   poly    : pptr;  {world}
                   dseg    : dgptr; {screen}
                   dpnext  : dpptr
                 end;

d_list_solid   = record
                   sld     : sptr;  {world}
                   dseg    : dgptr; {screen}
                   dsnext  : dsptr
                 end;
```

The display list segment record (D_LIST_SEGMENT) contains the actual two-dimensional information for depicting the transformed and clipped image of a world segment. This information is stored as two points. In addition, it stores points to the display list polygon (DPOLY) or display list solid (DSOLID) to which the display segment belongs and to the world segment or edge, which it depicts. These pointers are used in picking segments, polygons, and solids, as discussed in Chapter 30.

☐ CREATING DISPLAY LISTS

The display lists are built by the modified display procedures that were discussed in Chapter 28. These operators still transform and clip their argument shapes, but instead of sending the resulting output to the screen, they store it in the appropriate display list records.

```
procedure display_segment (g : gptr; w : wptr;
                           d_poly : dpptr; d_solid : dsptr);
{Transform, clip, and add the line connecting the two vertices
 bounding segment g to the display polygon d_poly or the display
 solid d_solid in window w, whichever is not nil}

var  v1,v2      : vptr;
     pnt1,pnt2 : point;
     dg         : dgptr;

begin
  v1 := g^.gvert; v2 := other_vertex (g);
  world_to_screen (v1^.form, pnt1, w);
  world_to_screen (v2^.form, pnt2, w);
  if clip_line (pnt1, pnt2, w)
    then begin
      new (dg);

      with dg^ do
        begin
          pnt[1] := pnt1; pnt[2] := pnt2;
          if d_poly <> nil
            then begin
              seg_of_poly := true;
              seg := g; dpoly := d_poly;
              dgnext := w^.d_poly;
              w^.d_poly := dg
            end
            else begin
              seg_of_poly := false;
              edg := g^.gedge; dsolid := d_solid;
              dgnext := w^.d_solid;
              w^.d_solid := dg
            end
        end
    end
end; {display_segment procedure}
```

```
procedure display_polygon (p : pptr; w : wptr);
{Transform, clip, and add all the segments of polygon p to the
 polygon display list of window w.}

var  dp : dpptr;

  procedure display_all_segments (glist : gptr);

  var  g : gptr;

  begin
    g := glist;
    repeat
      display_segment (g, w, dp, {ds =} nil);
      g := g^.gnext
    until g = glist
  end; {display_all_segments procedure}

begin
  if p <> nil
    then begin
      new (dp);
      dp := w^.dp_list;
      w^.dp_list := dp;
      dp^.poly := p;

      display_all_segments (p^.glist);
      if not p^.hole
        then display_polygon (p^.child, w)
        else display_polygon (p^.pnext, w)
    end
end; {display_polygon procedure}

procedure display_solid (s : sptr; w : wptr);
{Transform, clip, and add all the edges of solid s to the solids
 display list in window w.}

  procedure display_all_edges (elist : eptr);

  var  e : eptr;

  begin
    e := s^.elist;
    repeat
      display_segment (e^.eseg[1], w, {dp =} nil, ds);
      e := e^.enext
    until e = nil
  end; {display_all_edges procedure}
```

```
begin
  if s <> nil
    then begin
      new (ds);
      ds := w^.ds_list;
      w^.ds_list := ds;
      ds^.sld := s;

      display_all_edges (s^.elist);
      if not s^.cavity
        then display_solid (s^.child, w)
        else display_solid (s^.snext, w)
    end
end; {display_solid procedure}
```

As can be readily seen from the display procedures, the intricate structure of polygons and solids as they are represented in the world is not maintained in the display lists. Even the identification of holes and cavities is abandoned. This is due to the purpose of the display lists, which is to store two-dimensional images for display only, rather than for the manipulation of the shapes. For this purpose the much simplified structure suffices.

□ SHOWING DISPLAY LISTS

The actual display of segments stored in the display lists is a simple matter of traversing the lists and applying procedure SHOW_LINE to the lines they store. Display, however, can take different forms: at times, only one or two segments must be displayed, such as in the case when the display is used to confirm the picking of a particular segment or a vertex. At other times, an entire polygon must be displayed or an entire solid. The display procedures must be designed so they allow for such selective display. Each one of the three entities in the display list data structure warrants its own display procedures: segments, polygons, and solids. As we have practiced throughout the book, these procedures will be hierarchically structured, as shown in procedures SHOW_SEGMENT, SHOW_POLYGON, and SHOW_SOLID. In addition, the entire display list of a particular window can be displayed through a procedure that combines all the others.

```
procedure show_segment (dg : dgptr);
{Show display segment dg.}

begin
  show_line (dg^.pnt[1], dg^.pnt[2]);
end; {show_segment procedure}
```

```
procedure show_polygon (dp : dpptr);
{Show display polygon dp.}

var  dg : dgptr;

begin
  dg := dp^.dseg;
  while dg <> nil do
    begin
      show_segment (dg);
      dg := dg^.dgnext
    end
end; {show_polygon procedure}

procedure show_solid (ds : dsptr);
{Show display solid ds.}

var  ds : dsptr;

begin
  dg := ds^.dseg;
  while dg <> nil do
    begin
      show_segment (dg);
      dg := dg^.dgnext
    end
end; {show_solid procedure}

procedure show_display_lists (w : wptr);
{Show display lists of window w.}

var  dp : dpptr;
     ds : dsptr;

begin
  dp := w^.dp_list;
  while dp <> nil do
    begin
      show_polygon (dp);
      dp := dp^.dpnext
    end;

  ds := w^.ds_list;
  while ds <> nil do
    begin
      show_solid (ds);
      ds := ds^.dpnext
    end
end; {show_display_lists procedure}
```

☐ MODIFYING DISPLAY LISTS

A need to modify the display lists arises when the shapes themselves are modified or when the window parameters are changed (i.e., when zooming or panning, when changing window boundaries, and when changing the projection). In the first case, the old shapes must be deleted from the display list, and the new (or modified ones) must be added. In the second and third cases, the entire display list must be regenerated with the new display parameters. Furthermore, because the same world entity may be displayed in multiple windows, the display lists of *all* the windows (regardless of whether they are currently displayed on the screen) must be searched to see if they must be altered.

The removal of a particular shape, given a pointer to the world entity itself, requires search of the display list to find the display entity that was generated from the modified shape. Such searches are implemented here by functions FIND_DISPLAY_SEGMENT, FIND_DISPLAY_POLYGON, and FIND_DISPLAY_SOLID.

```
function find_display_segment (g : gptr;
                                 dg_list : dgptr) : dgptr;
{Search display list dg_list and return pointer to the display
 segment that was generated from world segment g, or nil if no
 such display segment.}

var  dg   : dgptr;
     stop : boolean;

begin
  stop := false;

  dg := dg_list;
  while not stop and (dg <> nil) do
    with dg^ do
      if seg_of_poly
        then if seg = g
               then stop := true else dg := dgnext
        else if (edg^.eseg[1] = g) or (edg^.eseg[2] = g)
               then stop := true else dg := dgnext;

  find_display_segment := dg
end; {find_display_segment function}

function find_display_polygon (p : pptr; w : wptr) : dpptr;
{Search polygon display list of window w and return pointer to
 the display polygon that was generated from world polygon p, or
 nil if no such display polygon.}

var  dp   : dpptr;
     stop : boolean;
```

```
begin
  stop := false;

  dp := w^.dp_list;
  while not stop and (dp <> nil) do
   if dp^.poly = p
     then stop := true else dp := dp^.dpnext;

  find_display_polygon := dp
end; {find_display_polygon function}

function find_display_solid (s : sptr; w : wptr) : dsptr;
{Search solid display list of window w and return pointer to the
 display solid that was generated from world solid p, or nil
 if no such display solid.}

var   ds   : dsptr;
      stop : boolean;

begin
  stop := false;

  ds := w^.ds_list;
  while not stop and (ds <> nil) do
    if ds^.sld = s
      then stop := true else ds := ds^.dsnext;

  find_display_solid := ds
end; {find_display_solid function}
```

When some world entity has been modified, the user interface control module of the program (which governs the creation of display lists as well as other functions of the system) will search all the windows and *remove* the display entities that correspond to that world entity. After the modification of the world entity has been completed, it will be *added* to the display lists of all the windows from which it has been removed (unless it is deleted from the world). This removal and addition of display entities is computationally more expensive than making changes to both display list entities and world entities, if the changes are minor. However, it guarantees that the display list entities always correspond to the world entities that they depict. It also eliminates the need to write a rather large set of operators to manipulate the display list and the need to decide which modifications can be handled by the display list and which cannot.

The display list thus becomes a transient, subservient, and dependent image of the world entities. It facilitates the rapid display and, as discussed in Chapter 30, the picking of the world entities it depicts. The display list does not, and must not, however, constitute a duplicate, redundant data structure of equal status to the world data structure.

30

PICKING

The process of interactive geometric modeling requires indicating particular locations on the screen, which are interpreted as selecting world entities to be modified and the manner of their modification. The fundamental concept associated with such transactions is *picking*.

Picking is a process that matches a particular world entity (solid, edge, polygon, segment, or vertex) with the screen location indicated by the designer, for the purpose of applying to it some design operation. The process involves mapping the screen location indicated by the user to a particular world location, as prescribed by the transforms of the window in which the point has been indicated, and searching the database to find the entity that is within some predefined range of that location. In cases where several entities fall within that range, a sorting process may be applied to identify the entity that is closest to the indicated point. This chapter discusses the concept and possible implementation of picking.

☐ PICKING VERTICES, SEGMENTS, POLYGONS, AND SOLIDS

Picking is an operation whose purpose is to translate the user's directive, expressed as a point registered on the screen of a graphic workstation, into a pointer referencing a particular data entity. For example, it may return a pointer to a vertex, a segment, a polygon, or a solid. This translation is typically implemented by *searching* pertinent parts of the data structure for an entity of the desired type (i.e., a vertex, a segment, a polygon, or a solid) that is *closest* and within some predefined *range* of the point registered by the user.

Given the display list mechanism discussed in Chapter 29, this search can be performed on the display list database, rather than in the world. Searching the display list simplifies picking and makes it more efficient. First, only a small portion of the world is searched—that which is visible through a particular window and, hence, only that which the user can identify graphically. Second, the user-indicated screen location need not be converted into world coordinates, because the search is performed entirely on the screen. Third, picking three-dimensional entities becomes possible: In the display list all the entities are two-dimensional. If there exists some ambiguity concerning which one of several overlapping entities has been picked, the user may also have to pick the desired entity in another window, and the result of both picks will determine the picked world entity.

We shall use two geometric proximity functions, POINT_DISTANCE and LINE_DISTANCE, which were first presented (in a slightly different form) in Chapter 6, to calculate linear distances between two given points and between a point and a line.

```
function point_distance (pnt1,pnt2 : point) : real;
{Return linear distance between points pnt1 and pnt2.}

var  dx,dy : real;

  begin
    dx := pnt1[x] - pnt2[x]; dy := pnt1[y] - pnt2[y];
    point_distance := sqrt(sqr(dx) + sqr(dy))
  end; {point_distance function}

function line_distance (pnt,pnt1,pnt2 : point) : real;
{Return shortest distance between point pnt and the line
 connecting points pnt1 and pnt2.}

var  dx,dy,dist : real;

begin
  dx := pnt2[x] - pnt1[x]; dy := pnt1[y] - pnt2[y];
  dist := sqr(pnt[x]*dy + pnt[y]*dx)/(sqr(dx) + sqr(dy));
  line_distance := sqrt(dist)
end; {line_distance function}
```

In addition, because segments make up bounded regions of lines, searching for the segment that is closest to the point indicated by the user also necessitates ascertaining that the point is within the region bounded by the segment, as depicted in Figure 30.1. Function IN_BOUNDS confirms this assertion. This function uses the global parameter RANGE, which can be set such that the user will not have to actually register a point on the segment itself, which is a rather difficult task. Instead, the user registers a point in the segment's close vicinity.

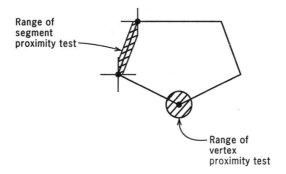

Range of
segment
proximity test

Range of
vertex
proximity test

Figure 30.1. Range of proximity tests for vertices and segments.

```
function in_bounds (pnt, pnt1,pnt2 : point) : boolean;
{Return true if point pnt is within the range of the segment
 connecting points pnt1 and pnt2.}

var  test_positive : array [coords] of boolean;
     ax            : coords;

begin
  for ax := x to y do
    test_positive [ax] :=
        ((pnt[ax] >= pnt1[ax] - range) and
        (pnt[ax] <= pnt2[ax] + range)) or
        ((pnt[ax] >= pnt2[ax] - range) and
        (pnt[ax] <= pnt1[ax] + range));
  in_bounds := test_positive[x] and test_positive[y]
end; {in_bounds function}
```

The search technique employed by the picking operators relies on traversing
the display list of a particular window and comparing the locations of its entities
with the location of the point indicated by the user on the screen. This technique
is implemented by functions PICK_VERTEX, PICK_SEGMENT, PICK_
POLYGON, and PICK_SOLID, which return pointers to the display list entities that were picked. Once a display list entity has been picked, its own pointers
can be used to identify the world entity it depicts.

```
function pick_vertex (dglist : dgptr; pnt : point;
                      var distance : real) : dgptr;
{Return pointer to the display segment in dglist which is
 closest to point pnt, and its distance from pnt. If all
 display segments in dglist are out of range, return nil.}

var  dg  : dgptr;
     dis : real;
```

```
begin
 {initialize search variables}
 pick_vertex := nil; dg := dglist; distance := range;

 while dg <> nil do {search}
   begin
     dis := point_distance (pnt, dg^.pnt[1]);
     if dis < distance
        then begin distance := dis; pick_vertex := dg end;
     dg := dg^.dgnext
   end
end; {pick_vertex function}


function pick_segment (dglist : dgptr; pnt : point;
                       var distance : real) : dgptr;
{Return pointer to the display segment in dglist which is
 closest to point pnt, and its distance from pnt. If all
 display segments in dglist are out of range, return nil.}


var  dg  : dgptr;
     dis : real;


begin
 {initialize search variables}
 pick_segment := nil; dg := dglist; distance := range;

 while dg <> nil do {search}
   begin
     dis := line_distance (pnt, dg^.pnt[1], dg^.pnt[2]);
     if (dis < distance) and
     in_bounds (pnt, dg^.pnt[1], dg^.pnt[2])
       then begin distance := dis; pick_segment := dg end;
     dg := dg^.dgnext
   end
end; {pick_segment function}


function pick_polygon (pnt : point; w : wptr) : dpptr;
{Return pointer to the display polygon in window w, one of whose
 segments is closest to point pnt. If all display polygons
 are out of range, return nil.}


var  dg             : dgptr;
     dp             : dpptr;
     dis, distance  : real;
```

```
begin
 {initialize search variables}
 pick_polygon := nil; dp := w^.dp_list; distance := range;

 while dp <> nil do {search}
   begin
     dg := pick_segment (dp^.dseg, pnt, dis);
     if dis < distance
       then begin distance := dis; pick_polygon := dp end;
     dp := dp^.dpnext
   end
end; {pick_polygon function}

function pick_solid (pnt : point; w : wptr) : dsptr;
{Return pointer to display solid in window w, one of whose
 segments is closest to point pnt. If all solids are out of
 range, return nil.}

var  dg            : dgptr;
     ds            : dsptr;
     dis, distance : real;

begin
 {initialize search variables}
 pick_solid := nil; ds := w^.ds_list; distance := range;

 while ds <> nil do {search}
   begin
     dg := pick_segment (ds^.desg, pnt, dis);
     if dis < distance
       then begin distance := dis; pick_solid := ds end;
     ds := ds^.dsnext
   end
end; {pick_solid function}
```

Extent Testing

As can be readily seen from the picking functions discussed here, picking is an inherently expensive operation, which linearly depends on the number of entities in the display list ($O(n)$). Because picking is one of the most frequently invoked operators in any modeling system, ways to minimize the search must be found. The scope of this book does not permit lengthy treatment of this topic.[†] One of the most useful search-minimizing techniques is *extent testing*. This method is based on the observation that although we cannot simplify the test, we can reduce the number of times it must be used. Such reduction is achieved through

---

[†]The reader is referred to Preparata and Shamos's book mentioned in the bibliography at the end of this chapter.

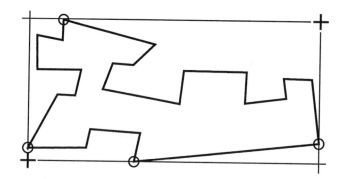

Figure 30.2. Boxing the vertices and segments of a polygon for extent testing.

"wholesale" testing of many entities at once, by enclosing them in an "extent box," as depicted in Figure 30.2.

The so-called extent box is calculated from the location of the extreme vertices of a display polygon or a display solid. Such calculation involves traversing all the vertices and storing the extreme coordinates of their bounding box (in the form of two points) with the display list record that stores the polygon or the solid. This calculation is time consuming; however, it must be done only once for each entity at the time it is created or changed. Picking, on the other hand, may be applied to the same set of shapes thousands of times. The investment in computing the extent box will, therefore, pay off in the long run.

Once an extent box has been computed, it can be used to trivially reject display polygons and solids in the picking process. The point indicated by the user is first tested to see if it is within the bounds of the extent box of the display polygon or the display solid. Only if the point is found to be within the box, the display polygon or solid themselves must be tested segment by segment. Otherwise, they were not picked.

Computing the extent of a display polygon or solid is a simple matter of traversing all its display segments and finding the extreme ones. It is demonstrated here by procedure EXTENT_BOX, which can be applied to the list of display segments of both polygons and solids. The results are stored in the display polygon and the display solid records, to which we must add the field EXTENT, an array of two points:

```
ext_box = array [(min,max)] of point;

d_list_polygon = record
                poly    : pptr;        {world }
                dseg    : dgptr;       {screen}
                extent  : ext_box;
                dpnext  : dpptr
              end;
```

```
d_list_solid =    record
                    sld     : sptr;      {world }
                    dseg    : dgptr;     {screen}
                    extent : ext_box;
                    dsnext : dsptr
                  end;

procedure extent_box (dglist : dgptr; var extent : ext_box);
{Compute the extent of the box bounding the list of display
 segments in dglist.}

var  dg : dgptr;
     ax : coords;
     i  : 1..2;

begin
  extent[min] := maxint; {a very large number}
  extent[max] := -maxint; {a very small number}

  dg := dglist;
  while dg <> nil do
    begin
      for i := 1 to 2 do
        for ax := x to y do
          begin
            if dg^.pnt[i][ax] < extent[min][ax]
               then extent[min][ax] := dg^.pnt[i][ax]
            if dg^.pnt[i][ax] > extent[max][ax]
               then extent[max][ax] := dg^.pnt[i][ax]
          end;
        dg := dg^.gnext
    end
end; {extent_box procedure}
```

Once the extent boxes of all display polygons and solids have been computed,
their extended picking can be avoided if the point indicated by the user is outside
that box. The inclusion of the point indicated by the user within the extent box of
any display polygon or solid can be tested with function IN_BOX. It uses function IN_BOUNDS that was used earlier to test if a point is in the bounds of a
segment.

```
function in_box (pnt : point; extent : ext_box) : boolean;
{Determines if point pnt is within range of extent box.}

begin
  in_box := in_bounds (pnt,extent[min],extent[max])
end; {in_box function}
```

Picking a Window

The identification of the window itself in which a point has been indicated is also subject to the picking process, although it requires less computation. As shown by function PICK_WINDOW, it is based on exploiting the flexibility of function IN_BOUNDS, which really tests if a point is within the boundary of a box mined by its diagonally opposite points, rather than if the point is properly on the line segment that connects them (which is the reason IN_BOUNDS must be used in conjunction with LINE_DISTANCE to determine if a point lies on a line segment itself).

```
function pick_window (pnt : point) : wptr;
{Return pointer to the window which contains point pnt.}

const range = 0; {the point must be properly inside}
var    w    : wptr;

begin
  w := wlist;
  while (w <> nil) and
   not in_bounds (pnt, w^.w_min, w^.w_max) do
     w := w^.wnext;
  pick_window := w
end; {pick_window function}
```

Highlighting

The combined effects of picking and display are used to visually confirm which entity was identified by the system in response to the user's indicating a point on the screen. First, the picking process must be completed. If it fails to return an entity of the type the user wished to pick (i.e., a vertex, segment, polygon, or solid), the user must be so notified. If, on the other hand, the search yielded a nonempty result, it must be visually differentiated from the other entities, to confirm whether the entity identified by the system is the one the user intended to pick. This is visually confirmed by redisplaying the entity in a different color, or by causing it to blink, or by any other method that will distinguish it from other, nonpicked entities. Both picking and highlighting are performed by using only the display list database, which contributes to the speed of the interaction.

Only after the picking and highlighting process has been completed to the satisfaction of the user, the actual modeling operation for which the entity was picked can be executed. Execution takes place in the world data structure, by following the pointer from the display list entity to the world entity from which it was generated. The modeling operation may, in turn, modify the world entity, and thereby require the removal of the corresponding display list entity from all the windows and the addition of the modified world entity to them.

☐ USER-INTERACTIVE GENERATION OF POLYGONS

By combining all the operators we have developed so far, the user can interactively MAKE, KILL, and otherwise MODIFY complex shapes. It is not possible to develop in this book a complete system. Still, procedures MAKE_POLYGON and KILL_POLYGON demonstrate how an interactive user interface for the purposes of geometric modeling can be structured. They assume that a global array of windows W_LIST, is maintained by the system, along with a variable LAST_WINDOW, which marks the number of windows. Using this information, procedures MAKE_POLYGON and KILL_POLYGON allow for the creation of a polygon and its deletion in *all* windows simultaneously. That is, the polygon can be initialized in any window, and vertices can be added to it through points indicated in any window, regardless in which window the previous point was indicated. Such multiple window entry of points facilitates the creation of complex polygons: one window can be zoomed in, allowing accuracy in detail, while another may be zoomed out, providing global visual reference. Procedure MAKE_POLYGON exploits the fact that adding a polygon to the display list does not automatically show on the screen. Instead, the newly created polygon is shown on the screen by using procedures SHOW_CROSS and SHOW_LINE. The entry of points in multiple windows to create a single polygon reinforces the idea of windows as the means to access a singular world. In the same way that a world entity can be displayed in many windows, it can be created and modified through multiple windows.

```
procedure make_polygon (var p : pptr);
{Create polygon p interactively, by reading user-defined cursor
 locations. The polygon can be entered and displayed in any
 window, and is displayed in all windows simultaneously. The
 completed polygon is added to the display lists of all
 windows, so it will become visible in subsequent operations.}


const  abort = 0;
       stop  = 0;


var  s_pnt0,s_pnt1,s_pnt2,            {screen points}
     w_pnt0,w_pnt1,w_pnt2 : point;    {world points}
     cmd                  : integer;  {menu option command
                                        code}
     i                    : integer;
     g                    : gptr;
     v                    : vptr;
     w                    : wptr;
```

```
begin
  {get user's first input point}
  get_input (s_pnt0,cmd);
  if cmd <> abort
    then begin
      {pick a window}
      w := pick_window (s_pnt0);

      {initialize Primitive Polygon}
      g := nil; v := nil;
      create_polygon (p,g,v);
      screen_to_world (s_pnt0,w_pnt0, w);

      v^.form := w_pnt0;
      {show vertex in all windows}
      for i := 1 to last_window do
        begin
          world_to_screen (w_pnt0, s_pnt0, w_list[i]);
          show_cross (s_pnt0)
        end;

      {get user input and add segments}
      w_pnt1 := w_pnt0;
      repeat
        get_input (s_pnt2,cmd);
        if cmd <> stop
          then begin
            {pick current window}
            w := pick_window (s_pnt2);

            {create new segment}
            g := nil;v := nil;
            add_segment (p^.glist, g, v);
            screen_to_world (s_pnt2,w_pnt2, w);
            v^.form := w_pnt2;
            place_segment (p^.glist);
            place_segment (g);

            {show new segment in all windows}
            for i := 1 to last_window do
              begin
                world_t_screen (w_pnt1, s_pnt1, w_list[i]);
                world_to_screen (w_pnt2, s_pnt2, w_list[i]);
                show_line (s_pnt1, s_pnt2)
              end;
            w_pnt1 := w_pnt2
          end
      until cmd = stop;
```

```
            {erase cross and complete display of polygons}
            for i := 1 to last_window do
              begin
                set_color (erase);
                world_to_screen (w_pnt0, s_pnt0, w_list[i]);
                show_cross (s_pnt0);

                set_color (normal);
                world_to_screen (w_pnt2, s_pnt2, w_list[i]);
                show_line (s_pnt2, s_pnt0)
              end;

            {add polygon to display lists of all windows}
            for i := 1 to last_window do
              display_polygon (p, w_list[i])
          end
  end; {make_polygon procedure}

procedure kill_polygon (plist : list_of_polygons);
{Delete polygon indicated by user-defined cursor location, and
 erase it from all windows.}

const  abort   = 0;
       confirm = 1;

var  w   : wptr;
     i   : integer;
     dp  : dpptr;
     p   : pptr;
     pnt : point;
     cmd : integer;

begin
  get_input (pnt,cmd);
  if cmd <> abort
    then begin
      w := pick_window (pnt);
      dp := pick_polygon (pnt, w);

          if dp <> nil
            then begin
              p := dp^.poly;

              {mark polygon p in all windows}
              set_color (mark);
              for i := 1 to last_window do
                begin
                  dp := find_display_polygon (p, w_list[i]);
                  show_polygon (dp)
                end;
```

```
                get_input (pnt,cmd); {to confirm}
                if cmd = confirm
                   then begin
                      {erase polygons from screen}
                      set_color (erase);
                      for i := 1 to last_window do
                         begin
                            dp := find_display_polygon (p,w_list[i]);
                            show_polygon (dp);
                            remove_display_polygon (w_list[i], dp)
                         end;

                      {delete p from the world}
                      delete_polygon (p)
                   end
            end
      end
end; {kill_polygon procedure}
```

☐ VERIFYING WELL-FORMEDNESS

The user interface should also handle the verification of well-formedness, as far as it depends on the user's actions. The verification of user-dependent actions is particularly important for functions that involve the assignment of geometry to topological entities, because the data structure and the operators developed throughout the book guarantee the *topological* well-formedness of the modeled polygons but cannot guarantee the shapes' *geometrical* well-formedness. More specifically, the data structure and the operators guarantee *closure* and consistent *orientation*. They cannot guarantee that the orientation complies with the right-hand rule, which was discussed in Chapter 3. They also cannot guarantee that polygons and solids will not self-intersect.

Compliance of the polygons' orientation with the right-hand rule is the basis for computing the polygons' area and for labeling holes as negative polygons. This property is also relied upon by the inter-polygon operators discussed in Chapter 7 and by applications such as the display of shaded solids or the elimination of their hidden lines. It is necessary, therefore, to test the orientation of all polygons constructed interactively by the user and, if necessary, "correct" them by reversing the pointers connecting their segments.

The non-self-intersection condition can be easily violated by the user in constructing a new polygon or in modifying existing ones, by placing a vertex such that the segments it bounds intersect some other segments of the same polygon or its holes. Self-intersection must, therefore, be tested, and if detected, it must be reported to the user. It could be tested every time a vertex is assigned a location to see if the two segments adjacent to it do not intersect other segments of the polygon. This test, however, is rather expensive in terms of computing resources. If the polygon has many segments or holes, the test may slow down the interaction with the user. Furthermore, self-intersection can be a temporary condition, to be corrected when the user has completed the polygon construction or modification transaction. If self-intersection is tested each time the user moves a vertex or a segment, the modeling transactions could become prohibitively expensive, because the test would be applied unnecessarily many times.

It may, therefore, be preferable to delay testing for self-intersection until the entire polygon has been outlined or its modeling transaction has been completed. Function SELF_INTERSECT performs this test. It performs the test for a single polygonal boundary, while employing the geometrical intersection function TEST_INTERSECTION, which was introduced in Chapter 7.

```
function self_intersect (p : pptr) : boolean;
{Return true if p self-intersects, otherwise returns false. Test
 the intersection of each segment with all other segments of
 the polygon. Note: This function only tests a single polygonal
 boundary!}

label  exit_loops;
var    gtest,g : gptr;
       pnt     : point;

begin
  self_intersect := false;

  {outer loop through all segments}
  gtest := p^.glist;
  repeat
    {loop through segments following successor of gtest}
    g := gtest^.gnext^.gnext;
    while (g <> p^.glist) and (g^.gnext <> gtest) do
      if test_intersection (gtest,g, {condition=} 1, pnt)
        then begin
          self_intersect := true;
          goto exit_loops
        end
        else g := g^.gnext;

    gtest := gtest^.gnext
  until gtest = p^.glist;

  exit_loops {destination of goto statement}
end; {self_intersect function}
```

The user must be notified when self-intersection is detected. Then the user can rectify and eliminate that condition, or override the system's well-formedness maintenance control at the risk of introducing semantic integrity violations in later design processes.

Error Handling

Detection of self-intersection is an example to conditions where the performance of certain operations cannot proceed unless the conditions are corrected. The detection and handling of such conditions are known as *error handling*. They determines whether the operations should be carried out or should be aborted. Often, their resolution requires user intervention, for which purpose the user must be apprised of their existence.

Because the operators are layered, errors can be tested at different levels of the hierarchy. Duplication of testing should be avoided, so when testing for errors, where should the test occur? Usually it is preferable to test for errors at the highest possible level in the hierarchy. This will prevent lower level operators from being invoked at all if error conditions persist and will possibly provide more meaningful error messages. In addition, if errors are checked at a very low level of the hierarchy before the user is consulted, certain steps may have to be "undone" if the user decides to abort the operation.

Obviously, the user interface to such high-level polygon operations includes many more functions that must be augmented by prompts and error messages. These and others issues related to the development of powerful and friendly user interfaces are left for the reader to explore.

□ BIBLIOGRAPHY

Eastman, C. M., "Fundamental Problems in the Development of Computer-Based Architectural Design Models," in *Computability of Design* Y. E. Kalay, ed., Wiley-Interscience, New York, 1987.

Kalay, Y. E., "WORLDVIEW: An Integrated Geometric Modeling/Drafting System," *IEEE Computer Graphics and Applications* 7(2):36–46, February 1987.

Shamos, I. M., and F. Preparata, *Computational Geometry*, Springer Verlag, New York, 1985.

31

EXERCISE 5: USER INTERFACE

Chapters 28 through 30 and Appendix C discuss many (but not all) of the issues concerning the user interface with a modeling system of the type described in this book. Some aspects of the user interface must have been implemented by the reader who implemented Exercises One through Four. Yet in all those exercises, the emphasis was on the modeling aspects themselves, rather than on the user interface.

In many respects, a proper user interface determines how useful a modeling system will be. It is the first thing buyers of modeling systems evaluate and what they see in trade shows. Furthermore, a good user interface may compensate for deficiencies in modeling, to some extent. A bad user interface, on the other hand, will hinder the use of even the most powerful modeling system. The development of the user interface deserves, therefore, as much effort and thoughtfulness as the modeling functionality of the system.

Using the concepts of windowing and display lists that were introduced in this part of the book, you are challenged in this exercise to implement an interface to the polygon and solid modeling operators that you have implemented earlier.

Specifically, the user of your modeling system should be able to create, modify, and delete windows. The user should be able to associate with each window a pair of transformations from world to screen and screen to world and be able to modify them through zooming, panning, and changing the projection (e.g., from top to side, from orthographic to perspective). Of particular interest will be the simultaneous use of *multiple windows* to facilitate such functions as the picking of a polygon for the purpose of its extrusion to a certain height. Because this operation requires three-dimensional input, a single window cannot support it (unless the third dimension is entered through the keyboard).

The linkage between the display and the world entities should be through display lists, which will enable the user to pick world entities and operate on them.

A menu structure of the kind discussed in Appendix C could be used to facilitate the presentation and selection of functions offered by the system, while grouping them in logical units.

In this exercise you will also have the opportunity to experiment with error handling and with prompting. Prompting is the means to direct the user's attention to specific required inputs and to guide the user through complex operations. Like error messages, prompts play an important role in making the system useful and helpful to casual users and in informing experienced ones of the status of the system.

Modeling suffers from a lack of standardization. It is wide open for experimentation with novel and more productive methods, which rely as much on technical skills as on understanding the psychology of the designer. There are even fewer "rights" and "wrongs" in user interface than there are in modeling. Feel free to experiment and discover the joy of clever user interfaces.

32

CONCLUSION

The goal of this book is to introduce the principles that underlie the ability of computers to assist in the design of physical artifacts through their representation in the computer's memory. A concept called *modeling*, which encompasses both *representation* and *manipulation* of symbol structures representing physical artifacts, has been introduced. As a *language of representation*, modeling stresses the importance of *mapping* between the arbitrary symbols and the real world or abstract phenomena they represent and endows the model with a particular *meaning*.

The study of modeling was introduced through understanding the general principles and techniques of representing physical artifacts in the computer. In particular, the technique of *abstraction* was presented as a method that allows the grouping of symbol structures, representing the modeled artifact, and the operators which manipulate them, into one computational entity. The technique of *hierarchical structuring* was presented as a method that facilitates modularity of model building, whereby abstract entities can be combined into larger, more complex entities, which can themselves be regarded as unitary elements of the model.

Objects and environments are composed of many attributes that include shape, location, materials, color, and cost. The book discussed many of these attributes, but has emphasized the modeling of *shape*, not only as the predominant attribute of physical artifacts but also as the one most difficult to model. The modeling of shapes has been pursued in the book at two levels: first in two dimensions, then in three. A *polygon-based* approach to shape modeling was used, which lends itself to both the representation and manipulation of area-enclosing shapes (polygons) and volume-enclosing shapes (solids). It also allows separate introduction of the concepts of topology and geometry and their interrelations to be explained.

Because most artifacts and environments are made of many, closely linked objects (both physically and functionally), the study of *assembly modeling* has been introduced, which relies on principles used in database management systems and in artificial intelligence (e.g., attribute inheritance and instancing).

Some issues concerning the *user interface* to geometric modeling were also introduced, although rather briefly. In particular, the concept of separating the *screen* display from the *world* database has been emphasized, and a technique called *display list* was introduced. As for many other topics discussed in this book, the treatment of these issues is not exhaustive. It is hoped that interested readers will, therefore, make use of the bibliographies at the end of each chapter.

The importance of modeling cannot be over emphasized: it is the basis on which all computer-aided design rests. Modeling provides the information used by application programs to evaluate the artifact's future performances, the information that is used by the designer to visualize and appraise the emerging artifact, and the database on which knowledge-based systems must rely if they are to offer advice to the designer. Modeling is also a means to its own end: It can relieve the designer from performing some tedious tasks, enhance the integrity and consistency of the designed artifact, and thus enable a more efficient design process and a better result.

APPENDICES

A

SET THEORETIC PRINCIPLES OF SHAPE MANIPULATION

The general concept of a set is of fundamental importance to many branches of mathematics, such as number theory, the theory of point sets, real functions, and topology. For a long time sets were regarded as being so intuitively clear as to need no formal definition. Cantor (1845–1918) was the first mathematician to subject them to systematic study, which yielded the so called "naive," or "intuitive" theory of sets. This theory was extended, when mathematicians like Russel, Frege, Zermelo, von Neumann, and others discovered contradictions in Cantor's "naive" theory of sets. Still, it is sufficient for establishing the general concepts that will be used throughout the following discussion.

☐ THE DEFINITION OF SETS

Cantor defined sets as follows:

A "set" is any assemblage, regarded as one entity M, of definite and separate objects m in some given context.

This definition allows us to gather into one "whole" M all the elements m that have some given property. In the context of our interest here we may, according to this definition, regard all the points in the Euclidean two-dimensional space as one "set," which we shall call *the universal set*.

The notation which we use to express the fact that x is an element of set A, is $x \in A$ (x is in A). Sets that contain the same elements are considered to be equal. Thus a set is determined by its elements, a quality known as *the principle of extensionality*. A set that has *no* elements is known as the *empty* set and is denoted by 0.

Set A is called the subset of B ($A \subseteq B$) if $\forall_x$ ($x \in A \rightarrow x \in B$) (for all x, x in A implies x in B). If in addition A is not equal to B, then A is known as the *proper* subset of B or is said to be *properly contained* in B.

The set C is called the *union* of sets A and B (denoted $A \cup B$), if $\forall_x$ ($x \in C \leftrightarrow x \in A \lor x \in B$) (for all x, x in C implies and is implied by x in A **or** x in B).

The set C is called the *intersection* of sets A and B (denoted $A \cap B$) if $\forall_x$ ($x \in C \leftrightarrow x \in A \land x \in B$) (for all x, x in C implies and is implied by x in A **and** x in B).

Two sets are *disjoint* if they have no common elements; that is, $A \cap B = 0$. The complement $NOT\,A$ of a set A is the set of all the elements in the domain of interest M which are *not* elements of A.

It is convenient to illustrate these concepts by means of the *Venn diagrams* (Figure A.1), named after John Venn who presented this technique in 1880.

☐ AN ALGEBRA OF SETS

The concepts introduced here define an *algebra of sets*, which includes, among others, the following laws:

1. The commutative laws:

$$A \cup B = B \cup A$$
$$A \cap B = B \cap A$$

2. The associative laws:

$$A \cup (B \cup C) = (A \cup B) \cup C$$
$$A \cap (B \cap C) = (A \cap C) \cap C$$

3. The absorption laws:

$$A \cup (A \cap B) = A$$
$$A \cap (A \cup B) = A.$$

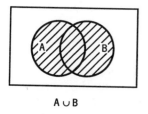
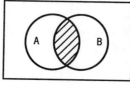
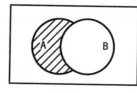

$A \cup B$ $A \cap B$ $A - B$

Figure A.1. The Venn diagrams representation of set-theoretic operators.

By imposing closure rules on these set-theoretic laws through the theory of relations, we can derive the so-called *propositional calculus of sets*, which was first put in algebraic form by George Boole (1847) and is known, therefore, as *Boolean algebra*. The axioms that underlie this algebra are isomorphic to the set-theoretic laws, some of which have been enumerated earlier, with the explicit definition of the *inclusion* property:

$$A \subseteq B \leftrightarrow A = A \cap B$$
$$B \subseteq A \leftrightarrow A = A \cup B,$$

and the *closure* property, which is defined as follows:

The operators $\cup$, $\cap$, *and* $\neg$ *are closed for subsets A, B, of a finite domain M if* $A \cup B$, $A \cap B$, *and* $\neg A$ *are defined for all elements of M.*

From the Boolean axioms, the inclusion rules, and the closure rules, it follows that for sets A, B, and C, which are elements of M, that:

$$(A \cap B) \subseteq A,$$
$$A \subseteq (A \cup B)$$

(A.1)

$$(A \subseteq B \wedge A \subseteq C) \rightarrow A \subseteq B \cap C$$
$$(B \subseteq A \wedge C \subseteq A) \rightarrow B \cup C \subseteq A.$$

(A.2)

Thus the sets $B \cap C$ and $B \cup C$ serve as *bounds* with respect to the inclusion relation $\subseteq$ of all elements of A (greatest lower bound and least upper bound, respectively). Every element x of A that is contained in B and C is also contained in their greatest lower bound $B \cap C$, and every element x of A that contains B and C also contains their least upper bound $B \cup C$. A domain M that complies with these Boolean axioms is called a *finite Boolean lattice*.

☐ SPATIAL SETS

It was discussed in Chapter 1 that polygons and solids can be considered subsets of the Euclidean two-dimensional (E2) and three-dimensional (E3) space, respectively. (In the following we shall discuss only polygons, but the concepts also apply to solids.) It was demonstrated in Chapter 2 that polygons can be represented by a one-dimensional subset (E1) of E2, called the *boundary* of the polygon, if that set complies with certain well-formedness conditions. (In Chapters 9 and 10 it is shown that a solid can be similarly represented by a well-formed subset E2 of E3.) In set-theoretic terms, a polygon can be represented as subset B in the domain E2, while the other points in E2 (which are not part of the polygon) can be represented by n disjoint subsets C_i, $i = 1 \ldots n$ ($n \geq 1$) of E2 (allowing for holes), as depicted schematically in Figure A.2.

It is easy to verify that the Boolean axioms hold for points in E2, and that E2 is, therefore, a Boolean lattice. Hence, a new polygon $p3$ theoretically can be produced by applying the operators $\cup$, $\cap$, and $\neg$ to two existing polygons $p1$ and $p2$. While complying with the definition of a finite Boolean lattice, however, the product of such an operation may not be well-formed, in terms of the conditions that were discussed in Chapter 2. In particular, the product shape may not be homogeneously continuous in E2. As an example, consider the product of intersecting two polygons that are coincident at a segment (Figure A.3). A segment is an E1 subset of E2 that does not enclose an area and, therefore, does not constitute a well-formed polygon.

In order to construct operators that can manipulate the boundary of polygons, which are logically equivalent to the set-theoretic operators of union, intersection, and difference, and which comply with the well-formedness rules, special attention must be paid to the set-theoretic properties of the *boundary* of shapes.

The Set-Theoretic Properties of the Boundary

Considered from a boundary representation point of view, the goal of the set-theoretic inter-polygon operators is to produce a new polygon whose boundary is made of the suitable parts of the boundaries of the two polygons that were used as operandi for the operation. Determining what constitutes a "suitable" part of each boundary depends on the desired operation and on the relative positions of the boundaries in relation to each other. In analogy to mathematical sets, the *union* of two polygons should produce a new polygon whose boundary is made of those parts of the boundary of each operant polygon that are *outside* the domain of E2 occupied by the other polygon. Their *intersection* should produce a new polygon whose boundary is made of those parts of the boundary of each operant polygon that are *inside* the domain of E2 occupied by the other polygon. The *difference* of two polygons should be made of those parts of the boundary of the

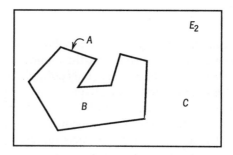

Figure A.2. A set-theoretic representation of a polygon.

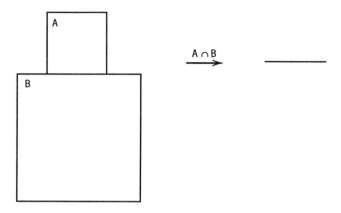

Figure A.3. An ill-formed product of intersecting two well-formed polygons.

first operant polygon that are *outside* the domain of E2 occupied by the second polygon, and those parts of the boundary of the second operant polygon that are *inside* the domain of E2 occupied by the first polygon. This last operation can be treated as an *intersection* operation, after the second operant polygon has been inverted inside-out by reversing its orientation, in analogy to the set-theoretic equivalence:

$$A - B = A \cap \neg B$$

This makes it possible for us to consider only the *union* and *intersection* operations of polygons, for most purposes of the following discussion.

Dealing with Coincident Segments

As discussed in Chapter 7, the unambiguous classification of segments of each polygon as being either inside or outside the other polygon is crucial to the proper identification of the parts of each polygon which will partake in the product of the set operation. This unambiguous classification is, nevertheless, complicated when the operant polygons coincide along one or more segments. In such cases the transition from the "inside" of one polygon to its "outside" is accomplished along a *line segment*, rather than a *point*, as in the well-behaved cases. Such line segments are neither "inside" nor "outside" either polygon, but rather "on" the boundary of both. Thus they do not conform to the set theoretic basis of the algorithm and may render it inapplicable.

In order to illustrate this point, consider the following two cases: Two rectangular polygons A and B (B larger than A) are positioned such that they coincide at a segment. In case 1 (Figure A.4a), A is outside B, whereas in case 2 (Figure A.4b), A is inside B.

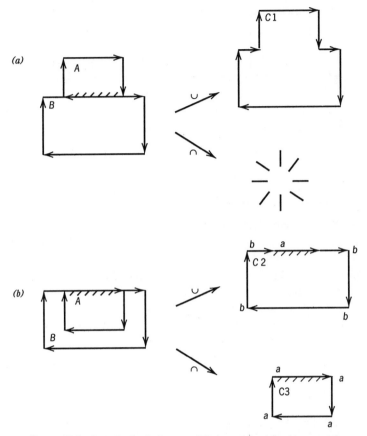

Figure A.4. A case study for considering coincident segments.

Considering the areas enclosed by the polygons, their *union* in case 1 (as expected) is a polygon $C1$, whose area is the sum of the areas of A and B. Their *intersection* is null (there are no points that are both in A and in B). In case 2, the *union* of A and B is a polygon $C2$, which is equivalent to B, and their *intersection* is a polygon $C3$ which is equivalent to A.

Let us now consider the points that make up the boundaries of the three polygons: the boundary of $C1$ (the product of unioning A and B in case 1) is made of the boundaries of both A and B, after the overlapping segment has been *excluded from both* in order to create the "gap" that connects the two areas. Thus *unioning* the polygons caused *exclusion* of some segments of the boundaries of both polygons from the product polygon.

Unioning A and B in case 2 produced a polygon $C2$ whose boundary is made exclusively of that of B; that is, the overlapping segment has been *excluded only once*. Their *intersection* produced a polygon $C3$ whose boundary is equivalent to that of A, where again the overlapping segment has been excluded once.

When we examine the overlapping boundary segment, it appears as if it is treated inconsistently: sometimes it is treated as part of the area enclosed by the polygons (union in case 1 and both union and intersection in case 2) and sometimes as part of the "void" outside the polygons (intersection in case 1). This seeming inconsistency can, however, be explained by applying the set-theoretic rules that were discussed earlier and depicted in Figure A.2. If we consider the boundary set A of a polygon to be an element in both subsets B and C (the "solid" and the "void" subsets of E2, respectively), then by rule (A.2) A is the *least upper bound* on the elements of B (the "solid"), which conforms with what is intuitively meant by a *boundary* or a "tight skin" of a polygon. At the same time, it is also the *greatest lower bound* of the "void" point-set outside the polygon. Recognizing this mathematical duality is central to constructing the spatial set operators. It provides the justification for associating the boundary of a polygon sometimes with the "solid" and sometimes with "void" about it.

Now that the mathematical justification for the different associations of the coincident boundary elements have been established, it is necessary to determine the particular domain of E2 with which coincident parts of the boundary shall be associated in every case. In order to do so, it is necessary to modify the rules that establish the nature of the parts of the boundary of each operant that partakes in the product polygons. A closer examination of the segment of A which coincides with the boundary of B, and which partakes in the product polygons C_i, reveals that by the right-hand rule it is always oriented toward the domain of E2 which is *inside* polygon B, as depicted in Figure A.4. This fact can be used to develop an algorithm for performing the set theoretic operations on polygons, according to the following rules:

1. The boundary of the product polygon resulting from a spatial *union* operation on two operant polygons consists of the noncoincident parts of the boundary of each operant that are *outside* the domain of E2 occupied by the other polygon.

2. The boundary of the product polygon resulting from a spatial *intersection* operation on two operant polygons consists of the noncoincident parts of the boundary of each operant that are *inside* the domain of E2 occupied the other polygon.

3. In addition to the above, those parts of the boundary of *one* of the operant polygons that are *coincidental* with the boundary of the other operant, and that are *oriented toward the domain of E2 that is outside the other operant*, also partake in the boundary of the product polygon (both for union and for intersection).

Rule 3 is a direct result of the above analysis and has been implemented in the algorithm for computing the spatial set operation product of two polygons, as discussed in Chapter 7. Furthermore, the principles discussed here are directly extendable to solids and thus constitute the basis for the shape operators discussed in Chapter 14.

☐ BIBLIOGRAPHY

Behnke, H., F. Bachmann, K. Fladt, and H. Kunle, eds., *Fundamentals of Mathematics*, MIT Press, Cambridge, MA, 1974.

Giblin, P. J., *Graphs, Surfaces, and Homology*, Chapman and Hall/Halsted Press, New York, 1977.

Harary, F., *Graph Theory*, Addison-Wesley, Reading, MA, 1969.

B

TREES: PRINCIPLES, DATA STRUCTURES, AND ALGORITHMS

A *tree* data structure consists of *nodes* and *edges*. It is thus a special case of graph-theoretic structures, with the added constraint that it contains no cycles. The relationships between the nodes of a tree are characteristic of "family trees," which portray parental relationships over generations: Each edge connects exactly two nodes in a directed way. The *direction* associated with the edge results in one node denoted as the *parent* and the other as the *child*. Each node may be the parent of many children, but it may be the child of at most one parent. All the children of the same parent are called *siblings*. Only one node in the tree has no parent; it is called the *root* of the tree. Nodes that have no children are called *leaves* or terminal nodes (Figure B.1).

In more formal terms, a tree is recursively defined as a finite set of one or more nodes, such that:

1. There is exactly one specially designated node called the *root* of the tree.
2. The remaining nodes (excluding the root) are partitioned into zero or more disjoint sets, each of which is, in turn, a *tree*, and is known as a *subtree* of the root.

This definition, given by Donald Knuth,† defines a tree in terms of itself. It is also the basis for most tree operations, which are recursive.

Tree structures come in many varieties: a *general tree* is one which has no particular restrictions on the number of children each parent may have. A *binary tree* is a tree where each parent may have exactly zero or two children. It is

---

†Knuth, D. *The Art of Computer Programming: Fundamental Algorithms*, Addison-Wesley, Reading, MA, 1973.

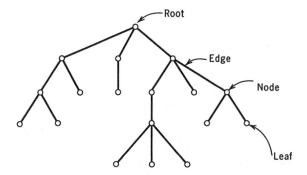

Figure B.1. The structure and terminology of trees.

thus the simplest tree structure (because a structure where each parent could have at most one child is a linked list, not a tree). A *quad tree*, which is often used in image processing applications, is a structure where each parent may have exactly zero or four children. In the following we shall restrict our discussion to binary trees because of their simplicity and universal applicability for our modeling purposes.

☐ THE REPRESENTATION OF TREES

Unlike linked lists, it is not obvious how tree structures can be represented computationally. In the case of general tree structures, each parent may have a variable number of children. If pointers are used to represent the relationships between each parent and its children, then a variable number of pointers is needed. A solution to the problem can be found if we consider "siblingness" as the primary relationship between nodes, rather than the parent-child relationships. In that case, it is possible to link-list all the siblings (nodes that have the same parent) and connect the list to the parent node by a single pointer. This method effectively transforms the representation of general trees into the simpler problem of representing binary trees (Figure B.2).

Binary trees are easy to represent computationally because the fixed number of children each node has permits their representation by a fixed record struc-

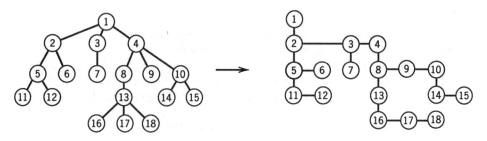

Figure B.2. Binary tree representation of a general tree structure.

ture. Each node of the tree represented in this manner is an element in two linked lists: a "horizontal" list and a "vertical" list each. Each horizontal layer describes the siblings of a node, and each vertical list describes its parent-child associations. To simplify some of the tree manipulation operators, which are described in the next section, each node of the tree also has a back-pointer to its parent node, as shown in Figure B.3, that is based on the following record structure (where the data contained in each node is simply an integer for the sake of simplicity):

```
type   nptr = ^node;
       node = record
                 name      : integer;
                 sibling,              {horizontal}
                 parent,               {vertical  }
                 child     : nptr      {vertical  }
              end;
```

□ MANIPULATION OF TREES

From Knuth's definition of tree structures, it can be determined that a *minimal tree* consists of a single node, called the root. In order to add nodes to the tree, we must also add an equal number of edges (which means that in a tree structure there is always one more node than there are edges). Similarly, when we delete a node, we also delete an edge. These principles can be embedded in a few primitive operations, which govern the manipulation of trees and from which all other operations can be composed. They are the following:

1. Initialize a tree (or subtree).
2. Add a node to a given parent.
3. Delete a node (and all its children).

A tree could thus be constructed by creating its root node, as demonstrated by procedure INIT_TREE, then adding more nodes as needed, using procedure INIT_TREE in conjunction with procedure ADD_NODE. New nodes are created as subtrees, then attached to the tree as children of specified parent nodes.

```
procedure init_tree (var root : nptr);
{Initialize a tree by creating the root node.}

begin
  new (root);
  with root^ do
    begin
      data := 0;
      child := nil;
      parent := nil;
      sibling := nil
    end
end; {init_tree procedure}
```

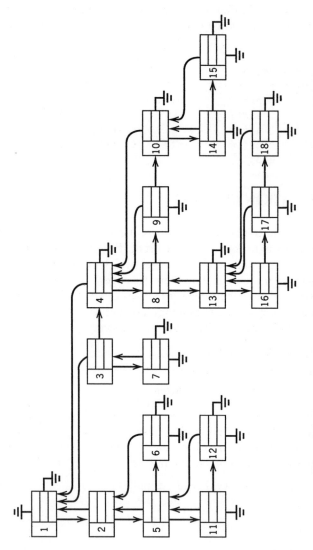

Figure B.3. A computational representation of the tree structure of Figure B.2.

```
procedure add_node (node, par : nptr);
{Attach node (which is the root of a subtree) to the child list
 of parent.}

begin
  node^.sibling := par^.child; {add node to sibling list}
  par^.child := node; {add node as child of par}
  node^.parent := par
end; {add_node procedure}
```

The deletion of a node from the tree is a matter of *removing* it from its sibling list of nodes, as demonstrated by procedure REMOVE_NODE, then disposing of it. The removed node may, however, be the root of a nonempty subtree, in which case all its children also must be deleted. Such deletion can be done recursively, as demonstrated by procedure DELETE_NODE. If the node to be deleted is the root of the tree itself, then its deletion amounts to deleting the entire tree.

```
procedure remove_node (node : nptr);
{Extract node from its sibling list.}

var  temp : nptr;

begin
  if node <> tree {if node is root then take no action}
    then begin
      {set temp to first node in sibling list}
      temp := node^.parent^.child;
      if temp = node {node is first in sibling list}
        then node^.parent^.child := node^.sibling
        else begin
          {find predecessor of node}
          while temp^.sibling <> node do
          temp := temp^.sibling;
          {bypass node in sibling list}
          temp^.sibling := node^.sibling
        end;
      node^.sibling := nil;
      node^.parent := nil
    end
end; {remove_node procedure}
```

```
procedure delete_node (node : nptr);
{Delete node and all its children, recursively.}

begin
  remove_node (node);
  while node^.child <> nil do
    delete_node (node^.child);
  dispose(node)
end; {delete_node procedure}
```

If the children of the deleted node are to be preserved rather than deleted, they must be reparented one by one before their parent node is deleted. Reparenting is a process that combines the operations of removing a node from the tree and adding it to a new parent. This operation is demonstrated by procedure MOVE_NODE.

```
procedure move_node (node, parent : nptr);
{Make node the child of parent. The children of node go with
 node.}

begin
  remove_node (node);
  add_node (node, parent)
end; {move_node procedure}
```

□ TRAVERSAL OF TREES

Unlike the traversal of linked lists, which is a simple matter of advancing a pointer from one element of the list to its successor, the traversal of a tree is more complicated: it requires that all the elements of a nonlinear structure be "visited" once and only once. We call the traversal of trees a "tree walk." It is typically implemented recursively and can take one of two forms:

1. Depth-first traversal
2. Breadth-first traversal

The first form, depicted in Figure B.4, uses the following recursive algorithm for traversing the tree:

1. Visit the node
2. Visit the child of the node
3. Visit the sibling of the node.

"Visiting" a node means applying to the node some operation (for which the traversal has been invoked), such as printing the data it contains, as demonstrated by procedure SHOW_TREE. In a depth-first search, the data in the

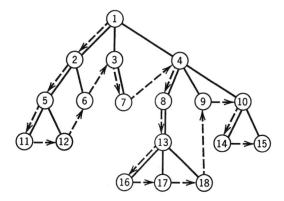

Figure B.4. Depth-first traversal of a tree.

root of the subtree is printed first, then the process is re-invoked and applied to the child of the root node. In this re-invocation, the child is considered the root of the subtree, and its data are printed. This process continues until the current root node has no children, at which time the process is re-invoked and applied to the sibling of the current node, considering it to be the current node. Its content is printed, and the process is invoked again, applied this time to the child of the current node (which is the sibling of the former node). The process recurses until all the nodes of the tree have been visited. It is known as "depth-first" tree walk because the *children* of a node are visited before its siblings.

```
procedure show_tree (node : nptr);
{Print tree recursively, using depth-first tree walk.}

begin
  write (node^.data);
  if node^.child <> nil
    then show_tree (node^.child);
  if node^.sibling <> nil
    then show_tree (node^.sibling)
end; {show_tree procedure}
```

The result of applying procedure SHOW_TREE to the tree depicted in Figure B.3 is:

1 2 5 11 12 6 3 7 4 8 13 16 17 18 9 10 14 15

Breadth-first tree walk is similar to depth-first tree walk except that the *siblings* of the current root node are visited before its children, as depicted in Figure B.5. This form of tree walk uses the following recursive algorithm:

1. Visit the node.

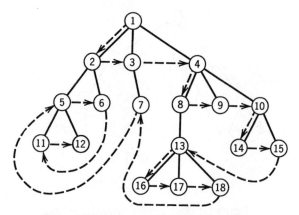

Figure B.5. Breadth-first traversal of a tree.

2. Visit the sibling of the node.
3. Visit the child of the node.

Breadth-first tree walk is demonstrated by procedure FIND_NODE, which searches the tree for the node whose data equals the given ID.

```
procedure find_node (tree : nptr; id : integer; var node : nptr);
{Search tree recursively to find a node whose data=id, using
 breadth-first tree walk.}

begin
  node := nil;
  if tree <> nil
    then if tree^.data = id
            then node := tree
            else begin
              if tree^.sibling <> nil
                then find_node (tree^.sibling,id, node);
              if (node = nil) and (tree^.child <> nil)
                then find_node (tree^.child, id, node)
            end
end; {find_node procedure}
```

The following sequence of nodes are those visited by procedure FIND_NODE in searching the tree depicted in Figure B.3 to find the node whose ID equals 12, using the breadth-first tree walk:

1   2   3   4   8   9   10   14   15   13   16   17   18   7   5   6   11   12

It can be readily ascertained that this sequence is different from the one produced by procedure SHOW_TREE while traversing the same tree using depth-first tree walk. Needless to say, if depth-first tree walk were used to find the node whose data equal 12 rather than breadth-first tree walk, the sought node could have been found in 5 steps instead of 18. However, using depth-first traversal to find the node whose data equal 11 would have required 17 steps, instead of only 4 using the breadth-first method. Hence the efficiency of the search does not depend on which tree walk we use, but rather on the distribution of the nodes in the tree. On the average, both methods will perform equally well.

Program TREE implements all the operators that were discussed in this appendix for a simple tree that stores integer values.

```
program tree (input, output);

type    nptr = ^node;
        node = record
                   data    : integer;
                   sibling : nptr;
                   parent  : nptr;
                   child   : nptr
               end;

var     tree    : nptr;
        stop    : boolean;
        counter : integer;
        k, space : integer;

procedure init_tree (var root : nptr);
{Initialize a tree by creating the root node.}

begin
  new (root);
  with root^ do
    begin
      data := 0;
      child := nil;
      parent := nil;
      sibling := nil
    end
end; {init_tree procedure}

procedure add_node (node, par : nptr);
{Attach node (which is the root of a subtree) to the child list
 of parent.}

begin
  node^.sibling := par^.child; {add node to sibling list}
  par^.child := node;          {add node as child of par}
  node^.parent := par
end; {add_node procedure}
```

```
procedure remove_node (node : nptr);
{Extract node from its sibling list.}

var   temp : nptr;

begin
  if node <> tree {if node is root then take no action}
    then begin
      {set temp to first node in sibling list}
      temp := node^.parent^.child;
      if temp = node {node is first in sibling list}
        then node^.parent^.child := node^.sibling
        else begin
          {find predecessor of node}
          while temp^.sibling <> node do
          temp := temp^.sibling;
          {bypass node in sibling list}
          temp^.sibling := node^.sibling
        end;
      node^.sibling := nil;
      node^.parent := nil
    end
end; {remove_node procedure}

procedure delete_node (node : nptr);
{Delete node and all its children, recursively.}

begin
  remove_node (node);
  while node^.child <> nil do
    delete_node (node^.child);
  dispose(node)
end; {delete_node procedure}

procedure move_node (node, par : nptr);
{Make node child of par. The children of node go with node.}

begin
  remove_node (node);
  add_node (node, par)
end; {move_node procedure}
```

```
procedure find_node (tree : nptr; id : integer; var node : nptr);
{Search tree recursively to find a node whose data=id, using
 breadth-first tree walk.}

begin
  node := nil;
  if tree <> nil
    then if tree^.data = id
            then node := tree
            else begin
              if tree^.sibling <> nil
                then find_node (tree^.sibling,id, node);
              if (node = nil) and (tree^.child <> nil)
                then find_node (tree^.child, id, node)
            end
end; {find_node procedure}

procedure show_tree (node : nptr);
{Print tree recursively.}

begin
  writeln (' ':space, node^.data);
  if node^.child <> nil
    then begin
      space := space + 4;
      show_tree (node^.child);
      space := space - 4
    end;
  if node^.sibling <> nil
    then show_tree (node^.sibling)
end; {show_tree procedure}

procedure add_new_node;

var   node,par : nptr;
      i        : integer;

begin
  write('enter name of parent node: ');
  readln (i);
  find_node (tree, i, par);
  if par = nil
    then writeln ('node ', i, ' does not exist.')
    else begin
      init_tree (node);
      add_node (node, par);
      counter := counter + 1; node^.data := counter;
      show_tree (tree)
    end
end; {add_new_node procedure}
```

```
procedure re_parent_node;

var    n_name, p_name          : integer;
       p_node, c_node, node : nptr;

begin
  write('enter name of node to be moved: ');
  readln (n_name);
  find_node (tree, n_name, node);
  if node = nil
    then writeln ('node ', n_name, ' does not exist')
    else if tree = node
            then writeln('node 0 is root')
            else begin
              write ('enter name of new parent: ');
              readln (p_name);
              find_node(tree, p_name, p_node);

              if p_node = nil
                then begin
                  write ('node ',p_name);
                  writeln (' does not exist')
                end
                else begin
                  {is new parent child of node?}
                  find_node (node^.child, p_name, c_node);
                  if c_node <> nil
                    then begin
                      write('new parent is ');
                      writeln('child of node')
                    end
                    else begin
                      move_node(node, p_node);
                      show_tree (tree)
                    end
                end
            end
        end
end; {re_parent_node procedure}

procedure kill_node;

var    n_name : integer;
       node    : nptr;

begin
  write('enter name of node to be removed: ');
  readln (n_name);
  find_node (tree, n_name, node);
  if node = nil
    then writeln ('node ', n_name, ' does not exist')
```

```
      else if node = tree
        then writeln ('node 0 is root')
        else begin
          delete_node (node);
          show_tree (tree)
        end
end; {kill_node procedure}


procedure help;

begin
  writeln;
  writeln('tree manipulation commands are:');
  writeln;
  writeln('0 - help');
  writeln('1 - re-initialize tree');
  writeln('2 - add new node to tree');
  writeln('3 - delete node from tree');
  writeln('4 - move node to a new parent');
  writeln('5 - show tree');
  writeln('6 - exit from program');
  writeln
end; {help procedure}


procedure get_command (var i : integer);
{Get a command from terminal.}

var   c : char;

begin
  write('tree> ');          {prompt user                }
  readln (c);               {read command as a character }
  i := ord(c) - ord('0')    {convert character to numeral}
  if not i in [0..6]        {test if command is legal    }
    then get_command (i)    {get new command, recursively}
end; {get_command procedure}

begin {main}
  counter := 0; space := 0; stop := false;
  init_tree (tree); show_tree (tree);
  repeat
    get_command (k);
    case k of
      0 : help;
      1 : begin
            init_tree(tree);
            show_tree(tree);
            counter := 0
          end;
```

```
      2 : add_new_node;
      3 : kill_node;
      4 : re_parent_node;
      5 : show_tree (tree);
      6 : stop := true
    end {case}
  until stop
end. {main program}
```

C

MODULAR MENU MAPPING AND HIT-TESTING

The single most frequent operation in any menu-driven interactive computer graphics system is determining the action to be executed next, based on a menu hit test. This operation typically comprises sensing the user-defined screen location of a cursor and matching it against a pre-defined set of menu boxes, each of which is associated with a particular action that can be performed by the system at that state. While multiple different actions may be associated with the same menu box at different states in the program, the box configuration itself in most cases is invariant, following the conventions of human engineering.

The act of associating the variant location of the cursor with the invariant set of menu boxes is known as *menu hit-testing*. It is an operation that is invoked each time the user interacts graphically with the system, whether to select a new action or to provide graphical input for an action in progress. For example, a line drawing sequence may be initiated through one menu hit test, while the location of the points that make up the line itself may be provided by subsequent hit tests. The line drawing sequence as a whole will determine when the point falls inside a menu box that represents a different action.

Menu hit-testing, itself a simple operation, comprises a major portion of run-time cost by virtue of its abundance. This appendix presents a function-based menu hit-testing method that reduces the cost of this operation to a constant. This is achieved by trading the search time with a look-up table, denoted *menu map*, and by defining a function that maps any cursor-defined screen location, thereby determining the action to be taken.

A choice between time or space is often a poor choice, in particular when the cost of either one of them is high. Therefore a hybrid method, where search is not completely eliminated but is significantly reduced, is also introduced. This method is made possible through *run-length encoding* the menu map and searching the run-length vector. Its added space requirements are much smaller than those for full mapping, and its search time is much smaller than that for no mapping at all.

The next section reviews traditional menu structuring and hit-testing. The third section presents the modular approach to menuing and hit-testing, and the fourth section introduces the run-length encoding method and examines the advantages and disadvantages of both methods.

Two example menus are used throughout the presentation: a simple one and a complex one. The advantages of modular menu mapping come forth only in more complex menus, but can be better explained on simple ones. Their apparent simplicity should, therefore, not be confused with the issues dealt with in this appendix.

☐ TRADITIONAL MENU STRUCTURING AND HIT-TESTING

Typically, a menu is displayed as a set of labeled boxes on a cathode-ray tube (CRT) screen or on a digitizing tablet.† The boxes provide the user with a frame of reference, a "button" to be hit with a cursor or a lightpen. The labels within the boxes denote the actions that are selectable by the user at the particular mode the system is in. Simple human engineering conventions recommend that the shape and location of the menu boxes be kept invariant, in order to maximize user familiarity and "muscle memory." The labels within the boxes may, and often do, vary according to the state (mode) the system is in, particularly when a hierarchical menu structure is used. Typical menus are depicted in Figures C.1 and C.2.

The menu boxes can be separated from their content (represented by the labels) by associating each box with a unique code, which is in turn associated with one or more actions. The codes thus act as buffers between the physical menu boxes and the actions they invoke. Such separation also facilitates the use of a single menu hit test, which returns the code associated with the selected menu box and is thus global to the entire menu structure.

The menu hit test can be implemented as a *serial*, box-by-box inclusion test or as a *hierarchical*, region-based inclusion test, where successive tests refine the gross location determined by earlier testing. For example, given a particular $<x, y>$ screen location, a hit test for the menu depicted in Figure C.1 can be implemented serially by the following sequence of statements:

```
if (x > 5) and (x < 165) and (y > 65) and (y < 95)
   then code := 111
   else if (x > 165) and (x < 325) and (y > 65) and (y < 95)
           then code := 112
           else ...
```

---

†The box contours may or may not be explicitly displayed, but they exist nevertheless virtually as boundaries for hit-testing.

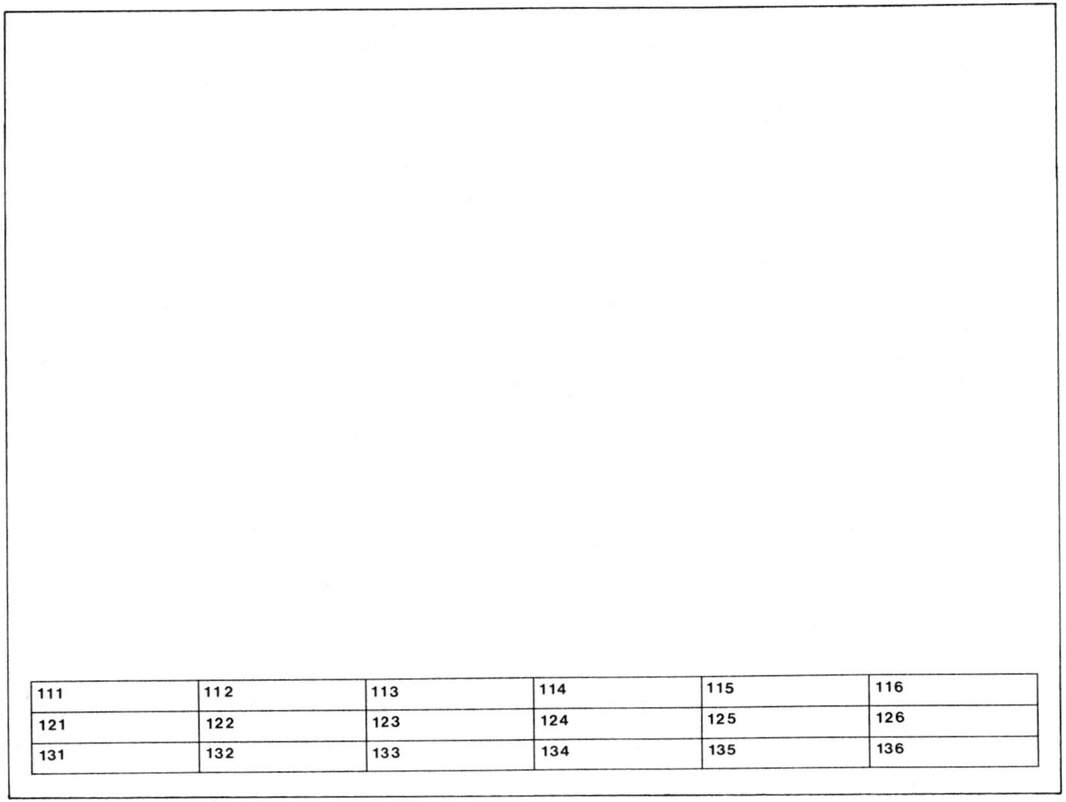

111	112	113	114	115	116
121	122	123	124	125	126
131	132	133	134	135	136

Figure C.1. A typical simple menu.

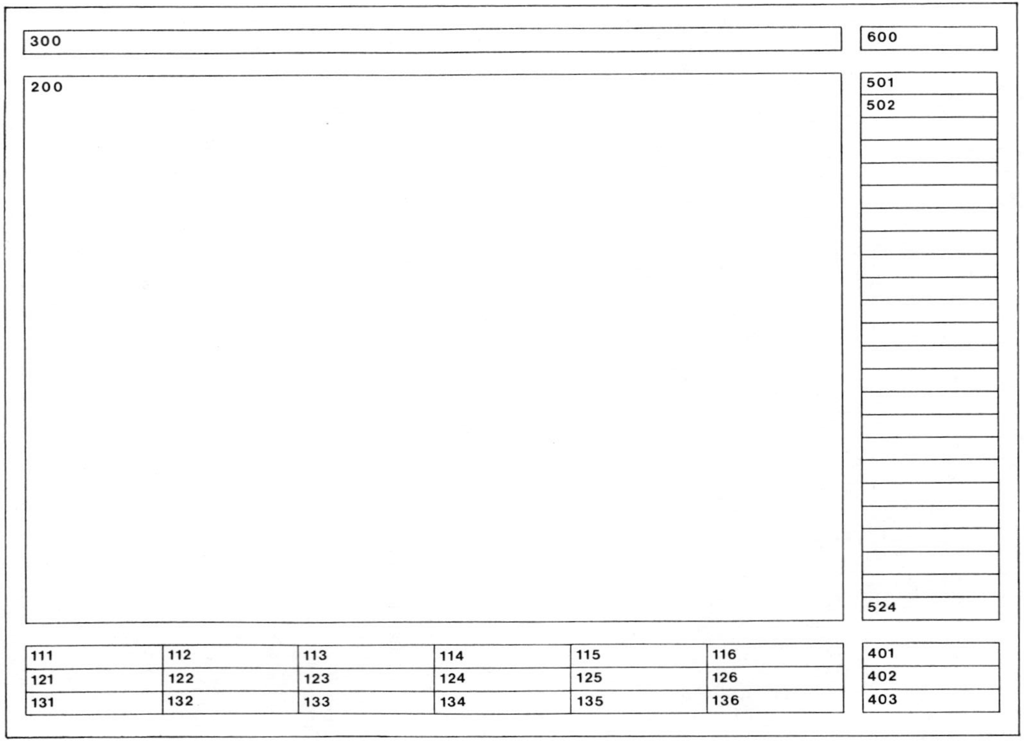

Figure C.2. A typical complex menu.

Alternatively, it could be implemented hierarchically as follows:

```
if (y > 65) and (y < 95)
  then if (x > 5) and (x < 165)
          then code := 111
          else if (x > 165) and (x < 325)
                  then code := 112
                  else ...
```

Even in a simple menu layout such as the one depicted in Figure C.1, hierarchical hit-testing requires at least eight decisions, assuming a particular encoding scheme was adopted. In more complex menus, such as the example depicted in Figure C.2, many more complex decisions are required (38, to be precise).

While such numbers of decisions are insignificant in themselves, they become prohibitively expensive when multiplied by the number of times they are invoked in the course of a typical interactive session. For example, if a typical architectural drawing consists of 10,000 lines, then the number of decisions concerning hit-testing alone would easily exceed one-third of a million!

☐ MODULAR MENU MAPPING

At the heart of rationalizing menu layouts and reducing the cost of hit-testing is *modularity*. Rather than define menu boxes at arbitrary screen locations, we can impose on them some ordering in the form of a *modular grid*. This grid can then be used as a *look-up table* (which we will call a *menu map*) for hit-testing. By associating each cell in the grid with the specific code that pertains to its superimposed menu box, hit-testing becomes a simple matter of determining the grid location of the cursor and reading off its associated code. If we define the grid in terms of its individual cell dimensions (*xmodule, ymodule*), then determining the grid location of the cursor, given its $<x, y>$ screen coordinates, can be done by means like the following statements:†

```
i := x div xmodule;
j := y div ymodule;
code := grid [i,j];
```

The above statements assume that the origin of the grid and the screen are the same, and that the grid starts at $<0, 0>$. To remove these restrictions, we can generalize the hit-testing by introducing a grid-to-screen translation, and by

---

†DIV is a PASCAL operator that returns the largest integer in the result of dividing two numbers, and is equivalent to truncating the result of their division.

adding a unit to each grid coordinate so that the grid will start at $<1, 1>$ rather than $<0, 0>$:

```
i := ((x - dx) div xmodule) + 1;
j := ((y - dy) div ymodule) + 1;
code := grid [i,j];
```

where Dx and Dy are the respective translations between the origin of the screen and the origin of the grid.

The grid cell size can be made equal to or smaller than the corresponding menu box sizes, and the grid as a whole may cover the entire screen area or the menu area alone, depending on the particular menu layout. In the case of a simple menu such as the one depicted in Figure C.1, a grid of 18 cells (the number of menu boxes), each of which is equal to the size of a menu box, will suffice. It will, however, require at least one decision to determine whether the cursor is at all in the menu area. To eliminate the necessity of decisions altogether, the grid can be extended so it covers the entire screen area, in which case its non-menu cells must be coded accordingly.

Encoding the menu map (grid cells) is a simple task that needs to be performed only once. For example, to encode the grid depicted in Figure C.3 such that it corresponds to the menu codes depicted in Figure C.1, we could use the following sequence of statements:

```
for i := 1 to 6 do
  begin
    for j := 3 downto 1 do
      grid [i,j] := 100 + 10 * (4 - j) + i;
    for j := 4 to 24 do
      grid [i,j] := 200
  end;
```

In case there are more complex menus, it may be desirable to make the grid spacing smaller than the smallest menu box. More precisely, it should be set to the size of the largest common module of spacing used in the layout. Such a grid, which corresponds to the menu depicted in Figure C.2, is shown in Figure C.4.

While the cost of hit-testing, in terms of time, is only a constant unit for such modular menus, the space required to store the menu map may be prohibitively large. The grid depicted in Figure C.4 requires 1,500 spaces, a number which may increase if an even finer grid is used. We shall now examine a hybrid method that uses more compact storage for the menu map and in return requires some search.

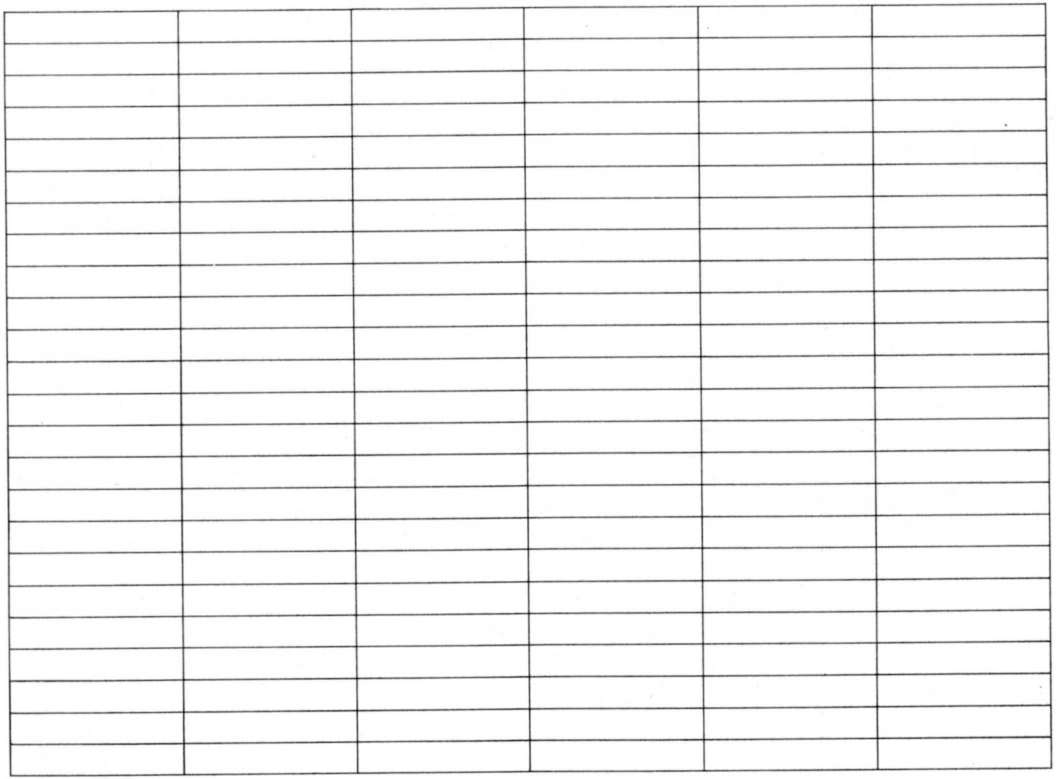

Figure C.3. The grid underlying the menu map of a simple menu.

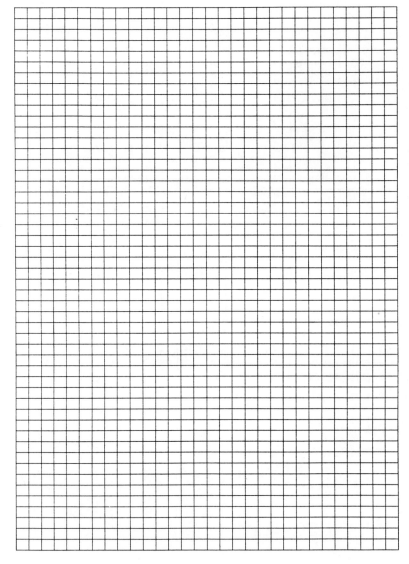

Figure C.4. The grid underlying the menu map of a complex menu.

□ RUN-LENGTH ENCODING

Compaction of the space required to store the menu map can be achieved by taking advantage of the similarity of many adjacent grid cells in terms of the menu code they represent. For example, in the menu map depicted in Figure C.3, all the grid cells from the fourth row up share the menu code 200.

Compact linear encoding of two-dimensional arrays has been developed as a means to store bit-mapped frame buffers in computer graphics. It uses a vector to store the run-length of each color when the frame buffer is scanned top-to-bottom, left-to-right. If large areas of the picture share the same color, this method then produces a much more compact stored image of the picture than the image produced by storing it pixel by pixel.

Run-length encoding can be adapted to store the menu map, which is essentially a large two-dimensional array, by replacing the colors with menu codes. The menu can be run-length encoded by scanning the grid bottom-to-top, left-to-right while counting and recording the number of grid cells that share the same menu code. These numbers are added up, so that each cell in the run-length vector contains the accumulated number of grid modules that share the same code, starting where the preceding cell left off (the cell starts from 1). Figure C.5 depicts the run-length encoded image of the menu depicted in Figure C.4. Procedure LOAD_RUN_VECTOR is a simple routine that converts a given menu map (grid) into a run-length encoded image (vector).

```
type runvector = array [1..101,1..2] of integer;

procedure load_run_vector (menu : menumap;
                           var menuvector : runvector;
                           var runcount: integer);

var   i,j,runlength,currentcode  : integer;
      stop                       : boolean;

begin
  {initialize}
  i := 0; j := 0; stop := 0;
  runlength := -1; runcount := 0;
  currentcode := menu[(i + 1), (j + 1)];

  repeat
    {determine run length of current mode}
    repeat
      runlength := runlength + 1;
      if (i = xscreensize) and (j = yscreensize)
        then stop := true
        else begin
          i := (i mod xscreensize) + 1;
          if i = 1 then j := j + 1
        end
    until (menu[i,j] <> currentcode) or stop;
```

#	MODULE	CODE	#	MODULE	CODE	#	MODULE	CODE
1	7	131	35	392	200	69	943	0
2	14	132	36	393	0	70	953	510
3	21	133	37	400	521	71	992	200
4	28	134	38	442	200	72	993	0
5	35	135	39	443	0	73	1000	509
6	42	136	40	450	520	74	1042	200
7	43	0	41	492	200	75	1043	0
8	50	403	42	493	0	76	1050	508
9	57	121	43	500	519	77	1092	200
10	64	122	44	542	200	78	1093	0
11	71	123	45	543	0	79	1100	507
12	78	124	46	550	518	80	1142	200
13	85	125	47	592	200	81	1143	0
14	92	126	48	593	0	82	1150	506
15	93	0	49	600	517	83	1192	200
16	100	402	50	642	200	84	1193	0
17	107	111	51	643	0	85	1200	505
18	114	112	52	650	516	86	1242	200
19	121	113	53	692	200	87	1243	0
20	128	114	54	693	0	88	1250	504
21	135	115	55	700	515	89	1292	200
22	142	116	56	742	200	90	1293	0
23	143	0	57	743	0	91	1300	503
24	150	401	58	750	514	92	1342	200
25	200	0	59	792	200	93	1343	0
26	242	200	60	793	0	94	1350	502
27	243	0	61	800	513	95	1392	200
28	250	524	62	842	200	96	1393	0
29	292	200	63	843	0	97	1400	501
30	293	0	64	850	512	98	1450	0
31	300	523	65	892	200	99	1492	300
32	342	200	66	893	0	100	1493	0
33	343	0	67	900	511	101	1500	600
34	350	522	68	942	200			

Figure C.5. The run-length vector of a complex menu.

```
{store in run length map}
runcount := runcount + 1;
menuvector[runcount, modules] := runlength;
menuvector[runcount, code]:= currentcode;
currentcode := menu[i,j]
    until stop
end; {load-run_vector procedure}
```

The advantage of this encoding method over full grid storage depends on the relative size of the grid cells and the number of different menu codes. In general, one vector storage space is required for each outside-in and inside-out transition between grid cells that represent different menu codes (except for the first and last modules). For example, the menu depicted in Figure C.3 can be run-length encoded in 19 spaces (compared with $7 \times 24 = 168$ grid cells), and the menu depicted in Figure C.4 can be run-length encoded in 101 spaces (compared with 1,500 grid cells). This saving increases proportionally to the inverse of the square of the grid cell sizes and decreases proportionally to the complexity of the menu in terms of number of different menu boxes.

The disadvantage of run-length encoding compared with the menu map is in having to decode the run-length vector for searching each hit test. In essence, decoding consists of searching the run-length vector to find the menu code that corresponds to a given cursor location. This is a two-step operation:

1. The cursor's screen location must be translated into grid modules.
2. The run-length vector must be searched to find the cell that corresponds to the smallest number of scanned grid modules that is larger than or equal to the translated cursor location.

The run-length vector can be searched by a simple recursive binary search that returns the vector cell (or its associated menu code) that matches the translated screen location of the cursor. Procedure BISEARCH is an example of such a routine.

```
procedure bisearch (address, high, low : integer;
                    var menucode : integer);

var  midrange : integer;

begin
  if high = (low + 1)
    then if address = menuvector [low, modules]
           then menucode := menuvector [low, code]
           else menucode := menuvector [high, code]
    else begin
           midrange := trunc ((low + high) * 0.5);
           if menuvector [midrange, modules] >= address
             then high := midrange
             else low := midrange;
           bisearch (address, low, high, menucode)
         end
end; {bisearch procedure}
```

The cost of such a search is, of course, $O(\log N)$, N representing the number of entries in the run-length vector. For the menu depicted in Figure C.3, this number is at most 5, whereas for the menu depicted in Figure C.4, it is at most 7.

While the search makes this hybrid method more expensive than the direct look-up in a menu map, as discussed in the previous section, it is still far less expensive than the search that would have had to be performed with no modular mapping at all. Furthermore, similar to run-length encoding, the relative efficiency of run-length decoding depends on the complexity of the menu and the size of the individual grid cells. And because it increases only at the rate of $O(\log N)$ while the number of grid cells increases at a rate of N squared, it is progressively more efficient than modular mapping when both factors (menu complexity and number of grid cells) increase, suggesting that overall, the hybrid method should be used for more complex menus, rather than simple ones.

□ SUMMARY

Menu hit-testing is an operation that comprises a large portion of run-time cost, by virtue of its abundance. This appendix introduced two methods that reduce this cost by more than an order of magnitude.

The first is called *modular menu mapping*. It rationalizes the menu layout by imposing on it a grid structure, which is also used for menu testing. It does, however, bring forth the classic time versus space trade-off, through substituting search time with a large stored look-up table.

As an alternative to complete substitution of space for time, a hybrid method was introduced that minimizes the added space requirements for storing the look-up table through *run-length encoding*, but requires some search. This search can, however, be made very efficient, taking advantage of the linearity and uniformity of the searched data.

The decision of which method to use depends on the relative complexity of the menu and the size of individual grid cells; run-length encoding seems appropriate for complex menus that are based on grids, whereas the look-up table approach seems appropriate for simple menus that by nature do not require fine grids.

It seems however, that most any layout and menu hit-testing can benefit from some form of modular menu mapping, rather than be left to a sequential or hierarchical decision tree search.

□ BIBLIOGRAPHY

Foley, J. D., and A. van Dam, *Fundamentals of Interactive Computer Graphics*, Addison-Wesley, Reading, MA, 1982.

Giloi, W., *Interactive Computer Graphics*, Prentice-Hall, Englewood Cliffs, NJ, 1987.

Newman, W. M., and R. F. Sproull, *Principles of Interactive Computer Graphics*, McGraw-Hill, New York, 1979.

INDEX

399